'Ice and Flame': Aleksandr Pushkin's *Eugene Onegin*

In the canon of Russian literature, few works have been as controversial, or as influential, as Pushkin's novel in verse, *Eugene Onegin*. Its critical history mirrors the changes in Russian political culture since its publication in 1833. Clayton traces that history and offers a new reading.

Nineteenth-century critics of *Eugene Onegin* saw it solely as a novel, and recognized its programmatic function in the creation of the Russian realistic novel. It was only in the 1920s that the Formalists perceived the ambiguous nature of the work as poem/novel and identified the metaliterary concerns that make *Onegin* the forerunner of Modernism. Later, Stalinist criticism brought a stultifying return to the realist view that had prevailed in the nineteenth century, but Soviet criticism after 1953 has produced a new and vigorous debate.

This new reading offered by Clayton encompasses all the contradictory features of form and content that have preoccupied successive schools of critical thought. He identifies a principle of 'flawed beauty' as central to an interpretation of the form, and examines the major characters of *Onegin* within this context. He explores the lyric burden of what is ultimately a profoundly moral work, in which the many opposites in the text are characteristic of Pushkin's poetic semantics.

Clayton concludes that *Eugene Onegin* is the first great work of Russian literature in which the moral values differ significantly from Western models; its moral sense, like its critical history, is uniquely Russian.

J. DOUGLAS CLAYTON is associate professor in the Department of Modern Languages and Literatures, University of Ottawa.

Ice and Flame

Aleksandr Pushkin's
Eugene Onegin

J. Douglas Clayton

UNIVERSITY OF TORONTO PRESS

Toronto Buffalo London

© University of Toronto Press 1985
Toronto Buffalo London
Printed in Canada

ISBN 0-8020-5655-5

Canadian Cataloguing in Publication Data

Clayton, J. Douglas.
'Ice and flame' : Aleksandr Pushkin's *Eugene Onegin*

Bibliography: p.
Includes index.
ISBN 0-8020-5655-5
1. Pushkin, Aleksandr Sergeevich, 1799–1837.
Evgeniĭ Onegin – Criticism and interpretation.
I. Title.
PG3343.E83C58 1985   891.71'3   C85-098991-4

The drawings by Pushkin reproduced on pages 71, 137, 159, and 194
are from A.S. Pushkin, *Sobranie sochinenii v desiati tomakh*, IV
(Moscow: Gosudarstvennoe izdatel'stvo khudozhestvennoi literatury,
1960), pages 11, 68, 29, and 40 respectively.

This book has been published with the help of grants from the
Canadian Federation for the Humanities, using funds provided by
the Social Sciences and Humanities Research Council of Canada,
the University of Ottawa, and the Publications Fund of the
University of Toronto Press.

for Merijean

Volna i kamen',
Stikhi i proza, led i plamen'
Ne stol' razlichny mezh soboi.

[*Wave and stone, verse and prose, ice and flame
are not as different from each other.*]

Contents

Preface

In this study I have used transliteration system II as described in J. Thomas Shaw, *The Transliteration of Modern Russian for English-Language Publications* (Madison: University of Wisconsin Press, 1967). Quotations from *Eugene Onegin* are marked in the following way: chapter written out, stanza in roman numerals, and line references in arabic, e.g., One: LX: 5-6. All quotations from Pushkin's oeuvre are taken from the 'Jubilee' edition A.S. Pushkin, *Polnoe sobranie sochinenii v shestnadtsati tomakh* (Moscow-Leningrad: AN SSSR, 1937-49), which is designated *PSS*. Quotations from Pushkin's letters are from Shaw's translation: A.S. Pushkin, *The Letters of Alexander Pushkin*, three volumes in one, translated with preface, introduction and notes by J. Thomas Shaw (Madison: University of Wisconsin Press, 1967). All other translations are my own unless otherwise indicated. Another source to which frequent reference is made is Nabokov's translation and commentary: *Eugene Onegin: A Novel in Verse by Aleksandr Pushkin*, translated from the Russian, with a commentary, by Vladimir Nabokov, revised edition in four volumes (Princeton University Press, 1975; Bollingen Series LXXII). This is referred to simply as 'Nabokov.' Notes in parentheses in the text refer to the bibliography, which is organized according to the author-date system. I would like to thank the editors of *Canadian Slavonic Papers* and the *Russian Language Journal*, for their kind permission to quote extensively from two of my articles on *Onegin* published in their journals (1980b and 1981).

'Ice and Flame'

Introduction

If there is one work which has above all others the key role in the formation of Russian literature as we know it, then it is surely Aleksandr Pushkin's *Eugene Onegin*. In it the reader recognizes for the first time in the evolution of the literature those features which were to typify the Russian novel. It contains, quintessentially, the whole of Turgenev and Tolstoi within itself, like a DNA molecule. What is more, Russians have generally recognized Pushkin as the greatest poet and even the greatest writer their country has produced, an accolade which is by no means inconsiderable. In Russia a vast amount of scholarship has been devoted to the researching and analysis of Pushkin's work, his life, and his role in the development of Russian literature. This effort continues undiminished today.

This may be surprising to the Western reader who, although he has heard of Pushkin, is generally unlikely to have read much of his work, and may be disinclined to consider him on the same level as Tolstoi or Dostoevskii. It is more so when one realizes to what extent he is an exception in Russian literature. This difference is widely commented upon, but perhaps never better expressed than in the words of Iurii Zhivago:

> What I have come to like best in the whole of Russian literature is the childlike Russian quality of Pushkin and Chekhov, their shy unconcern with such high-sounding matters as the ultimate purpose of mankind or their own salvation. It isn't that they didn't think about these things, and to good effect, but that they always felt that such important matters were not for them. While Gogol, Tolstoy and Dostoevsky worried and looked for the meaning of life and prepared for death and drew up balance-

> sheets, these two were distracted, right up to the end of their
> lives, by the current, individual tasks imposed on them by their
> vocation as writers, and in the course of fulfilling their tasks
> they lived their lives, quietly, treating both their lives and
> their work as private, individual matters, of no concern to
> anyone else. And these individual things have since become of
> concern to all, their work has ripened of itself, like apples
> picked green from the trees, and has increasingly matured in
> sense and sweetness. (Pasternak 1958, 259)

While an English-speaking reader might be surprised at the solemn
tone of the passage (which in itself seems very un-Pushkinian), it seems
to me that the point of Zhivago's comment is undeniable: that Pushkin
was able to endow the apparently trivial with extraordinary meaning;
and that the nature of Pushkin's strength as a poet is very elusive. It
is to be found in the laconicism, in the irony, in the value which his
work acquires through the years – in spite of itself, almost.

It is this elusiveness that has led to Pushkin's being understood only
imperfectly, or with difficulty. He himself was aware of the fact and
shuddered to think of the critical fate which his works would receive
at the hands of the 'ignoramus' (*nevezhda*) or the 'fool' (*glupets*), to
use his own terms from 'The monument' ('Pamiatnik'). Intimate, personal, elusive, Pushkin is, to quote a cliché that appears apt here, a
'poet's poet,' appreciated most by the Pasternaks, the Mandel'shtams,
and the Akhmatovas of this world. In the critical literature, which I
survey in chapter one of this study, Pushkin has generally met with
everything but understanding at the hands of his critics; his worst fears
were justified. He quickly became an object of national veneration, an
icon to be fought over, to be praised or blasphemed, but rarely to be
understood. It is my central thesis in this book that what constitutes
in one sense the importance of *Onegin* – its 'programmatic' function,
which I described above – has led generations of critics to misapply to
it the criteria of realist aesthetics, that is to say of Russian literature
of a generation later. (It goes without saying that by 'realism' I understand the poetic which formed the Russian prose novel of the 1850s
through the 1870s and which strove to invoke in the reader a willing
suspension of disbelief and acceptance of the fictive reality as a 'reflection' of the real world. I do not, therefore, use the term in the loose
sense in which Soviet critics employ it to mean all works which have
a mimetic basis, or even all works which they find ideologically
acceptable.)

My own interpretation of *Onegin* fits into the process of rejecting the 'realist' reading which has gone on intermittently in Russia since the 1920s, and which has acquired a special vigour in the past two decades in the work of the Structuralists. It should therefore not be surprising to the reader if I borrow their insights and terminology at various points in my analysis. I aim, however, to go beyond them in striving to determine what *Onegin* can be seen to mean in the historico-literary and personal-biographical circumstances of its creation.

This is still a slightly unusual undertaking in the English-speaking world, where the tendency has been very much to read *Onegin* in the tradition of the Russian realist novel, the thing we 'know best' (a tendency which is no doubt reinforced by the strong tradition of the realist novel in British and American literature). This a posteriori imposition of the poetics of the realist novel is clear even in the latest translation of the work into English (by Charles Johnston), from which Onegin's Journey is totally omitted. Recent Soviet critics have echoed Tynianov's persuasive argument that the Journey forms a true coda to the work. It is a view that I share and which I shall elaborate in the following study. Clearly, to omit it totally is to deform the text in a very important way. This 'realist' bias in the view of the work is reinforced by John Bayley's introduction to the translation, which, while containing very useful insights, still manages to talk about the work very much as a novel in which we are totally absorbed in the fates of the characters.

If one reads *Onegin* with the expectations of the realistic novel in mind, one is likely to end up puzzled or even find one's expectations of that genre unmet and reject the work in toto. This was the logical conclusion to which the nineteenth-century Russian critic Pisarev came, in a rare moment of outspoken iconoclasm. In a sense he was right in dismissing *Onegin* – right, that is, according to his lights. If the objections which Pisarev had to the work are to be answered, then we must find an interpretation which does justice to both aspects of the work – the poem and the novel – and which permits us to account for the importance the work has been recognized to have by the vast majority of Russian and foreign critics. An attempt must be made to deal with more than technical aspects of the text. This is my intention in this book.

This book has been written with more than a narrow spectrum of specialists in mind. I assume that the reader is familiar with the text of *Onegin*, whether in translation (preferably that of Nabokov, if only for the wealth of background given in the commentary) or in the original, and has, in addition, some background in nineteenth-century Russian literature. Quotations are given in the original Russian with my own prose translations beneath to serve as a crib. Titles and quotations from Russian critics are translated with the original Russian given in parentheses if necessary. I have tended to quote more at length from recent Soviet critical commentary on *Onegin*, since it is precisely that which is likely to be unfamiliar even to some working in Russian literature, and therefore of the most interest.

The book which follows is the product of some five years of intermittent research. I am all too aware of certain inconsistencies and changes in opinion which I have undergone in the course of thinking about *Onegin*, and hope that these are not too evident in the final result. The reader will find six chapters of unequal length. The first, and longest, is devoted to the evolution of criticism on *Onegin*. Subsequent chapters are devoted to aspects of the work that seemed important for the illustration of the central thesis of the book. I am aware that in choosing to focus on certain topics I have neglected others – the analysis of the poetry being one, and the history of the writing another. However, these questions are adequately covered by others, and it did not seem useful to go over ground which they had already covered so well.

Finally, I would like to express my thanks to the Social Sciences and Humanities Research Council of Canada (formerly the Canada Council) for the generous grants which have made it possible for me to undertake this research, to the Faculty of Arts of the University of Ottawa for the time and facilities, and to my colleagues Z. Folejewski, J. Thomas Shaw, Henry W. Sullivan, and Andrew Donskov, whose advice and support I have found invaluable. I would like to record my gratitude to my assistants Madeleine Guérin, John Kwak, Caroline Lussier, and Phil Houston for help with various stages, and also offer special thanks to Mr Doug Geddie and the staff of the Office of External Relations at Brock University for kindly letting me use their word-processor for the final revision of the text. Most of all this work stands as a monument to the patience and encouragement of my wife and family, to whom the volume is dedicated.

May 1984 University of Ottawa

1

The Repainted Icon:
Criticism of *Eugene Onegin*

Khvalu i klevetu priemli ravnodushno ...
[*Receive praise and insult with equanimity ...*]

Of all the celebrated authors in Russian literature, Pushkin has been
and is the object of the greatest mass of writing in Russian – critical,
biographical, popular, and even fictional. In part we may attribute this
to the position that Pushkin is seen to occupy as the 'progenitor of
Russian literature,' and to the role he has played of 'national poet' (a
title first given to him by Gogol' in 1835); but perhaps the most com-
pelling reason is his enigmatic nature – at once supremely Russian in
his superstitions, his use of folk motifs, his loving depictions of Russian
nature and life, his command of the Russian language, and at the same
time 'foreign' in his lack of concern for deep philosophical problems,
his playful, insouciant attitude towards his art, his Gallic brevity and
wit, his formal perfection. In this complex literary personality generation after generation of Russian critics and scholars have found the
material for a lifetime of study, and the results, in terms of sheer
volumes of insights, trivia, polemics, and analysis, form a formidable
barrier reef for the new student of Pushkin to cross.

There is something supremely ironic in this mass of exegesis – much
of it mediocre, having more to say about the writer than about Pushkin
himself – compared to the brevity, elegance, and brilliance of the works
which gave it birth. And yet there is also much that is of interest. No
important critic or thinker in Russia has not had something to say
about Pushkin. In the literature on Pushkin we can trace all the major
developments in Russian thought. Even the foreign critic, who comes
to his reading of Pushkin from a different tradition and with different
premises, ignores at his peril the critical image that has been drawn
of the writer by one hundred and fifty years of study and thought.

Since it is the goal of this study to respond to (though not necessarily to echo) the Russian views of *Onegin*, it follows that we must review the critical literature, and define the varying attitudes.[1] As the American Pushkinist J. Thomas Shaw has pointed out, the definitive history of Pushkin studies still remains unwritten (1966, 67). There exist, however, a number of sketches which, though incomplete and at times biased, can give the reader some idea of the field.[2] There is also a dissertation in English on early Pushkin criticism – up to and including Belinskii, as well as scattered articles on different – more or less spectacular – moments in the criticism of *Onegin*.[3]

By and large the stages in the history of *Onegin* criticism correspond to the development in the history of Pushkin criticism as a whole. This history has proceeded under the influence of two types of impetus. First, it has formed a natural and important part of the evolution of Russian intellectual and literary thought as a whole. As B.V. Tomashevskii put it: 'there is not a single historico-literary work concerning the nineteenth century in which we do not find in one form or another an evaluation of Pushkin's works or their reflection in the subsequent development of Russian literature' (1961, 444). Thus, Pushkin criticism is an important element in the Belinskian school, in symbolist criticism, in formalism, in Soviet realist criticism, and in the criticism of structuralist poetics. A secondary but still vital factor in the history of Pushkin criticism in Russia is the *prazdnik* phenomenon – the celebration of an anniversary of the poet's birth or death. This began seriously in 1880 with the unveiling of the Pushkin monument in Moscow. Although it did not mark a significant anniversary, this event was a festival of historical importance that confirmed Pushkin's reputation as Russia's national poet. It was followed shortly by the fiftieth anniversary of the poet's death – 1887, which year also saw the extinguishing of the Pushkin family's rights to the poet's work and hence was marked by the beginning of a spate of cheap editions of the poet's works. Of supreme importance also was the centenary of the poet's birth in 1899, which was the cause of innumerable celebrations, speeches, and symposia throughout the Russian empire. Since the Revolution, the most significant event of the *prazdnik* type has been the hundredth centenary of the poet's death, celebrated in 1937. These festivals are an important feature of Russian cultural life and are closely bound up with the perception of Pushkin as a part of the national identity. They have lead to the growth of the Pushkin 'industry' which – especially in the first two or three decades of the twentieth century – created a huge wealth of factual information on the poet's life, his texts, his sources. Frequently lacking in these endeavours was an attempt at a critical understanding or appreciation of the poetry: a national cult object must be venerated, not treated critically as literature. True, it is to the initiation of Pushkin studies, and hence to the national festivals, that we owe the creation of such indispensable tools as the Academy edition of the complete works and the Pushkin dictionary. In general, however, the significant advances in criticism of *Onegin* have taken place independently of the festivals, in response to the natural development of literary thought in Russia.

For the purposes of the analysis contained in this chapter, the following periods have been identified in the development of *Onegin* criticism. 1. The criticism of *Onegin* up to 1840. This includes the criticism of the individual chapters as they appeared, as well as the reception of the collected works which appeared in 1837, immediately after the poet's death. 2. The criticism of Belinskii and his successors in the 'civic' school of criticism, up to Pisarev. 3. The alternative school of Grigor'ev and Druzhinin, culminating in Dostoevskii's speech. 4. Symbolist criticism of *Onegin*. 5. The formalists. 6. Soviet realist criticism. 7. Soviet structural poetics. In addition, we will examine finally some of the important foreign criticism of *Onegin*.

CRITICISM OF *ONEGIN* BY PUSHKIN'S CONTEMPORARIES UP TO 1840

Contemporary criticism of *Onegin* is useful on two counts. First, it tells us something about the immediate impact of the work, and hence about its meaning in the contemporary historico-literary context. This does not mean that contemporary criticism is necessarily the most important and valuable, although allusions to contemporary events, personalities, and cultural phenomena can certainly have much more force and immediacy on the contemporary reader. The subsequent critic is obliged to reconstruct for himself both the context and the meaning within that context. In this he may be more or less successful than the poet's contemporary. It is certainly a much more conscious process. Secondly, contemporary criticism is useful because it tells us a considerable amount about the state of criticism in Russia (or lack of it, as Pushkin thought) in the 1820s and 1830s.

This problem, which concerns us only indirectly, has been admirably described by Paul Debreczeny, who analyses the criticism that appeared in the literary journals and almanacs of the period into three tendencies (1969, 403). The first of these is composed of the 'conservatives,' who rigidly applied the classical genre-system and conservative linguistic norms to Pushkin's works. The second group were the romantics, who were interested in defending what they perceived as the romantic breaking of norms by Pushkin. Debreczeny sums up this critical opposition as follows: 'While the conservatives felt themselves delegated to voice the dissatisfaction of society with new trends in poetry and thought, the romantics did their best to justify and popularize these trends. The conservatives spoke for the public to the author, the romantics for the author to the public.' The third group that Debreczeny singles out is the Moscow circle known as the *liubomudry* or 'philosophers' – a group influenced by idealist German philosophy who were engaged in the quest for a Russian identity and read Pushkin's work in this light.

Debreczeny's classification is useful in that it clarifies the polyphony present in Russian criticism of the time. The situation is complicated by the fact that *Onegin* was being published, chapter by chapter, against the background of the evolution of Russian criticism and literary society. Russian literature, which until approximately 1825 had been dominated by verse and was practised and read by a small group of noblemen, was being taken over by a mass audience and was simultaneously undergoing a shift towards prose. The career of Pushkin, a nobleman who tried to earn his living from literature, and whose output changes its centre of gravity from verse (1820s) to prose (1830 onwards), reflected this shift. As a writer who was at first idolized, then treated with considerable disrespect by the critics, Pushkin was vitally interested in the practice of criticism in Russia, and we find among his critical and publicistic writings a number of essays published or in draft form on the subject. Essentially, it was Pushkin's position that Russia did not yet have her critics. Thus, in an unpublished review of Bestuzhev's 'Survey of Russian literature for 1824 and the beginning of 1825' he writes: 'Do we have criticism? Where is it then? Where are our Addisons, our Schlegels, our Sismondi? What have we analysed? Whose literary opinions have gained national acceptance, to whose criticisms may we refer, on whose may we base our arguments?' (*PSS*, XI, 26). This was in reply to Bestuzhev's assertion that there was Russian criticism, but no Russian literature. Pushkin remarks further (in a note published in *Literaturnaia gazeta*, 1830): 'Criticism in our journals either is limited to dry bibliographical information, satirical remarks, and more or less witty, general, friendly praise, or simply turns into a domestic correspondence between the publisher and the collaborators, proof-reader, et al.' (*PSS*, XI, 89). Certainly, Pushkin's treatment at the hands of critics during his lifetime gave him little reason to be satisfied with the standard of the profession as practised in Russia. The principles of criticism as he perceived them are laid out in an unpublished note (attributed to 1830): 'It is based on a perfect knowledge of the rules which an artist or writer follows in his works, on an in-depth study of the models, and on an active observation of noteworthy contemporary phenomena. I do not even speak of dispassionateness – whoever in criticism is motivated by anything save a pure love for art descends to the level of the rabble, which is motivated by base, greedy impulses. Where there is no love for art there is no criticism' (*PSS*, VI, 320).

Although such principles might seem self-evident to the point of banality, in the context of the reception of Pushkin's work by certain critics the assertion carries a note of emotional protest. This protest carried over into print in several instances when Pushkin felt constrained to reply, notably in the notes to *Onegin* and in the forewords to the initial publications of Chapters One and Eight (the forewords were dropped when the work was published in its entirety for the first time). Pushkin begins his running battle with the critics with an ironic taunt: 'Farsighted critics will notice, of course, the absence of a plan. Everyone is free to judge the plan of an entire novel, having read its first chapter. They will also criticize the anti-poetic character of the protagonist, who resembles the Prisoner of the Caucasus, as well as certain strophes, written in the tiresome style of the latest elegies' (*PSS*, V, 638).

These remarks, placed in the foreword to the original publication of Chapter One, suggest the poet's extreme sensitivity to the potential critical fate of his new work. *Onegin* was not simply another book – it was a continuing literary phenomenon surrounded by passionate partisanship and controversy. The nature of the phenomenon itself changed spectacularly as chapter after chapter appeared.

Pushkin's response to his critics in the forewords and notes varies. In some cases he ironically echoes them, even quoting them verbatim (with tongue in cheek). At other times he attempts a learned rebuttal (e.g., when the criticism is of a particular expression or lexical item). Although the 'polemic with critics' mode of *Onegin* is considerably softened in the final version by the elimination of the forewords in question, it is still there in the footnotes and forms one aspect of the overall literary dimension which the work possesses; as such it merits close attention.

The foreword to the original publication of Chapter One is written in the third person and mimics the tone and style of an editor. The poker-faced irony of the introduction amounts almost to parody. Thus the 'stamp of gaiety' which the verses bear is attributed to the 'influence of favourable circumstances' – a sarcastic reference to the trials and tribulations of Pushkin's exile in the South. As a ruse the foreword was effective in that Pushkin succeeded through it in 'preprogramming' some of the critical discussion which ensued. This was clearly the effect for which he was aiming – to discredit the critics by putting words in their mouths. The points which Pushkin was feeding to his critics may be listed as follows.

1. The work may never be finished and therefore the first chapter may be read as a fragment, especially since it 'has a certain unity.' He then tantalizes the critics with the thought that several chapters are already finished and with the reference to 'the plan of the whole novel,' about which he invites them to speculate on the basis of one chapter.

2. The work is gay, but satirical, a 'humorous description of manners' (Pushkin subsequently denied any satirical intent). The reference to 'strict decency' in its execution was a veiled reference to other works in Russian literature which the critics were to seize on.

3. It is reminiscent of *Beppo* – 'a humorous work of gloomy Byron.'

4. The ambiguity of genre in the subtitle is maintained in the reference in one place to 'a large poem' – using the word *stikhotvorenie* rather than the usual *poema* ('epic poem') to heighten the confusion – and to 'cantos, or chapters.'

5. The reference to 'the tiresome style of the latest elegies, in which a *feeling of despondency [unynie] has consumed all else'* invites a discussion of romanticism without mentioning the term. It was reinforced by the discussion of a poet's role, of inspiration, and so on, in the poem 'Conversation of a Bookseller with a Poet' which accompanied Chapter One.

To read the reviews of the first chapter is to realize how effective Pushkin's device was. True, most of the reviews were superficial in nature and, typically for the time, contented themselves with a little indiscriminate praise, some lengthy excerpts, and criticism of grammatical 'errors.' However, the appearance of Chapter One prompted one review – that of N.A. Polevoi – which led to a considerable polemic with D.V. Venevitinov. Polevoi's review, which was by far the most thorough and serious, raised a number of fundamental questions.[4] Polevoi, as an enthusiastic supporter of the romantic school, was unstinting in his praise of the new work. His first remarks represent a refutation of 'certain critics' who attacked *Onegin* because of its contravention of the classical laws of genre. Unfortunately, as Venevitinov subsequently pointed out, these critics were almost entirely a figment of

Polevoi's imagination.[5] Nevertheless, Polevoi does make a brave attempt to define the genre of the new work, which he sees in the tradition of the humorous poem – an observation which is clearly derived from the reference in the foreword to the 'indecency' of the precursors. In a later refutation of Venevitinov, Polevoi specifies the burlesque travesties of Maikov and Shakhovskoi. One wonders whether he did not also have in mind a bawdy poem by Pushkin's uncle V.L. Pushkin, 'The Dangerous Neighbour' ('Opasnyi sosed,' 1811), describing a riotous visit to a brothel, which circulated in manuscript form and which he would presumably not wish to mention in print.

Polevoi's review shows the influence of the foreword in a number of ways. He remarks, for example: 'We agree that it is impossible to judge the plan.' In his discussion of the genre he follows up on the hints in the foreword at a 'humorous poem,' although he suggests that Pushkin has developed the genre, making it more profound and meaningful. Other catchwords that Polevoi adopts from the foreword are 'gaiety' (*veselost'*) and 'despondency' (*unylost'*): 'His gaiety blends into despondency' (14). The formula seems to be derived straight from Pushkin's foreword.

In the most original part of his review Polevoi denies anything more than a casual similarity between *Onegin* and the Western 'models' – Byron's *Don Juan* and *Beppo*. The importance of *Onegin* lies, Polevoi suggests, in its *narodnost'*: 'Onegin is not copied from the French or the English; we see our own scenes, hear our native speech, behold our own quirks' (15). The concept of *narodnost'* – best rendered here as 'Russianness' – implies in general the specific qualities which single out a literature and make it an expression of the national identity. The doublet *natsional'nost* betrays the French origin of the word, and was for some critics interchangeable with the Russian calque which subsequently took over; Polevoi's emphasis on this question is a reflection of the romantic quest for a national literature.

In his comment on the character of Onegin, Polevoi likewise touched a chord by asserting that Onegin is a link between the scenes rather than a character (although we might see an echo here of the reference in the foreword to the 'anti-poetic' character of the hero). Polevoi's review, despite its pedestrian qualities and irritating critical habits (e.g., the ritual enumeration of 'mistakes') and despite the fact that it was to a considerable extent 'preprogrammed' by Pushkin's foreword, did touch on a number of the key issues which have since dominated *Onegin* criticism: genre, *narodnost'*, the character of Onegin, and the relationship of the work to foreign models.

The reasons for the 'anticritique' which Venevitinov wrote in reply to Polevoi have to do with the history of Russian criticism rather than the evaluation of *Onegin*. Venevitinov, as a member of the *liubomudry*, saw in Polevoi a mediocre vulgarizer of romanticism, who had rejected the classical approach to criticism without replacing it with a new system: 'As regards Mr. Polevoi's article – I would like to find in it criticism more based on positive rules, without which all judgements are shaky and inconsistent' (227). Venevitinov's review, which seems to have been provoked by a certain aesthetic embarrassment at the enthusiasm of Polevoi, was sufficiently inaccurate and inflammatory for Polevoi to write an effective rebuttal, although the polemic (enlarged by the contribution of two other critics) was by this time degenerating into fruitless attacks by both critics on real or asserted inaccuracies of phrase and grammar in the other's Russian. One aspect of Venevitinov's side of the argument which is of interest is his deepening of the concept of *narodnost'* which, in his view, 'is reflected ... in the very feelings of the poet, who is nourished by the spirit of one people and lives, so to speak, in the development, the achievements, and the separateness of its character' (237). It is perhaps this application of a more profound set of values in Venevitinov's article that prompted Pushkin's reported remark that 'This is the only article which I read with affection and attention. All the rest is either abuse or sugary nonsense' (quoted in Venevitinov 1934, 477). Venevitinov, who was to die in 1827, left only one further brief comment on *Onegin*, published posthumously in *Moskovskii vestnik*, in which he gave, apropos the second chapter, a precise description of Onegin: 'Experience did not implant in him either a tormenting passion or a bitter and active annoyance, but boredom, an outward dispassionateness, characteristic of Russian coldness (not to speak of Russian indolence)' (1827, 238-9).

' The criticism which greeted the appearance of Chapters Two through Six assumes a fairly monotonous pattern of ecstatic praise, some retelling of the content of the chapter in question, and numerous (often lengthy) quotations. One of the few exceptions to this rule is the review of Chapters Four and Five in *Atenei*. The reviewer finds fault with the improbable storyline (e.g., the fact that Tat'iana falls in love with Onegin, having seen him only once briefly), and criticizes a large number of the expressions in the text, especially the neologisms in the description of Tat'iana's dream (*khlop*, *top*, etc.).[6] Pushkin refuted the latter criticism in footnote 31 of the final text with the laconic comment: 'One should not impede the freedom of our rich and beautiful language' (*PSS*, VI, 193-4). The review of the same chapters in the *Moskovskii vestnik* assumes the form of a series of comments purportedly overheard by the critic concerning the novel.[7] The comments are interesting in only one respect – they illustrate the wave of interest, popularity, and speculation that accompanied the chapters as they appeared.

This wave was to crest and break spectacularly with the appearance of Chapter Seven, which was greeted with a chorus of disappointed – or even malicious – criticism. Thus, the *Moskovskii telegraf* critic found the 'principal idea' – to 'cast a sardonic eye' on salons, young gentlewomen, and on fashionable young men – 'tiresome both for him [Pushkin] and the readers.' However, the attempt (in a work called *Evgenii Vel'skii*) to imitate *Onegin* 'proves only how difficult it is to imitate Pushkin,' whom it was impossible to parody. This review can be credited with the notion, which quickly spread, that the work was 'a collection of disparate, unlinked notes and thoughts about this and that, inserted into one frame' (Zelinskii, III, 1-4). The *Telegraf* review was accompanied by others in *Literaturnaia gazeta* and *Galateia*, which were likewise more or less negative. The critic of the latter periodical reproaches Chapter Seven for the lack of action, the deficiencies in the Russian, the 'tirades' (for example, the list of utensils in Seven: XXXI), and the 'unsuccessful combination of colloquial and Slavonic words' (Zelinskii, III, 4-12 [11]).

The most severe blow was dealt Pushkin by F.V. Bulgarin in *Severnaia pchela*. Bulgarin, whose 1826 review of Chapter Two had been tentative, but not negative, now launched a vitriolic attack upon Chapter Seven: 'This Chapter ... is blotched with such verse, such tomfoolery that in comparison with it even *Evgenii Vel'skii* seems something like a business-like work. Not a single thought, not a single emotion, not a single scene worthy of attention! A complete fall, *chute complète!*' (Zelinskii, III, 12-18 [12-13]). Bulgarin went so far as to attack the egoism of the poet and the descriptions of *byt* (such elements from everyday life as the domestic utensils), and to express his disappointment at the descriptions of Moscow and the ball.

It has been pointed out that Bulgarin was inspired to attack *Onegin* by a highly critical review of his own novel *Dmitrii Samozvanets* which had appeared in *Literaturnaia gazeta* and which he had (wrongly) attributed to Pushkin. Some sources point, in addition, to Bulgarin's role as editor of the semi-official newspaper *Severnaia pchela* and his connections with the secret police.[8] The logic of this last factor would suggest an official conspiracy to attack *Onegin* and Pushkin himself. This appears exaggerated, since it is hard to see in *Onegin* a seditious document, or in the (relatively compliant) Pushkin of the late 1820s an enemy of the state; but Bulgarin's personal reaction to the critical review of his own work does seem a likely factor. The fact remains, however, that the review (although mockingly chided by Nadezhdin) was feasible on the basis of Chapter Seven and did not contradict, but rather echoed, the tone of most other reviews.

In the draft of a foreword which Pushkin intended to place before an (unrealized) edition of Chapter Eight and the Journey, he comments: 'When Canto VII appeared the journals on the whole viewed it extremely unfavourably. I would willingly have believed them, had their judgment not contradicted what they had said about the previous chapters of my novel' (*PSS*, VI, 539). Characteristically, he goes on to quote verbatim Bulgarin's review, including the parodistic verse:

> Nu, kak rasseiat' gore Tani?
> Vot kak: posadiat devu v sani
> I povezut iz milykh mest
> V Moskvu na iarmanku nevest!
> Mat' plachetsia, skuchaet dochka;
> Konets sed'moi glave – i tochka.

> [*Well, how can one allay Tania's grief? This is how: the girl will be put on a sleigh and shipped from her beloved haunts to Moscow to the bride market. The mother weeps, the daughter is bored; there's an end to the seventh chapter: period!* (*PSS*, VI, 540)]

In response Pushkin noted: 'These verses are very fine, but the criticism they contain is unfounded. The most insignificant subject may be chosen by the poet; criticism does not need to analyse what the poet describes, but how' (ibid.).

The reaction of the critics is, in fact, not totally incomprehensible when we look at the situation, not, as we do now, from the perspective of a knowledge of the complete novel, but as critics confronted by yet another separately published chapter of *Onegin*. The first point in the chapter's disfavour is the absence of three of the four central characters: Onegin, Lenskii, and Ol'ga have gone, apparently (for all the critic knows) never to return. As the critic of *Literaturnaia gazeta* put it: 'A reading of Chapter Seven of *Onegin* has the same effect on one as the sight of some haunts which were once dear to one, but which have been abandoned by those persons who animated them' (Zelinskii, III, 4-6 [4]). Although one might add that this is precisely the effect for which Pushkin strove, nevertheless the critic perceives it as a defect.

As important as the absence of three main characters is the fact that the critics were not aware that the novel would end soon. Thus Nadezhdin, in *Vestnik Evropy*, expects another seven chapters, and another reviewer, discussing the publication of Chapter Eight (1832), writes in the *Moskovskii Telegraf*: 'few thought to see so soon the end of this tale' (Zelinskii, III, 18-37 [36]; 124-9 [125]). Clearly, those critics who assailed Chapter Seven for its lack of action expected to see the work continue indefinitely to appear, chapter by chapter, becoming more and more unstructured and devoid of action. Such an assumption finds support in the foreword to a separate edition of Chapter One (which the reviewers would have had to read to survey the work to date – the foreword was dropped only when the work appeared in a single volume in 1833), in which Pushkin notes that the work will 'probably not be completed' (*PSS*, VI, 638). Ironically, at the time when these reviews were appearing, the concluding Chapter Nine (subsequently renumbered Eight) was in its final stages of preparation.

There were, perhaps, additional factors which contributed to the less than ecstatic reception of Chapter Seven. Among these is the fact that the public had already seen substantial parts of the chapter (stanzas XXXV-LIII, published in *Moskovskii vestnik* and then in *Severnaia pchela* in 1828, and I-IV in the almanac *Severnye tsvety*, in December 1829). This practice of Pushkin's of publishing excerpts from a work before it appeared had the effect, in this case, of making the appearance of Chapter Seven anticlimactic. There might also be the suspicion that Pushkin was milking *Onegin* for more than it was worth. Thus one critic, writing in the *Moskovskii telegraf* on the occasion of the publication, in 1833, of the complete text under one cover, noted that this new edition cost the reader only twelve roubles, rather than the forty roubles which he had had to pay to buy the novel piecemeal, as it appeared.[9] The posthumous (1837) edition was even cheaper at five roubles.[10]

Another final, more profound, factor which must be considered in our efforts to understand the critical reception of Chapter Seven has to do with the change of taste in the reading public. Pushkin, in the unpublished foreword to Eight (already quoted), takes issue with the notion that the times and 'Russia' have left him behind: 'If an age can advance, and the sciences, philosophy and civic consciousness can be perfected and change, poetry remains in the same place, and does not age or change. Its goal is the same, as are its means ... works of true poets remain fresh and eternally youthful' (*PSS*, VI, 540-1). Pushkin fails here to sense the true movement in the reading public, which was not progress, but a shift to a coarser, less esoteric popular literature (historical novels and romantic adventures). The public no longer understood (if it ever did) the subtlety of the verse, the hidden allusions, the irony (one critic was indignant at Onegin's remark 'that stupid moon on that stupid horizon').[11] Pushkin was not repentant: 'However it may be, I have decided to try its [the public's] patience once more. Here are two more chapters of *Eugene Onegin* – the last, at least for print ... Those who would look in them for entertaining events can be assured that they contain less action than all the preceding ones' (*PSS*, VI, 541).

Chapter Eight and the Journey appeared in 1832 without the foreword quoted above, and were generally greeted favourably. Thus the reviewer 'P.S.' wrote in the *Severnaia pchela*: 'Such an ending to *Onegin* will reconcile everyone with the author' (Zelinskii, III, 124). Another reviewer noted in *Teleskop*, 1832: 'Each chapter of *Onegin* revealed with ever greater clarity that Pushkin did not have the ambition to fulfil the gigantic plan ascribed to him' (Zelinskii, III, 131). It was the public, in the view of this critic, that had had exaggerated expectations which Pushkin would not, and did not, realize. As regards the genre, the same critic noted: '*Eugene Onegin* was not, and was not in fact intended to be, a novel, although this description, under which it appeared originally, has remained for all time at the head of it ... It cannot be bound by all the artificial conventions which criticism has a right to expect of a real novel' (ibid.). This important insight was to be lost as the subsequent generations entered the age of the realistic novel, of which *Onegin* was to be perceived to be the precursor.

The view that *Onegin* would not be judged by novelistic standards was developed by the critic of the *Moskovskii telegraf*, discussing the complete edition of *Onegin* in 1833, who saw it as an open-ended, unstructured work: 'the Poet was not thinking of completeness. He simply wanted to have a frame into which he could insert his opinions, scenes, heart-felt epigrams and madrigals to friends ... What is the underlying thought? None' (Zelinskii, III, 152). 'When he began to write, he did not know how to finish it, and when finishing it he could have written as many chapters again without damaging the integrity of the work, because there is none' (ibid.). Such an extreme perception of the work as a loose framework is balanced by the remarks of the critic in the *Literaturnye pribavleniia k Russkomu invalidu*, 1832, who develops the idea of the characters in the novel as types: 'A writer ... observes all the characteristics, all the features and peculiarities of a person and creates from them his heroes, his dramatis personae. This is how the character of *Eugene Onegin* is created, perhaps from a multitude of different characters whom the poet chanced to meet and who in his imagination assumed the form of a single ideal, the ideal of a cold egoist, exclusively self-centred, hungry for all worldly fame, though outwardly oblivious to it.'[12] Such a dichotomy of opinion – whether to treat the novel as novel or as framework for the poet's self-indulgences – has been a persistent feature of *Onegin* criticism.

The appearance of the complete edition of *Onegin* in 1833 marks the end of the work as a contemporary literary phenomenon surrounded by the critical birds of passage and modified, at least in details, by the reaction of the author to criticism, and the beginning of its new and eternal function as an event in literary history. Pushkin was not unaware of the importance of this change. In saying farewell to his novel in verse, he was also, in a sense, making a truce with the critics. He responded to this with a stanza which several critics were disposed to quote and comment on:

> Kto b ni byl ty, o moi chitatel',
> Drug, nedrug, ia khochu s toboi
> Rasstat'sia nynche kak priiatel'.
> Prosti. Chego by ty za mnoi
> Zdes' ni iskal v strofakh nebrezhnykh,
> Vospominanii li miatezhnykh,
> Otdokhnoven'ia l' ot trudov,
> Zhivykh kartin, il' ostrykh slov,
> Il' grammaticheskikh oshibok,
> Dai bog, chtob v etoi knizhke ty
> Dlia razvlechen'ia, dlia mechty,
> Dlia serdtsa, dlia zhurnal'nykh sshibok,
> Khotia krupitsu mog naiti.

[*Whoever you might be, O my reader, whether friend or foe, I would like us to part now on friendly terms. Farewell. Whatever you sought here as you followed my careless stanzas – be it rebellious memories, repose from your labours, lively pictures or witticisms, or errors of grammar – God grant that you found at least a crumb – for your amusement, for daydreaming, for the heart, or for squabbles in the journals.* (Eight: XLIX: 1-13)]

For critics, contemporaries, acquaintances, and friends reading them in the 1837 edition of *Onegin* or in the first volume of the posthumous *Collected Works* of 1838, these lines must have been fraught with a particular, poignant significance. The critics reviewing the *Collected Works* (the 1837 edition of *Onegin* did not attract any reviews in its own right) were keenly aware of the fact that not only *Onegin* but now Pushkin too had passed into history, and their comments are frequently intended to provide an overview of the poet's oeuvre and its significance for Russian literature.

The first attempt to survey Pushkin in this fashion dates from an earlier period: 'On the character of Pushkin's poetry' was published by I. Kireevskii in 1828. Kireevskii, a member of the *liubomudry* group, later became known as a philosopher. He sets out his goals at the beginning of his essay in a rhetorical question: 'Why has no one until now undertaken to determine the character of his [Pushkin's] poetry as a whole, to evaluate its beauties and its defects, to show the position which our poet has succeeded in occupying among the first-class poets of this age?' (1). While noting that the variety of Pushkin's work made it difficult to see the unity in it, Kireevskii attempts some generalizations, including the first attempt at periodization of Pushkin's work. Significantly, Kireevskii clarifies three periods which he distinguishes in terms of external influences, 'the Italo-French school' and 'the echo of Byron's lyre' constituting the first and second periods. It is only in the later chapters of *Onegin*, of which Kireevskii had read five, and in *Boris Godunov*, of which he had read one scene, that the critic sees the original Pushkin appearing. Kireevskii discusses the difference between Pushkin and Byron in terms of their heroes: 'Childe Harold has nothing in common with the mob of ordinary people: his sufferings, his aspirations, his pleasures are incomprehensible to others; only lofty mountains and naked crags reply to him with their secrets which he alone can hear ... Onegin, on the other hand, is a perfectly ordinary and insignificant creature' (11). If in *Onegin* the character and the form of the work are Byronic in inspiration, the other characters, in Kireevskii's view, show Pushkin's originality and independence. At the point when Kireevskii was writing, there was little more to be said. His tendency to view *Onegin* in terms of Byron's work was one from which most subsequent critics felt obliged to distance themselves. The critic, however, was also careful to stress Pushkin's Russianness, his *narodnost'*: 'But all the innumerable beauties of the poem: Lenskii, Tat'iana, Ol'ga, Petersburg, the countryside, the dream, winter, the letter etc. etc. – belong to our poet alone. Here he clearly revealed the natural bent of his genius' (12).

Ten years later, the appearance of the posthumous *Collected Works* provoked a number of panoramic reviews, most notably those by a

German critic Varnhagen von Ense, published in translation in *Syn otechestva*, 1839, by S. Shevyrev, in *Moskvitianin*, 1841, and an anonymous review in *Biblioteka dlia chteniia*, 1841.[13] All three of these critics agree that Pushkin is not an imitator in *Onegin*. The question had to do with the *narodnost'* or *natsional'nost'* of the poet. Thus Shevyrev writes: 'Eugene Onegin himself is loftier than all the heroes who were inspired in Pushkin by Byron's muse, because in Onegin there is a truth extracted from Russian life' (205). For Shevyrev it is Russian life that is influenced by the West: 'He is typical of Western influence on our people of society, a current type, encountered everywhere: this is our Russian apathy, inspired in us by an aimless acquaintance with Western disillusionment' (ibid.). The notion of Onegin's typicality is not entirely new, but Shevyrev repeats it with renewed force. From his reading of Onegin's character it is but a step to the Oblomovs and Rudins that are the commonplace characters of the Russian nineteenth-century novel.

All three reviews typically stress the 'truth' and 'naturalness' of the work. They see in Pushkin a 'national' or *narodnyi* poet, and they stress Pushkin's freedom from Byron. They all take for granted the form of the work, and have nothing but a few banalities to say on the subject of the verse. True, the critic of *Biblioteka dlia chteniia* does attempt some further account of the personal aspect of the work: 'we see in *Onegin* a secret but sincere, frank confession by the poet. He has revealed himself before us in his entirety, with all his passions and weaknesses, and has divided his character into two persons: one, the dark side of this character, was transposed into Onegin, the other, bright side animated Lenskii' (156). Such an interpretation is hopelessly schematic and sets up an artificial opposition that is scarcely vindicated by the irony with which Lenskii is portrayed, nor by the affection and sympathy that Onegin evokes at certain points (to say nothing of the presence of the poet as a character in the work). The reality of *Onegin* is much more complex than this simplistic formula. The critic was right, however, in drawing attention to the intimate, 'confessional' aspect of the work.

The criticism published during a poet's lifetime is important because it is — or can be — a two-way street. This aspect of *Onegin* criticism was enhanced by the fact that the work appeared chapter by chapter, so that it was a continuing phenomenon on the pages of Russian journalism rather than a single event. Although Pushkin stated in one place that he only skimmed the criticism of Chapter Seven, it is clear that for the most part he paid attention to the critics and frequently took time to refute them, reply to them, and attack them. It is less clear whether Pushkin actually modified the work substantially because of criticism. The answer is almost certainly not – although the literary dimension of the novel is enhanced by the ironic asides directed at the critics in text, forewords, and footnotes.

The criticism that appeared during Pushkin's lifetime and in the first years after his death permit one to discern a number of problems and critical truisms which were to become of prime importance in subsequent *Onegin* criticism. Foremost among these are the relationship of the work to foreign models (specifically Byron, although others were mentioned; Benjamin Constant, for example); the problem of Onegin's character; the *narodnost'* of the work; the question of the form / genre – a novel or a 'frame' for a series of random 'pictures'; the excellence and importance of Tat'iana's character and of the poetry. It remained for a critic of stature to undertake a detailed analysis of these problems and to give the critical discussion the necessary depth and scope.

BELINSKII AND HIS SUCCESSORS

If the first criticism of Pushkin and specifically of *Onegin* consisted of more or less inspired reviews of the various editions as they occurred, the years 1843-6 saw, in the eleven articles published by V.G. Belinskii in *Otechestvennye zapiski* on Pushkin, the first real literary criticism of lasting value. The articles taken together, although they were entitled 'The Works of Aleksandr Pushkin' and were provoked initially by the publication of three additional volumes of the *Collected Works*, represent a sweeping critical monograph that laid the basis for much subsequent nineteenth-century and twentieth-century Soviet Pushkin criticism, and essentially created the 'Pushkin myth' in Russian life and letters. Whether one is studying Pushkiniana or Pushkin, after the oeuvre itself one reads Belinskii.

The reader of the articles is immediately struck by their scope. The first three articles cover the major developments in Russian literature (especially poetry) before Pushkin, so that it is only in the fourth article that Belinskii, having placed the poet in his literary and historical context, actually focuses on the subject himself. It is this awareness of the historical perspective that sets apart Belinskii's criticism from the efforts of his predecessors. He expresses his critical credo early in the first article: 'the task of healthy criticism consists in determining the importance of a poet both for his own age and for the future, his historical and his undoubted artistic importance' (132). Noting that 'in

Russia everything grows not by the year, but by the hour, and five years for her are almost an age,' Belinskii, writing some six years after the poet's death, finds Pushkin is no longer a contemporary but a historical figure: 'All have come to feel that Pushkin, while not losing in the present and in the future his importance as a great poet, was nevertheless also a poet of his time, of his epoch, and that that time has already passed' (132). Later Belinskii confesses that it is only with the passing years that his own views on Pushkin have crystallized to the point that he has a clear understanding of Pushkin's significance (136). This understanding is, for Belinskii, rooted in his reading of Russian literature, since 'to write about Pushkin means to write about the whole of Russian literature' (137). To sum up Belinskii's view of Russian literature, it is that it had, until Pushkin, consisted of empty imitations of foreign models: 'In the twenties of the present century Russian literature moved from imitation to originality: Pushkin appeared' (449-50). In doing so, literature had a vital social role to play: 'literature, by bringing together and making friends of people of different classes through the bonds of taste and the desire for the noble pleasures of life, turned a *class* into a *society*' (449; Belinskii's emphasis). Thus, Belinskii's sense of the historical development of Russian literature is complemented by his awareness of the sociological processes in Russia and their relationship to literature.

The sociological dimension is very important in Belinskii's criticism, and much space is devoted to the discussion of Russian society as it is reflected in *Onegin*. Belinskii's view of society – and hence his interpretation of literature – is permeated by a radical determinism. Thus he writes, discussing the *narodnost'* of *Onegin*: 'The primary reason for the particularity of a tribe or people lies in the soil and climate of the land it occupies: are there many lands on the globe which are identical as to geology and climate?' (439). Belinskii puts a finer point on his definition of the circumstances surrounding the creation of the individual in a subsequent statement: 'Man may be created by nature, but he is developed and educated by society. No circumstances of life can save or protect a man from the influence of society; there is nowhere for him to hide or escape from it' (484). This determinism has an important role to play in Belinskii's interpretation of the characters in *Onegin*. It is clear, from the bitter sketches which Belinskii draws of Russian society, that he is profoundly alienated from it. We have, in a phrase or two, the simplistic logic of revolutionary Russia: to make the people better, one must change the society.

In Belinskii's view, the problem of Russian society is the same as that of Russian literature: 'Our society, which consists of the educated classes, is a fruit of the reforms [i.e. of Peter the Great]. It remembers the day it was born because it existed officially before it existed in reality, and because, finally, this society for a long time consisted not in the spirit, but in the cut of the dress, not in enlightenment, but in privilege. It began, like our literature, with the imitation of foreign forms without any content' (485). The role of literature, for Belinskii, is to create and describe the national spirit, the *narodnost'*, which would be the content of the literature and of the society. In his discussion of the problem Belinskii (like Polevoi before him) rejects the notion that *narodnost'* – national content – consists in folkloric peasant motifs: 'The secret of the national spirit of each people consists, not in its dress and cuisine, but, so to say, in the way it understands things. In order to depict a society, one must first understand its essence, its particularity – and this can only be done by discovering factually and evaluating philosophically the sum of rules by which the society is maintained' (445). It is precisely this task which Belinskii believes Pushkin to have accomplished in *Onegin*: '*Onegin* is a depiction of Russian society at a certain point in time which is poetically true to reality' (445).

This position, which Belinskii defends in his study of *Onegin*, was to become axiomatic in much of subsequent Russian criticism, in which 'true to reality' is transformed into 'realistic.' Belinskii's approach is most defective in that it ignores the ambiguous nature of the text of *Onegin* and reads the work as a *novel* pure and simple. Thus he writes:

> The first national-artistic work was Pushkin's *Eugene Onegin*. In this determination of the young poet to represent the moral physiognomy of the most European class in Russia one cannot help but see proof that he was, and profoundly felt himself to be, a national poet. He understood that the time of the epic poem was long past, and that to depict contemporary society, in which the prose of life had so deeply penetrated the very poetry of life, he needed a novel, not an epic poem. He took this life as it was, rather than simply extracting its poetic moments; he took it with all its coldness, all its prose and vulgarity. Such boldness would be less surprising, if the novel were written in prose; but to write such a novel in verse at a time when there was not a single decent prose novel in Russian – such boldness is undoubted testimony to the genius of the poet. (443)

Belinskii's argument is exposed at its weakest here: he does not perceive the profound difference in intent and in effect between a prose novel and a 'novel in verse.' If it is true that the poet's aim was to depict the 'prose of life' and if, as Belinskii argues, prose of life equals prose in literature (in fact an empty formula: 'prose' and 'poetry' in life are figures of speech that have nothing to do with literary genres) then Pushkin would surely have written in prose. Throughout his discussion Belinskii discusses the work as a novel in which everything unfolds, and is susceptible to analysis, in the manner of a realist prose novel. In doing so he begs the question of the genre (did Pushkin choose verse simply to demonstrate his 'boldness' and hence his 'genius'? – surely not) and ascribes to the poet those goals which Belinskii would like him to have in terms of his own premises. Even if Pushkin does depict certain features of Russian life, one cannot take this to be the sole purpose of the work, to the neglect of its other features, without distorting the total effect which the work has on the reader.

The criterion which Belinskii assumes to be cardinal in Russian literature – 'faithfulness to reality' – colours the entire historical perspective in which he views literature: 'He [Pushkin] was concerned not with resembling Byron, but with being himself and being faithful to that reality which until his time had been unperceived and untouched, and which begged to be described. And it is for this reason that his *Onegin* is a highly original and national Russian work. Together with the contemporary creation of Griboedov's genius – *Woe from Wit* – Pushkin's verse novel laid a firm foundation for a new Russian poetry, a new Russian literature' (444). Belinskii's view of literature is teleological, progressive. He sees works of literature as stepping stones in a chain of development towards greater profundity, and towards a 'more national' literature. The problem with this view is that it tends to stress the ephemeral, the transient aspects of a work and ignores that which is universal, which exists, eventually, outside time (compare Pushkin's view quoted above that art does not change). Certainly, one cannot deny that there are traces of *Onegin* in subsequent Russian literature, although they are much more oblique than Belinskii would have us believe, and the work proved, ultimately, inimitable. Rather than laying the foundation for the new Russian poetry, in many ways *Onegin* proved to be the final expression of the old. Belinskii's historical and sociological approach, though well and seductively argued, does not, in the final analysis, succeed in doing justice to the work.

Most of Belinskii's analysis of *Onegin* is taken up with the study of the characters of Onegin and Tat'iana, whom the critic sees as equal in importance. Belinskii offers a psychological analysis, interpreting them as sociological portraits in a novel that is endeavouring to present an image of what is typical in Russian society. Characteristically, he refers to the characters as 'persons.' Thus, in discussing Onegin, Belinskii adopts a view which grows out of his determinism and his negative view of Russian society: 'The greater part of the public denied absolutely the existence of any heart or soul in Onegin, seeing in him a person who was cold-hearted, dry and an egoist by nature. It is impossible to have a more perverse or erroneous understanding of a person! This is not all: many honestly believed and believe that the poet himself wished to portray Onegin as a cold-hearted egoist' (455). It is Belinskii's thesis that Onegin, far from being a 'cold-hearted egoist,' is an 'involuntary egoist,' a 'suffering egoist' (459) because he does not live in 'a society which gives each of its members the possibility of working in his line of activity towards the realization of the ideal of truth and well-being' (460). According to Belinskii, it is society which is responsible for Onegin's egoism: this is his *fatum*, the lot which society has imposed on him.

The discussion of Tat'iana which takes up Article Nine – the second part of the analysis of *Onegin* – begins with an impassioned discussion of the state of women in Russia: the superficial education, the goals (to marry successfully), the arranged marriages, the fantasy life in literature. Tat'iana is, in Belinskii's view, typical of this milieu. For Belinskii, the Tat'iana of Chapters Two to Six lives in a fantasy world: 'for Tat'iana the real Onegin did not exist; she could neither understand him nor know him' (488). The Onegin whom she falls in love with is a literary creation, borrowed from her reading. It is only when she reads the books in his library in Chapter Seven that she understands him. The world of 'other interests and sufferings' revealed by these books is a revelation which 'frightened her, horrified her and obliged her to regard the passions as the destruction of life, convinced her of the necessity of submitting to reality as it is, and, if one is to live the life of the heart, then secretly, in the depth of one's heart, in the silence of withdrawal, in the gloom of a night spent in grief and sobbing' (495-6).

In attempting to account for Tat'iana's psychological development Belinskii is breaking new ground. For the most part he fleshes in the laconic strokes of Pushkin's portrait with a plausible motivation, and asks himself questions that other critics had not thought to consider. One finds it difficult, however, to agree with his analysis of the final scene between Tat'iana and Onegin. Belinskii takes at face value the reproaches which Tat'iana makes to Onegin that he loves her only because she is an object in society and 'now the desire for a scandalous fame brings him to her feet' (497). Most surely there is an intended irony in her reproaches; she senses the real passion behind Onegin's advances, a passion that dooms them to frustration, for the practised seducer knows one cannot succeed if one is sincere. Belinskii is scornful of Tat'iana's decision to remain faithful to her husband: 'Faithfulness to those relationships which constitute a profanation of feelings and feminine purity, because relationships not sanctified by love are highly immoral' (498). It is his conclusion that it is the opinion of society, the 'strict fulfilment of the external obligations' that motivates Tat'iana's rejection of Onegin's advances. Again, Pushkin's spare sketch is inscrutable. Yet one finds it difficult to believe that Tat'iana would be driven to her refusal by mere public opinion – more likely it is her rejection of that romantic belief in the happy ending. In her refusal is contained the entire logical sequence which later leads to the destruction of Anna Karenina. Although Belinskii accepts Tat'iana's refusal of Onegin, he attributes it to the fact that she is the 'typical Russian woman' who 'cannot ignore the opinion of society' (499). Rather, one would tend to see in her refusal a lack of typicality: most women would refuse for fear or yield to the moment's passion. Tat'iana, neither fearful nor impulsive, refuses out of a sense of principle, a very different matter.

If Belinskii's analysis of *Onegin* concentrated on the historico-literary aspect and treated the work almost exclusively as novel, the critic nevertheless is conscious of the artist in Pushkin. The work is, the critic insists, an *artistic* reproduction of reality. For Belinskii, the artist as artist remains, despite the 'progressive,' 'sociological' bias of his criticism, an indispensable part of the work – the expression of that 'genius' which he enthusiastically, even ecstatically, praises, but does little to investigate. Another aspect of the poet of which the critic is aware is his aristocratism. Belinskii takes considerable pains in the articles to refute the notion, expressed in a review in *Galateia*, that Pushkin is merely a writer about and for the nobility who has nothing to say about the lower classes. Belinskii's response, which strongly anticipates that of later Russian Marxist critics such as Plekhanov, is essentially to say that the upper classes offered, at that point in Russia's history, the only meaningful subject: 'Our poetry ... must find its materials almost exclusively in that class which, by its way of life and customs, is more developed and intellectually active' (437). Belinskii's defence of Pushkin's aristocratism is based on a tacit belief in the organic nature of the national spirit, which may be expressed by any class which has the necessary cultural baggage and intellectual consciousness. Belinskii's social generosity was not to be shared by all his followers, and his characterization of the poet was to be seen as accurate but damning: 'the personality of the poet which was so fully and brilliantly expressed in this poem is always so fine, so humane, but at the same time primarily artistic. Everywhere one sees in him a man who belongs heart and soul to a basic principle which is the essence of the class he depicts; in brief, everywhere one sees the Russian landowner ... He attacks everything in that class which contradicts humanity, but the principle of the class is for him an eternal truth' (499-500). To be above all an artist, to be above all a proponent of the landowning class – such credentials were not likely to render Pushkin and his work popular with a literary intelligentsia that was moving towards an infatuation with progress, class struggle, and the requirement that literature be *engagé* and progressive rather than artistic. Belinskii reconciles very disparate opposites in his analysis in which an instinctive love for literature comes together with a growing social and historical awareness.[14]

FROM BELINSKII TO PISAREV

The underlying contradiction in Belinskii's approach to Pushkin was to manifest itself, in the course of the next twenty years, in an increasingly strident polemic between two schools of critics, one of which, represented by Druzhinin, Katkov, and Grigor'ev, was to espouse the 'artist as artist' aspect of Pushkin. The other camp – Chernyshevskii, Dobroliubov, and Pisarev – proposed a 'utilitarian' concept of art which emphasized the transient, socio-critical role of the writer and was to bring Pisarev, ultimately, to attack both Pushkin and Belinskii. Paradoxically, both these groups owed much to Belinskii.

The years following the appearance of Belinskii's articles were relatively quiet as far as Pushkin studies are concerned. We may note, in passing, the appearance of A.P. Miliukov's *Outline of the History of Russian Poetry* (1847). Miliukov's sober academic study has little new to say on the subject. He stresses the influence of Byron's *Don Juan* on *Onegin*, and underlines the satirical intent ('a satire on the vacuousness of society, with all its ritual and conventions, opinions and pronouncements,' 171). After some by now commonplace praise of the character depiction, especially of Tat'iana, Miliukov comes to the conclusion that 'Pushkin is not a world poet, and is important only for his fatherland' (187).

The next significant event in the history of Pushkin studies was the publication in 1855 of a new edition of *Collected Works* with a companion volume, *Materials for a Biography of Pushkin* by P.V. Annenkov. The appearance of this new edition, and especially the wealth of biographical material given by Annenkov, prompted a number of reviews and stimulated renewed interest in Pushkin, who had in general suffered from the swing towards prose in the tastes of the Russian reading public.

In his reviews, published in *Russkii vestnik* (1856), Katkov defends the position of that camp which insisted on the primacy and independence of art: 'poetry, in its true sense, is cognitive thought directed on that which is not susceptible to abstract reasoning' (166). This quotation is taken from his first review, which is entirely devoted to questions of poetic theory. In his subsequent review, in which he discusses certain concrete works, Katkov shows his debt to Belinskii. Thus, Belinskii's assertion that *Onegin* was 'an act of consciousness for Russian society' finds its echo in Katkov: 'Before him [Pushkin] poetry was a matter of schools; after him it became a matter of life, its social consciousness' (284). Belinskii's benign view of Onegin is also reflected in Katkov, for whom Onegin is 'an empty fop, but still a nice chap, who could turn into something more useful' (303).

Concerning the form of *Onegin*, about which Belinskii had had little to say, Katkov emphasizes what he considers the lack of unity: 'Everywhere there are individual moments, depictions of individual events; nowhere is there a coherent development, for the whole is broken up into episodes, and the narrative serves only as a thread on which is strung a wonderful series of pictures, sketches, images and lyrical passages' (292). Katkov's remark shows his awareness of how far the poem is from the realistic novel that Belinskii had read it to be. There is, however, a note of critical condescension, almost annoyance. Rather than read it for what it was, critics were still inclined to impose on the piece a preconceived formal conception.

Another article inspired by the new edition and devoted to the notion of Pushkin the poet was that of A.V. Druzhinin, 'A.S. Pushkin and the latest edition of his works' (1855). Druzhinin reviews the literary life of Pushkin on the basis of Annenkov's *Materials* and attacks a number of preconceived ideas – for example, that Pushkin was 'lazy' and had written his best pieces by the time of his death and that poetry is merely a youthful activity. Rather, Druzhinin sees in the last works of Pushkin the 'embryo of something great' that would have made him an 'all-European poet.' Most important, Druzhinin attacks the notion that Pushkin's prose is weak (a feature of Belinskii's criticism), seeing in it 'an object of useful study for the most recent writers' (61). In Druzhinin's view, Pushkin offers an alternative to the contemporary trend in Russian literature: 'The poetry of Pushkin can serve as the best weapon against that satirical style to which we have been brought by the immoderate imitation of Gogol'' (60). It is in this stressing of Pushkin's poetic vision that the interest of Druzhinin's article lies. He has little to say about *Onegin* itself.

A third critic who was to discuss Pushkin (though not in the form of a review of the new edition) was Apollon Grigor'ev, who in his article 'A View of Russian Literature since Pushkin's Death' (1859) attempted to bridge the critical gap. Again, Grigor'ev owes much to Belinskii, whom he quotes extensively. He notes: 'The Pushkin problem has advanced little towards its resolution since the times of the 'Literary Reflections' [by Belinskii], – but if we do not solve this problem we cannot understand the actual situation of our literature. Some would see in Pushkin an aloof artist since they believe in some kind of aloof art, remote from life and not born of life, others would make the prophet "seize a broom" and serve their conventional theories.'[15] Grigor'ev's argument is conducted on a very general plane, and his famous observation on Pushkin the type is of little help to our present purpose: 'Pushkin is our spiritual physiognomy, realized for the first time, in outline, but fully and wholly; a physiognomy which is already clearly distinct and separate from the mass of other national, typical physiognomies ... He is our original type' (167). It is in this abstract and, to the modern reader, nebulous vein of discussion of 'national' (*narodnyi*) types and features that much of the debate of the middle decades of the nineteenth century was conducted: ''In Pushkin's great nature, which excluded nothing, neither the disturbed romantic element, nor the humour of common sense, nor passion, nor the northern contemplativeness – in this nature, which reflected everything, but reflected as a Russian soul should, – is found the justification and the reconciliation for all our present, apparently so hostilely divided sympathies' (ibid.). Both the tone and the sense of this passage foreshadow Dostoevskii's view of Pushkin as a figure who can heal the divisions in the nation and (through his Protean spirit) in humanity itself.

The debate that was provoked by the appearance of the edition of 1855 and Annenkov's *Materials* was waged, on one side, by the proponents of an independent art ('art for art's sake'). Their theories rested on the notion of the eternal importance of art – the perception of artistic beauty and the international, universal meaning of great art. This criticism, which stressed the poetic aspect of Pushkin and the irreducibility of the poetic mode, was derived, at least in part, from that Belinskii, who waxed ecstatic in praise of Pushkin's 'genius' and stressed his 'artistic' reproduction of reality. The notion that poetry did not need any external justification, that it had a unique and important artistic function, found its basis in the poetry of Pushkin in such themes as 'poetic inspiration' and 'the poet and the rabble.' Belinskii's observation on Pushkin's aristocratism (quoted above) is not without importance here, since in Russia lyric poetry had been – and in the 1850s continued to be – largely the preserve of an aristocratic élite. One important aspect of the 'aesthetic' criticism of the 1850s was the fact that it bore the seeds of a more profound interest in poetic technique (e.g., already Katkov shows such an awareness of Pushkin's transformation of language). Sooner or later critics would feel obliged to go beyond ecstatic praise of Pushkin's 'talent' and examine the specifics of his poetry.

Ranged against this 'aesthetic' criticism were those critics who developed the socio-critical aspect of Belinskii's study. Their interest was in that Pushkin who was a historical, obsolescent figure and who had occupied a certain place in the development of the national consciousness. In their view, Pushkin was of limited importance for the present day, since the society which he described was a restricted one and his satire had been superseded by Gogol''s. As we have seen, Pushkin had himself used the term 'satire' only to withdraw it subsequently. The hybrid nature of *Onegin* – novel (and hence reproduction of reality) and verse (poetry with the lyrical, inspirational, and intimate properties that entails) – is, furthermore, ambiguous. The ambiguities were, inevitably, compounded into contradictions in the criticism of Belinskii, and the result was the critical dichotomy of the 1850s.

An additional factor in the debate (and one of some importance for both parties) was the question of *narodnost'* – of Pushkin's 'Russianness.' As we have seen, this question went back, through Belinskii, as far as the Polevoi-Venevitinov polemic. As it was a question of the vitality of the national spirit and the originality of Russian literature in the face of foreign influences, this problem appealed to critics of both parties. Related to the *narodnost'* problem was the perception of 'types.' The typicality of Tat'iana and Onegin as representatives of the national spirit was to become axiomatic in Russian criticism. Onegin, for example, was assimilated to the growing gallery of 'superfluous men' – Pechorin, Rudin, Oblomov, et al. – who were perceived to be a 'national type.' The analyses of criticism were here provoked by the demands of realistic art. The 'realistic' interpretation of the Onegin / Tat'iana 'novel' became a source of inspiration for the prose novelist.

The years 1855 to 1865 saw a growing disaffection among the 'utilitarian' critics for Pushkin. As has been recently demonstrated by the Soviet critic S.S. Konkin, the attack on Pushkin and Belinskii by Pisarev in 1865 was no isolated outburst, designed to damage the 'aesthetic' critics, but rather the culmination of a process which had begun with Belinskii (Konkin 1972, 58, 61ff.). For the latter critic Pushkin's role as a poet and an artist was acceptable, even desirable. By Pisarev's time, Pushkin had become the rallying point of the aesthetic criticism and, hence, anathema. As Konkin demonstrates, Chernyshevskii, in his review articles on the 1855 edition, and Dobroliubov, writing subsequently, were both inclined to see in Pushkin a man of the past, who had made his contribution largely in the area of poetic form. Chernyshevskii writes: 'Pushkin carried out completely his great task – that of introducing into Russian literature poetry as beautiful artistic form, and having discovered poetry as form, Russian society could go further and seek a content in this form' (1855, 516).

Although he had abandoned Belinskii's historicism and organicism, so that his criticism was much cruder, Chernyshevskii still relied heavily on Belinskii in his review articles, as had Dobroliubov who, in an article entitled simply 'Aleksandr Sergeevich Pushkin' (1858a), writes: 'if we were to engage on a detailed account, we of course could say nothing new after the remarkable essays on Pushkin written by Belinskii.' Dobroliubov's view of Onegin is likewise derived from Belinskii: 'His Onegin is not simply a society fop; he is a man with great strength of soul, a man who understands the emptiness of that life to which he is called by fate, but who does not have sufficient strength of character to tear himself out of it' (300). The contradiction inherent in this formula of a character who has 'strength of soul' but not 'strength of character' are so apparent that little in the way of critical reasoning was needed for Pisarev to reject the Belinskii interpretation of Onegin as a 'nice chap' which had motivated Dobroliubov to trap himself in the formula. In another 1858 article, 'On the degree of participation of *narodnost'* in the development of Russian literature' (a review of a second edition of Miliukov's *History*), we see Dobroliubov's growing disenchantment with Onegin: 'if in Russia such talented natures as Aleko and Onegin were in the majority, and if, being so numerous, they still remained such worthless fellows as these gentlemen – Muscovites in Childe Harold's cloak – then it would be a sad look-out for

Russia' (1858b, 260). In the same article Dobroliubov concurs with Chernyshevskii's view that Pushkin had mastered only 'the *form* of *narodnost'*: its content remained inaccessible even to Pushkin' (ibid.). Pushkin, Dobroliubov maintains, had neither the inclination, the education, nor the character to go further.

Essentially, Chernyshevskii's and Dobroliubov's bromides were simply an intermediate stage in that development which led from Belinskii to Pisarev. The latter's essay on *Onegin* (published with a second part on Pushkin's lyrics under the title 'Pushkin and Belinskii,' 1865) represents the first major study of the work since Belinskii. It is also one of the most controversial statements on *Onegin* in a literature that is full of heated controversy, and is still a cause of debate and interpretation that can be read with profit and enjoyment.[16] The criticism that Pisarev makes, however, has to be read against the background of the polemic between the *engagé* progressive critics, of whom Pisarev is the most logical and radical, and the aesthetes, or 'philistines' and 'romantics' as Pisarev prefers to call them. Although Pisarev's article is a direct refutation of Belinskii's interpretation, he stresses his appreciation of Belinskii: 'While we diverge from Belinskii in our evaluation of certain facts, finding him overly credulous and too easily impressed, we still come much closer to his basic convictions than do our adversaries' (1865, 364). As we have seen, this ambivalent attitude is the consequence of the ambiguities in Belinskii's own criticism.

The positions from which Pisarev attacks *Onegin* are typical of the 'civic' strain of criticism. Pisarev had seen, in Turgenev's *Fathers and Sons* and *Rudin*, and before that in Griboedov's play *Woe from Wit*, what he interpreted as an *engagé*, realist art. Thus he seeks to find in *Onegin* 'answers to those questions which are posed by real life' (306). Having found those answers lacking, his conclusion is inevitable (and again reflects the expectations of the critic):

> the 'favourite child' of Pushkin's muse must have acted on its readers as a sedative, thanks to which a person forgot that which he should have constantly remembered, and reconciled with that against which he should have struggled untiringly. The whole of *Eugene Onegin* is nothing but a bright and shining apotheosis of the most dismal and ridiculous status quo. All the pictures in this novel are drawn in such bright colours, all the filth of real life is so carefully moved to one side, the massive absurdities of our social mores are described in such a majestic manner, minute peccadilloes are mocked with such

> unperturbed good humour, the poet himself leads such a
> merry life and breathes so easily, that the impressionable reader
> must inevitably imagine himself to be the fortunate denizen
> of some Arcadia, in which tomorrow must inevitably bring
> a golden age. (357)

The conclusions that Pisarev sarcastically draws suggest clearly his demand for a 'progressive' literature, didactic, moralistic, and, above all, critical of society's defects.

The attack that Pisarev makes on *Onegin* is concentrated on the depiction of Onegin and Tat'iana. At the outset of the discussion of Onegin, Pisarev quotes Belinskii's characterization: 'Onegin is a nice chap, and at the same time he is different. He will never be a genius, and has no pretensions to greatness, but inactivity and the emptiness of life are suffocating him' (306). Pisarev's discussion is directed at discrediting this view, which he assumes Pushkin shares, and demonstrating that Onegin, far from being admirable, is in fact a despicable egoist. In a reductio ad absurdum of Belinskii's determinism, Pisarev sarcastically attributes Onegin's spleen to overindulging in rich food and wine: 'This boredom is nothing but the physiological consequence of a very dissolute life' (311). Money and seduction of other men's wives are shown to be the other two mainsprings of Onegin's self-indulgent and wanton existence. Pisarev attacks what he sees as the fatalism in Onegin (the fatalism that becomes Belinskii's determinism – cf. the discussion of *fatum* above): 'To unload in this fashion all the guilt on the fateful laws of nature is, of course, very convenient and even flattering for those people who have not become accustomed and do not know how to reason and who, as a result of this delegation of responsibility, can with no further ado promote themselves from the ranks of layabouts to exalted natures' (315).

Pisarev's impatience with Onegin's immorality and lack of will is closely linked to his espousal of a different 'type' of hero. Thus, Pisarev believes Pushkin lets Onegin off lightly when the latter kills Lenskii in the duel: 'he [Pushkin] should have ridiculed, denigrated, and stamped into the ground without the slightest sympathy that base cowardice which obliges an intelligent man to play the role of a dangerous idiot in order not to be subjected to the timid and oblique gibes of real idiots worthy of total contempt' (329). Pisarev's ideal hero, by contrast, would have been oblivious to the opinion of society, would have taken a moral stand, and would have been actively engaged in useful pursuits: 'of course, Onegin's intellectual capabilities are very mediocre and completely spoiled by inactivity' (532). In his espousal of such a hero – and in consequent attacks on Onegin – Pisarev imposes on the text the criteria of the realist novel, and in assuming that it is Pushkin's goal to hold up Onegin as a tragic figure he ignores the irony with which Pushkin treats his hero. It is true that *Onegin* has important defects and contradictions if treated as a psychological novel. The question is – should the critic treat it as such? It is an error which goes back to Belinskii.

Pisarev's sarcasm in the criticism of Onegin is equalled by the contempt with which he treats Tat'iana: 'Belinskii places Tat'iana on a pedestal and ascribes to her high qualities to which she has no claim and with which Pushkin, despite his superficial and childish view of life in general and womankind in particular, would not and could not endow the favourite creation of his imagination' (351). For Pisarev, the fact that Tat'iana falls in love with a man after seeing him once (and not talking to him) and the fact that she acquiesces in the arranged marriage make her ineligible for the admiration she receives. He is also critical of her rejection of the man she loves, although Pisarev is the first critic to visualize the consequences of an acceptance: 'If this woman had thrown herself at Onegin and said to him: "I am yours for my whole life but, whatever the cost, take me away from my husband because I will not and cannot act a low farce with him" – then Onegin's protestations of love would have cooled very sharply in a minute' (351). If she had eloped with Onegin, the consequences would have been dire: 'The business would have finished with her running away from him, having learned to despise him to the bottom of her heart; and, of course, the poor, humiliated woman would have had to die in the most terrible poverty, or be dragged against her will into the most pitiful debauchery' (351).

Pisarev's approach to the analysis of *Onegin* is to present a sarcastic, depoeticized retelling of the events and characters from the point of view of the psychological novel. An important device is the invocation of a naive, gullible reader whose acceptance of the (to Pisarev) ridiculous assumptions in the text is ascribed to the seductive qualities of the poetry. In the space of forty years a poem which, when it was written, challenged the tastes and prejudices of the reader had become a mainstay of the conservative canon to be challenged in its turn by the new consciousness. In some ways we may see Pisarev's essay as performing an analogous function to the original text. It was Pisarev's function to educate the Russian reading public, to raise its consciousness. For this, as I have suggested, he imposes (in a deliberately

tendentious and perverse way) the criteria of the realistic novel on
Onegin. May we then assume that Pisarev is unaware of other approaches? Interestingly, there is a hint of another view in a remark
contained in the conclusion of the article in which, discussing Belinskii's paeans in praise of *Onegin*, he describes that work as 'an old
temple in which there is much food for the imagination and in which
there is no food for the mind' (363). Although for Pisarev 'the mind' is
positive and 'imagination' is pejorative, in another context his reference
to 'imagination' might prove a useful starting point for the appreciation
of the poetic qualities of the novel. In any case, his essay was an
important event in the history of the criticism of *Onegin* in Russia
and a challenge to the reader lulled by Belinskii's enthusiasm.

THE PUSHKIN MYTH 1880-99

The Pisarev article was to place a vast obstacle in the path of further
evaluation of *Onegin* by leftist or 'progressive' critics. Pisarev's denial
of the importance or relevance of *Onegin* for Russian society was to
reverberate until well into the Soviet period with greater or lesser
intensity, and *Onegin* and Pushkin became the property more of the
'aesthetic' trend in criticism in the last third of the nineteenth century.
It was to the articles by Grigor'ev and Katkov that Strakhov turned in
a series of articles on Pushkin (1866-77), later republished in book form
under the title *Notes on Pushkin*. Strakhov picks up where Katkov's
study of Pushkin's relationship to language left off. He examines such
questions as parody, imitation, and Pushkin's lack of innovation. Although he has little to say specifically about *Onegin*, Strakhov's *Notes*
are a stimulating change of focus and attention and foreshadow later
work on questions of poetics.

The year 1880 saw the first of the great Pushkin *prazdniki* with the
unveiling of the Pushkin statue in Moscow, accompanied by three days
of religious celebrations, performances, and speeches. Strakhov has left
us an account of the events of those three days, which were charged
with emotion and excitement and assumed the proportions of a national event (Strakhov 1888). Intellectually, Russia was divided into
several camps. There were the Slavophiles, the Westernizers, and a
number of people who did not fit easily into either group. With the
notable exception of Count L.N. Tolstoi, the Great Men of Russian
culture were present. In the emotional atmosphere the speech-making
assumed the importance of a competition, ultimately, between two
men, Turgenev and Dostoevskii. Turgenev, who spoke first, somewhat

disappointed his audience. His speech essentially continues the line of Belinskii's historical criticism. Thus he emphasizes the role of Pushkin as the 'first Russian poet-artist' who had the double task of 'establishing the language and creating the literature' (Turgenev 1880, 71). In response to the rhetorical question whether he was a 'national poet in the sense of universal' like Shakespeare, Goethe, and Homer, Turgenev replied: 'This is a monument to our teacher!' The carefully drawn historical perspective and the equally carefully calibrated discriminations of Turgenev's speech were too cerebral and sober for the audience and the occasion. They did not want to hear that 'only recently has the return to his poetry become noticeable' or that 'who knows, perhaps a new, as yet unknown chosen one will appear who will outdo his teacher and will fully earn the title of national-universal poet which we do not feel able to give Pushkin – though we do not dare deprive him of it' (75).

It was on the next day, in the speech of Dostoevskii, that the celebrations reached the emotional climax the audience had been seeking. This speech proved an important event in the interpretation of *Onegin* in Russia, since the first two points which were made involved the work. Firstly, Dostoevskii saw in Onegin and in Aleko, the hero of 'Tsygany' ('The Gypsies'), 'that traditional Russian wanderer so divorced from the people, whose appearance in our society was so historically necessary' (1880, 511). Dostoevskii's depiction of Onegin the 'dreamer,' 'wanderer,' 'terrestrial sufferer' owes more than a little to Belinskii. Onegin was, to Dostoevskii, 'our negative type, a restless and unreconciled man who believes neither in his native soil nor in its native strength, ... who ultimately denies Russia and himself, who does not wish to have to do with others and sincerely suffers' (500). With this 'negative type,' Dostoevskii contrasts the 'positive type' of Tat'iana, 'the type of positive beauty, the apotheosis of Russian womanhood' (515). The sentimental scheme which Dostoevskii imposes on *Onegin* reaches its apogee in his interpretation of Tat'iana's rejection of Onegin. For this it is necessary for him to see in Prince N 'simply an honest old man, the husband of a young wife in whose love he believes blindly, although his heart does not know her at all, loves her, is proud of her, is happy with her and at peace' (518). Typically, Dostoevskii sentimentalizes Tat'iana's relationship with her husband and, by making her husband a doting old man, drains it of any sexual content: 'No, this is what her pure Russian soul decides: "So what if I alone am deprived of happiness, if my unhappiness is immeasurably greater than the unhappiness of this old man, if, finally no one, not

even this old man, will ever learn of my sacrifice and appreciate it, –
I will not be happy through the destruction of another" ' (518). In these
lines the transformation of *Onegin* into a Dostoevskii novel is complete.

Dostoevskii's view of Tat'iana stresses in her the *narodnyi* element:
'He [Onegin] has no soil, he is a blade of grass, blown by the wind. She
is not so at all: even in her desperation, even in her suffering consciousness that her life has been ruined, she still has something firm
and unshaken on which her soul rests. This is her memories of childhood, memories of her place of birth, the rural backwoods in which
her humble, pure life began, and "the cross and shadow of the branches
above the grave of her poor nanny" ' (519). It is in this interpretation
of *Onegin* that the cliché becomes dominant and the reality is lost in
a scheme of 'types' that serve an ideological programme. *Onegin* had
become an icon, to be painted and repainted in versions ever more
remote from the original and darkened by the votive lamps of the
reverent. To a considerable extent we have to live with the consequences of Dostoevskii's icon-painting.

Turgenev's reluctance to give Pushkin the title of national or world
poet and his careful eschewal of hyperbole were not shared by Dostoevskii, who stressed (following Grigor'ev) what he saw as Pushkin's
'ability to respond to all the world and transpose himself almost completely into the genius of other nations' (501). This ability Dostoevskii,
incredibly, sees as a profoundly Russian trait, and he develops it into
a messianic pan-Russian philosophy: 'To become a true Russian, to
become totally Russian perhaps means only (ultimately, underline this)
to become the brother of all men – a pan-man, if you like.' In such a
messianic vision Dostoevskii tries to unite both the Slavophile and
Westernizing tendencies in a new synthesis. Pushkin, Dostoevskii suggests, took this vision with him to the grave; 'now without him we
are divining this great secret' (527). As I have suggested, the Dostoevskii
speech tells us more about its deliverer than its victim. Nevertheless,
it was an uproarious success and continued to influence Russian thought
on the subject long after. It signalled a new epoch in the history of
Pushkin criticism in Russia – an epoch of myth and misunderstanding.

The year 1887 – the fiftieth anniversary of the poet's death – followed
too closely on the heels of the 1880 celebrations to produce much
criticism of lasting worth. The historian V.O. Kliuchevskii delivered
a speech, subsequently published in 1887 under the title 'Eugene Onegin and His Forebears,' in which he traced the 'types' of the generations
(from Peter onwards) preceding Onegin. His essay, written from the
point of view of the historian, has little to say about the novel except

for reminiscences about its personal significance for Kliuchevskii and those of his generation who grew up immediately after Pushkin's death.

Despite the rather disappointing harvest of 1887 in terms of criticism, it was to prove a significant date in another respect: now anyone could print Pushkin's works, and cheap mass editions began to appear. The growth of interest thus engendered gave rise to a great increase in publications on Pushkin. Many of these, to be sure, were ephemera – textbooks for high schools, public lectures, articles in newspapers – but some were of more lasting significance – e.g., the articles which began to appear in scholarly journals on different aspects of Pushkin's life and works. In addition, in 1899 the nation celebrated the centenary of Pushkin's birth with hundreds of celebrations, great and small, throughout Russia. The anniversary was the cause for a huge quantity of publication. Again, much of this was of a highly ephemeral character, such as speeches given at high schools and poems composed by schoolboys for the occasion, but there were, in the 1890s, a number of publications that merit attention.

Some of the critics maintained what must be seen as a normative approach to *Onegin*, which had coalesced out of the writings of Dostoevskii, Grigor'ev, and, above all, Belinskii. The basic positions were clear: the work is interpreted as a realistic novel (seen as the 'progenitor' – *rodonachal'nik* – of the chain of novels in Russian realism – Lermontov, Goncharov, Turgenev, Tolstoi – which was by now complete); the characters are seen as 'types'; Tat'iana is interpreted as the sublime incarnation of Russian womanhood, with her roots in the Russian folk; Onegin is the first of the great 'superfluous men' of the novel tradition; the poetry comes in only for some vague, but generally ecstatic, praise. The critic A.I. Nezelenov, in an essay on *Onegin* published in 1890, offers only very minor variations on these themes (Nezelenov 1890). Thus, he imposes the criteria of psychological realism on the work to the extent of perceiving 'errors.' For example, he makes a great fuss over the fact that Pushkin, in Chapter One, does not tell us the effect which Onegin's reading had on him, or which books he read, an 'error' which Nezelenov attributes to the fact that Pushkin wrote the chapter in 1823 when his talent was not fully developed. Nezelenov's rather pompous, condescending tone and line of criticism continue when he finds another 'error' in the fact that Pushkin had 'left out' the 'period of romanticism' in describing the development of Onegin's character. Nezelenov's criticisms have nothing to do with Pushkin's intentions or procedures, but do illustrate how firmly the 'realistic novel' interpretation had established itself in the Russian critical consciousness.

The year 1897 saw the appearance of a book which, though short enough to be little more than a long essay, must be regarded by the impartial observer as an important event in the intellectual assimilation of Pushkin: D. Merezhkovskii's *Eternal Companions (Pushkin)*. Merezhkovskii, who is anathema to Soviet critics, develops an interpretation of Pushkin which, with its stress on the poet's anti-democratism and his cult of Peter the 'superman,' is a challenge to the basic assumptions of realist criticism. It is Merezhkovskii's thesis that Pushkin – almost alone in Russian literature – was able to express and hold in creative tension the two elements of great art (which had been realized in the art of the Renaissance): the superhuman and heroic, and, opposed to it, the forgiveness of one's enemies, charity.

Merezhkovskii's interpretation of the meaning of Pushkin's oeuvre is based upon the integrated reading of the works which (although other critics had made some comparisons, e.g. of Onegin and Aleko) are seen for the first time as repeated attempts to solve an aesthetic problem in artistic terms. Where Belinskii sees Pushkin mainly in a social and historical context, Merezhkovskii places him in the aesthetic context of world literature, something which had been made possible by the achievements of such writers as Gogol', Turgenev, Dostoevskii, and Tolstoi, but which for Belinskii, of course, was only a dream. It was this perspective that permitted Merezhkovskii to compare Pushkin to such giants as Dante, Shakespeare, and Goethe, which Belinskii had declined to do. By deepening the intellectual understanding of the meaning of Pushkin's art, Merezhkovskii takes the traditional statements on Pushkin and makes them precise. Thus, he sets out the importance of *Onegin* for subsequent Russian writers: 'In *Eugene Onegin* Pushkin described the horizon of Russian literature, and all subsequent writers had to move and develop within this horizon' (1897, 43). In this sense, we must see Pushkin as the initiator. Here the Russian writer is passive: Pushkin has created the world in which he must function. However, as Merezhkovskii also points out, that part of the Russian writer which is consciously acting in the Pushkin tradition betrays it: 'The tragedy of Russian literature lies in the fact that, although it with every step moves further away from Pushkin, it nevertheless considers itself the true guardian of Pushkin's legacy' (79). Merezhkovskii might have mentioned here the role of the critic as distorter.

The sharpness of focus with which Merezhkovskii redefines issues applies to *Onegin* as well. The critic places the novel in verse in the same context as 'The Gypsies' and 'The Prisoner of the Caucasus,' seeing in the Tat'iana/Onegin relationship an extension of the problem of the simple, innocent native and his relationship to the 'contemporary man' who is 'capable of neither love, friendship, contemplation nor action' (38). Thus, Merezhkovskii takes the by now accepted interpretation of Tat'iana as the simple country girl with her origins in the folk, but, again, deepens and sharpens the focus by placing the notion in a broader intellectual context. The figure of Onegin is one that has constantly exercised critics. It is, perhaps, best explained by placing it, as Merezhkovskii does, against the broader background of other similar works by Pushkin. Merezhkovskii offers a criticism of the result: 'The deficiency of the poem lies in the fact that the author does not fully separate the hero from himself, and therefore does not relate totally objectively to him' (36). It is difficult to agree with the critic here, although his comment is understandable when one considers the brevity of his analysis – he does not, for example, discuss the character of the poet/narrator at all.

If the problem of Onegin's character is a continual concern in Russian criticism, then the other question which may be considered an 'index' of the critic's orientation is his interpretation of the dénouement. Does Onegin love Tat'iana? Does she love him? How are we to interpret her refusal of his approaches? Merezhkovskii comes closer than most critics to an understanding of the irony and fittingness of the final scene: 'Only now does Onegin understand that pride which obliged him to despise a divine gift – simple love – and reject Tat'iana's heart with the same cruelty with which he stained his hands with Lenskii's blood. ... All the horror of the punishment strikes him when he realizes that Tat'iana loves him as before, but that this love is as sterile and dead as his own' (41). In his understanding of the symmetrical retribution which is meted out, the studied elegance of the finale, and the attribution of a poetic motivation to Tat'iana's rejection – in all of this Merezhkovskii reaches out beyond a psychological/realist interpretation of the novel.

It is impossible to agree fully with Merezhkovskii's generalized and schematic view of Pushkin's oeuvre. He cannot, and does not, go into the kind of detail necessary to do justice to the text. His essay must be seen as a sharp corrective, the critic distancing himself from a current of thought which he finds odious. But by emphasizing the poet's disdain of the 'rabble,' and his fascination with the strong type, the self-willed egoist, as expressed in variation after variation in work after work, Merezhkovskii made an important (though unfortunately often reviled and unheeded) contribution to the understanding of Pushkin. Most important, Merezhkovskii realized that Pushkin was a great thinker (contrary the common image of him as a frivolous poet incapable of philosophical depth), that he was an artist who sought aesthetic solutions to aesthetic problems, and that he must be read and evaluated in those terms.

Merezhkovskii's revision of the Belinskian interpretation of *Onegin* was, at least in part, echoed by the critic K.F. Golovin (Orlovskii) who, in his book *The Russian Novel and Russian Society* (1897), attacks Belinskii's desire to 'paint Onegin in liberal colours' (62). Concerning the interpretation of the finale, Golovin, too, is prepared to understand rather than judge Tat'iana's actions: 'She did not, however, cease to love him, but it was no longer the former ecstatic obeisance to an idol, but a bitter love to which was added not a little disappointment' (ibid.). Golovin also shares Merezhkovskii's view of the cult of the strong man in Russian literature: 'From Pushkin until the present day Russian literature has been searching for a strong man, ready to admire his egoism' (63). Onegin falls short of this ideal in that his 'excellence is fruitless.'

The jubilee of 1899 was, as I have said, marked by a great volume of Pushkin studies, mostly of a general character – Pushkin's meaning for Russian literature, Pushkin in Russian criticism, and so on. The atmosphere of civic pride and formal speechifying at various celebrations (e.g., at the universities) was hardly conducive to the emotional distance necessary for good criticism. The most interesting aspect of the jubilee was the position of the symbolists who, as poets and critics, tried to coopt Pushkin in an issue of the *World of Art* magazine. This event, and the polemical attack by V.L. Solov'ev that ensued, are important in the history of the literary climate of the time, but did not really contribute anything to the study of *Onegin*.[17]

The one essay of the jubilee that is worth noting is that by V.V. Sipovskii entitled 'Onegin, Lenskii and Tat'iana' (1899b). In an earlier essay 'Pushkin, Byron and Chateaubriand' (1899a), Sipovskii had attacked the commonly held view that Pushkin was 'influenced' by Byron, especially in the long poems written in exile. Sipovskii demonstrated that Chateaubriand was an at least equally important inspiration for those poems. The methodology is pushed further in the study of *Onegin*, where Sipovskii demonstrates that the character of Tat'iana is largely a pastiche of a number of characters in French and English literature – e.g., Pamela and Delphine – and that certain passages in her letter make much better sense if one realizes that they are taken from Western sources. The effect of the argument is to challenge the 'realistic novel' model still further and place a new stress in the study of *Onegin* on the literary plane. Sipovskii's argument discredited likewise the notion of Tat'iana's *narodnost'*: 'What is Russian about her, about this "ideal Russian woman"? Only that she was superstitious, loved Russian folktales, Russian nature, and the Russian troyka!' (326).

Sipovskii analyses the characters of Onegin and Lenskii in a similar manner. In Onegin he sees, in addition to the influence of Chateaubriand's René, Richardson's Lovelace and Grandison, and Byron's Childe Harold, and examines the role of Pushkin's friend A.N. Raevskii, the supposed original of Pushkin's poem 'The Demon,' as possible 'model.' Sipovskii's study proved important in that it demonstrated the necessity of literary scholarship as well as critical acumen for the interpretation of *Onegin*, which in his essay ceases to be a realist sociopsychological novel and becomes rather a palimpsest of literary allusions and echoes, in which the characters are as much parodies as types, and in which the details of the composition and motivation (e.g., Tat'iana's love for Onegin) cannot be interpreted simply as events in a narrative.

BEFORE OCTOBER

The jubilee celebrations of 1899 bore fruit in a number of ways. The scope and the fervour of the celebrations established (if there had been any doubt) the importance of Pushkin in Russian literature and the Russian consciousness. The years that led up to the Revolution were marked by a number of important developments. Of these, the most significant was the establishment of 'Pushkin studies' on an academic and scientific basis. The Imperial Academy of Sciences began the process of publishing an authoritative edition of Pushkin's works, and of concentrating manuscript and other material into one archive (to become, later, the 'Pushkin House'). A scholarly journal, *Pushkin and His Contemporaries*, was started to publish the mass of biographical, textual, and documentary material as it came to light, and the first university seminars devoted to Pushkin took place (under S.A. Vengerov) in Petersburg, preparing a generation of Pushkin scholars whose activity lasted into the 1950s.

The new scholarly impetus of the first decades of the twentieth century brought new insights to the study of *Onegin*. Many of these were minor – N.O. Lerner, in a series of articles, suggested, for example, new (literary) sources for *Onegin*, as well as possible models for Tat'iana among Pushkin's acquaintance.[18] But the publication in 1910 by P.O. Morozov of deciphered material which he attributed to a tenth chapter of *Onegin* was to have long-lasting implications. It suggested the existence of an entire clandestine chapter, and even that the canonical text of *Onegin* was only a modified version of a suppressed text or plan. The debate begun by the publication of Morozov's research will perhaps never be resolved. It had the effect, however, of politicizing the interpretation of *Onegin*. In particular, Morozov's article, and the inferences which could be drawn from it, were to play an important role in the formation of the Soviet view of the work.

Another development which must be mentioned here, and which was to prove of importance in the critical activity of the period during and shortly after the Revolution, was the interest shown by symbolist poets, especially Briusov and Belyi, in Pushkin's poetics.[19] Their studies (which may be traced back to Strakhov and Katkov) were the forerunners of Russian formalist criticism. Although their contribution was of a general kind, and little work was done specifically on *Onegin*, the growing interest in poetics must nevertheless be rated a significant factor in the pre-revolutionary scene, which was becoming polarized into 'aesthetic' and 'poetic' criticism on the one hand and 'realist' and sociological criticism on the other.

That there was an increasingly complicated critical situation in Russia in the period leading up to the revolution is true. One cannot speak, however, of a 'crisis,' as does the Soviet critic B.S. Meilakh.[20] On the contrary, the study of Pushkin was acquiring a new sophistication, and the perspective of time (marked by the jubilee) and new documentation placed new tasks before the critics. The most successful study of the period in question (and one which Meilakh – revealingly, perhaps – passes over in silence), was the article *'Eugene Onegin'* by Ivanov-Razumnik, which appeared in a special multivolume collection of texts and essays edited by Vengerov (Ivanov-Razumnik 1909).

Ivanov-Razumnik's essay is sober and thoughtful in tone, for the most part without the hyperbolic praise and panegyric outbursts that some critics felt necessary. Ivanov-Razumnik tries to appreciate *Onegin* on its own terms, without imposing external criteria. His arguments are strengthened by a good grasp of the detail, not only of the work itself, but also of Pushkin's poetry as a whole. In addition, Ivanov-Razumnik had studied the preceding critics on the subject, and attempts to synthesize the views of a considerable number of them.

The basic position of Ivanov-Razumnik may be characterized as 'neo-Belinskian.' A considerable part of the essay is devoted to sociological aspects of *Onegin* – the history and subsequent development of the Onegin and Tat'iana 'types' in Russian society. This sociological approach, inspired by Belinskii and Kliuchevskii, is taken about as far as

it can go by Ivanov-Razumnik. Thus, in the study of Onegin he distinguishes three social groups among the young men of that generation:
the affected (those who adapted to the régime), the disaffected (who
became the Decembrists), and those in between – disaffected, but un-
fired by the revolutionary ideals of youth. To this third group, Ivanov-
Razumnik suggests, belongs Onegin. In addition he takes the Tat'iana
'type' and sketches in an 'ancestry' for her (i.e., the 'types' of preceding
generations out of which she grew) just as Kliuchevskii had done for
Onegin. The problem with these arguments is that they are based upon
the concept of the 'type,' which is unquantifiable and must ultimately
be taken on trust. Ivanov-Razumnik is himself uneasy with the term.
Following Kliuchevskii he speaks of Onegin as a 'typical exception' –
'he is too typical to be an exception and sufficiently exceptional to be
a type' (213). This paradoxical remark is illustrative of the problems
that the sociological approach can get into. Another paradox results
from Ivanov-Razumnik's insistence that Onegin and Tat'iana, although
types, are also individuals. The approach begs a number of questions
about the work under study: did Pushkin intend to create 'types'? Was
a true sociological portrait of Russian society his goal or even the effect?
Does not the sociological interpretation contradict the image of Onegin
as literary parody of Western romantic heroes sketched by Sipovskii?

Whatever were the artist's intentions, it is certain that subsequent
Russian writers found in the work those 'types' and situations which
they sought, and Ivanov-Razumnik makes hay in his observations on
the impact of Onegin the 'superfluous man' (and even Tat'iana the
'superfluous woman') on subsequent writers. As he notes, the 'contrast
between the weak man and the strong woman' becomes a standard
feature of the Russian novel, which spawns 'Onegins' and 'Tat'ianas'
and the disease of 'oneginism' (*oneginstvo* – cf. Dobroliubov's similar
term for the Russian social disease of *oblomovshchina*) (217). Ultimately, the decision whether to accept Ivanov-Razumnik's line of argument depends on whether one believes that it is the function of art
to provide a sociological portrait of a society (leaving aside the question
of the accuracy of such a portrait). That this was the goal of certain
later realist prose writers in Russian is clear. But it is important, for
Ivanov-Razumnik's argument to succeed, that Pushkin be attached to
this group. Hence, he emphatically describes him as a 'great realist'
and equally emphatically declares: 'He was never a romantic; his Byronic pseudo-romanticism was therefore only a transitory and narrow
phenomenon even in this work of the years 1820-24' (216-17).

The sociological part of Ivanov-Razumnik's essay is the 'missing link' between nineteenth-century 'civic' criticism and the position which Soviet criticism was to adopt in the middle 1930s. The key words were *rodonachal'nik* (progenitor: Pushkin as the progenitor of Russian literature, Onegin as the progenitor of the superfluous men); 'realism' (Pushkin assimilated to the realist school, denial of romanticism as a negative, alien phenomenon); 'overcoming' (Pushkin 'overcame' [*preodolel*] the ideological content of Onegin the sceptic – in Soviet criticism this is reduced to the 'overcoming' of romanticism).

The insistence on the social role of the artist (and of all members of society) is an essential feature of Russian culture and, as such, runs counter to the desire of the individual artist for self-expression and artistic freedom. Ivanov-Razumnik is aware of this contradiction, which frequently is expressed in Russian criticism by ecstatic praise of the artist's 'genius' – a belated genuflection towards the importance of artistic individuality after social relevance has been proven – and he treads a fine line. Thus, in his essay he turns, after treating the historical and sociological aspects of the work, to questions of Pushkin's world-view, or 'world sense' as Ivanov-Razumnik modifies the term. This is the most interesting and original section of the essay. Here the critic links the writing of *Onegin* with the philosophical development of the poet. He interprets Lenskii as the incarnation of the naive optimism for humanity and the romantic longings of the Decembrist poets (in particular, Vil'gel'm Kiukhel'beker), and Onegin as a sceptical denier and a nihilist – representative of a phase which Pushkin went through during his exile in the south and which was expressed in the poem 'The Demon.' Ivanov-Razumnik describes the result of this searching for a philosophical view: 'the Demon had fulfilled its role – with the "cold poison" of his scepticism he had killed the "romanticism" of Pushkin-Lenskii; there is nothing of value, he had whispered – everything in life is equally senseless, everything is equally unnecessary, absurd, aimless.' The assimilation of this view leads, in *Onegin*, to a new attitude in the poet: 'Pushkin opposed to the denial of the objective value of life a recognition of its great subjective value – to the denial of the objective sense of life he opposed the recognition of its great subjective sense' (232). It is here that Ivanov-Razumnik sees the meaning of *Onegin*: 'In Pushkin victory went to the elemental, bright, sunny, unconscious acceptance of life, the fullness of existence. And at this height nothing is fearful – neither sufferings, nor evil, nor death itself' (233).

The perception of this meaning in *Onegin* – a meaning which is aesthetic and is achieved through poetic means – is Ivanov-Razumnik's contribution to the study of *Onegin*. He asked himself a question which had not been asked before by other critics, and his answer goes a long way towards the truth. He does not, in my opinion, sufficiently consider that tone of melancholy which suffuses the work (especially the last two chapters), nor does he give sufficient weight to the importance of art as mode of existence for Pushkin. What must be reckoned important is that here, in this discussion, he treats the work intrinsically, as opposed to the extrinsic discussion that informs and vitiates the major part of his essay. There are many other aspects of the work which Ivanov-Razumnik neglects totally – questions of poetics, tone, point of view, structure. What is more striking is that the extrinsic, 'Belinskian' elements and the intrinsic, original discussion are at odds with each other. As we have seen, this is a dichotomy which may be traced back to Belinskii himself.

Another critic whom one might also describe as 'neo-Belinskian' – although much less successful than Ivanov-Razumnik – was N.A. Kotliarevskii, who devotes a chapter (326-58) of his book *Literary Trends of the Alexandrian Period* (1907) to *Onegin*. In general, Kotliarevskii hews to the established line of 'types' and realism. He explains the choice of types as an 'opposition of a "romantic" nature to two sentimental ones' (i.e. Onegin versus Lenskii and Tat'iana); as well as symbols, however, Kotliarevskii insists that the characters are 'people and people of that time.' Interestingly, Kotliarevskii has some doubts about the genre of *Onegin* (which had generally been treated, since Belinskii, as a novel): 'Indeed, in essence, is it a novel? Does there not lie beneath this novel the purest lyrical confession?' (212). Further on, Kotliarevskii uses the phrase 'a diary in verse' to describe *Onegin*; the term is echoed later by the Italian critic Ettore Lo Gatto. Another little-discussed question that Kotliarevskii touches upon is the completeness of the work. In most critics the question is ignored and one is left with the impression that they did indeed consider it finished. Kotliarevskii insists on the opposite view: 'as we know, he broke off his work in the Eighth Chapter and never returned to it' (210).

One of the important establishment critics of the period was D.N. Ovsianiko-Kulikovskii. The chapter (331-76) on *Onegin* in his book *A History of the Russian Intelligentsia* (1906) covers ground already well tilled – the social basis of the Onegin 'type.' Like Belinskii, Ovsianiko-Kulikovskii tries to explain why Onegin was 'superfluous' and a failure. He suggests – with a stern moralistic tone – Onegin's 'bad psychological organization' and his 'alienation of personality from the environment' as the reasons. They appear to be little more than Belinskii's determinism.

Certainly, the discussion here has nothing to do with *Onegin* as literature and is totally extrinsic.

In contrast, another analysis of *Onegin* by the same critic in his monograph *Pushkin* (1909) is of much greater interest (85-112). Ovsianiko-Kulikovskii analyses the text of the work in terms of the presence of 'subjective' and 'objective' lyrics. By 'subjective' lyrics he means the lyrical presence of the author in the novel as manifested in the tone of the narrative and the lyrical digressions: 'True, he does not introduce himself onto the stage, but he frequently speaks about himself and, so to speak, is present in the novel, if not in the form of a dramatis persona, then as author' (85). Echoing Kotliarevskii, Ovsianiko-Kulikovskii sees the work to a significant degree as 'a poet's confession.' The division into objective and subjective is important because it hints, almost for the first time, at the complex structure of the text and the importance of the figure of the author. The critic gets into difficulties, however, when he treats other sections of the text as 'objective lyrics' – such a term might stretch to cover Tat'iana's dream, but it is totally misplaced when used to describe the specimens of Lenskii's poetry inserted into the text.

If one had to characterize the period leading up to the Revolution in one sentence, then one would say that the writing on *Onegin* was assuming an increasingly scholarly character. The critical interpretation established by nineteenth-century critics was so well entrenched that it needed a considerable effort of will to break out of it. Nevertheless, the critics whom we have discussed did offer certain new insights. In particular, the questions of poetics touched upon by Ovsianiko-Kulikovskii chimed in with a growing emphasis on the study of the poetic text (as opposed to the Belinskian emphasis on sociology and history) that was manifesting itself in Russian literary studies overall.

AFTER OCTOBER

The revolution of October 1917 brought to a head the changes that had been underway in literary criticism. A new society with a new ideology presupposed – or so many thought – a new approach to literature. The history of Soviet literary criticism in the first fifteen years is the history of the struggle of competing schools and approaches: formalism, Marxism, Freudianism, sociologism. It is a feature of Russian culture that it abhors disunity. Present-day Soviet scholars therefore tend to look back on the period negatively as a chaotic interregnum that took place before Soviet criticism was able to develop a single, unified line. Although it is true that the period did not produce any large-scale works of Pushkin scholarship, it did give birth to some of the most stimulating and thoughtful work that has been written to date, with the emphasis on criticism and poetics rather than on formal academic study.

The revolution had the initial effect of calling into question the usefulness and relevance of Pushkin for the modern, revolutionary period. The problem was posed by Boris Eikhenbaum in his article 'Problems of Pushkin's Poetics' (1921): 'Everyone is troubled by the question – after all that we have gone through in life and in art, is Pushkin alive? And if so, what has he become for us?' (11). Eikhenbaum's remarks were prompted by the Futurists' demand to throw Pushkin 'off the steamship of the modern age.' For the extreme avant-garde, Pushkin's art was the effete product of an exploiting class. But even those who were prepared to recognize and study Pushkin felt dissatisfaction with Pushkin criticism as it existed. Thus, Eikhenbaum continues: 'Up to now Pushkin was too close to us, and we perceived him badly. We talked about him in a dead, schoolboy language, repeating a thousand times over Belinskii's hasty and fuzzy words. But there it is – everything that is schoolboyish and dead that can be said in the Russian language about Pushkin has been said and learned off by heart. We have said and repeated an endless number of times that word which is limp on our modern lips and easy for everyone because it does not bind one to anything: "Genius." And what happened? – Pushkin has become, not a monument, but a plaster-of-paris statuette' (157). Eikhenbaum's outburst – in a language in which literary criticism tends to be guarded, circumspect, hemmed in by many constraints – is refreshing in its unwillingness to take anything for granted.

The article which these remarks prefaced (or, rather, the lecture, for this, like a number of the most important critical statements of the 1920s, was first delivered at a 'Pushkin evening' in the House of Littérateurs) touches only obliquely on *Onegin*, but in its theme it tackles one of the major topics in Pushkin criticism of the time: the shift from poetry to prose in Pushkin's work. It was a topic that grew naturally out of the interest in poetics that had become known as the 'formal method' or 'formalism' (a pejorative term in the later Soviet period). In the process of Pushkin's shift towards prose *Onegin* had an important role to play, as Eikhenbaum pointed out: '*Eugene Onegin* was the preparation for this transition. It is an album of lyrics, but also the beginning of subject structures which do not require verse' (161).

Eikhenbaum's call for a rereading of *Onegin* was brilliantly answered by two critics. The first of these – Viktor Shklovskii – creates an entire shift in the way *Onegin* is viewed in the space of twenty-one pages in his article '*Eugene Onegin* (Pushkin and Sterne),' published in Berlin in 1923. Even the form of the essay is extraordinary: a dishevelled zigzag of breathless insights and aphorisms that adopt an ironic stance towards traditional 'coat and tie' scholarship. Footnotes are conspicuous by their absence and the text has an ironical 'shimmer of errors' – to use Nabokov's phrase – again, an expression of disdain for the paraphernalia of scholarship? Characteristically, Shklovskii dismisses previous criticism – e.g. the concept of 'types' – in a few casual sentences at the end of the essay – almost as an afterthought. In fact, rather than refuting previous critics, Shklovskii ignores them. His essay uses the new terminology of the formal method with its emphasis on poetics rather than content or literary and social 'environment': the work is seen, to use Shklovskii's own formula, as the 'sum of all stylistic devices employed in it.' The comparison between the author of *Tristram Shandy* and Pushkin is used largely as an initial insight to set the argument in motion. Shklovskii notes the allusion to Sterne in *Onegin* (in footnote 16), before drawing attention to the way both *Tristram Shandy* and *Onegin* begin in medias res – without the traditional introduction, which is inserted in the text much later (in *Onegin*, at the end of Chapter Seven).

Discussing the structure of the novel, Shklovskii notes: 'The plot [*siuzhet*] of the novel is itself extraordinarily simple! The action is braked by the fact that when Tat'iana loves Onegin, Onegin does not love her and when he falls for her, Tat'iana rejects him' (209). The critic is led to conclude that this banal plot – so common, as he notes, in literature – is not the *raison d'être* of the work, and stresses the importance of the 'digressions': 'The true plot of *Eugene Onegin* is not the story of Onegin and Tat'iana, but the manipulation of this situation [*fabula*]. The main content of the novel is its own constructive forms, the plot form being used as real objects are used in Picasso's pictures' (211). Such an insight represents a quantum leap not only in the way literature is discussed, but in the philosophy of art. The distance between Belinskii and Shklovskii is (to use the latter's 'device' of analogy from the visual arts) the distance between Repin's *Volga Boatmen* and Malevich's *White Quadrilateral on White*.

Shklovskii's line of argument leads him to the conclusion that '*Eugene Onegin* is full of parodic devices.' He examines a number of these – vocabulary, verse structure, rhyme, footnotes, similes – and, although his approach is impressionistic, he makes a good argument for their parodic intent. The weight of these arguments leads him to ask: 'Indeed, this is an interesting question: was *Eugene Onegin* written with serious intent? To put it crudely, did Pushkin cry over Tat'iana, or was he joking? Russian literature, headed by Dostoevskii, assures us that he cried' (214). Shklovskii does not immediately answer his own question, although the ironical way it is framed and his switching the subject to the question of parody suggests that he does not share Dostoevskii's opinion. Later he remarks: 'True, Pushkin himself appears to relate seriously and sympathetically to Tat'iana. [Here he quotes from the poet's professions of sympathy for the heroine.] But the tone of these extracts is undoubtedly Sternian. It is sentimental play and a play on sentimentalism. The description of Tat'iana, so suspicious in its archaic vocabulary, must be parodic' (218). Inasmuch as the 'seriousness' of the work depends on Tat'iana's lack of parody, Shklovskii has, perhaps, proved his point. This suggests that if we wish to find a serious intent, it must be sought elsewhere, at a deeper level.

Shklovskii's argument concludes with another 'question': 'why it is that *Eugene Onegin* takes the form of a parodistic Sternian novel. The appearance of *Tristram Shandy* is explained by the petrification of the devices of the old adventure novel. All the devices had become completely ineffective. The only way to revive them was parody. *Eugene Onegin* was written, as Professor B.M. Eikhenbaum has shown, on the eve of the appearance of the new prose. The forms of poetry had already grown old. Pushkin dreamed of a prose novel. Rhyme bored him' (219). Thus Shklovskii, like Eikhenbaum, proposed a new historical perspective to replace the Belinskian one. Instead of seeing *Onegin* as the 'progenitor' of 'new Russian literature' he proposed to see it as the last event in the literature of classicism, a view which he captures in a remarkable and characteristic image: '*Eugene Onegin* is like a mimic who comes on stage at the end of a variety show and acts out all the trade secrets of the previous numbers' (219).

The second formalist critic whose work is of fundamental importance in the criticism of *Onegin* is Iu.N. Tynianov. The year 1974 saw the first publication in Russian of an article written (although only in draft form) by Tynianov in 1921-2 and entitled 'On the Composition of *Eugene Onegin*.' The appearance of this article may be reckoned an event of major importance in Russian criticism of *Onegin* (especially since Shklovskii's article has never been printed in the USSR), as may be adjudged from its initial appearance in the journal *Monuments of Culture* (along with reports on archaeological finds).[21] Despite its draft form, the line of argument is – typically for Tynianov – densely knit and logical with none of Shklovskii's imagery or aphoristic fireworks.

Tynianov approaches the question of composition from the point of view of the prose/verse opposition. This was a question which concerned him (and other formalist critics) a great deal (and which he discussed in the monograph *The Problem of Verse Language*, published in 1924). Tynianov sees the opposition of prose and poetry to be rooted in the contrast of sound and semantics in the word. The argument is summed up in a typical formulation: 'Deformation of sound by the role of meaning is the constructive principle of prose; deformation of meaning by the role of sound – is the constructive principle of poetry. Partial changes in the correlation of these two elements are the motive factor of both prose and poetry' (56). The definition of this principle has important implications for the interpretation of poetry in general, since 'speaking of poetic semantics we have to remember that we have to do with a sense which has been deformed' (56). The argument, though abstractly put, relates directly to *Onegin* in that 'We are wrong to relate to the semantic elements of verse speech in the way we do to the semantic elements of prose speech. Such an error occurs most easily when a genre which is usually for prose (e.g. a novel) and is closely linked to the constructive principle of prose is thrust into verse.' Without saying so directly, Tynianov here calls into question the entire tradition of what he called the 'naive realistic' interpretation of the novel, that tradition which read *Onegin* simply as a novel without considering the verse factor and the deformation of the novel which that brought.

The correlation of prose/verse was, as Tynianov shows, a continuous problem for Pushkin: the two forms had very different requirements. With regard to *Onegin*, Tynianov remarks: 'It was necessary to combine an entire prose genre with verse – and Pushkin oscillates. For him *Eugene Onegin* is sometimes a novel, sometimes a poem; the chapters of the novel turn out to be cantos of a poem; the novel, which parodies the usual strategies of novels through compositional play, oscillating, intertwines with the parodic epic' (64). The device of the combination of novel and verse had, as Tynianov shows, profound effects on various elements in the novel structure. First, and most important, it deformed the levels of plot and action: 'Pushkin did everything possible to stress the verbal plane of *Eugene Onegin*. By publishing the novel chapter by chapter with intervals of several years, he quite clearly destroyed all emphasis on the plane of the action, on the *siuzhet* and the *fabula*; the dynamic of the semantic signs was replaced by the dynamic of the *word* in its poetic meaning, the development of the action by the development of the verbal plane' (64). As Tynianov indicates, the dominance of the poetic element over the novelistic (prose) element is expressed in the characters – who lose their prime role as participants in the action – in the role of the digression, and in the device of the omission (which becomes an ambiguous sign in the composition of the work).

Tynianov's emphasis on the 'verbal dynamic' of the poetry as dominant feature leads him to a highly intriguing observation on the vexed question of whether *Onegin* is finished. Since the verbal plane is the decisive, 'levelling' element, the true ending of the novel is not Chapter Eight: LI; it is the last line of the 'Extracts from Onegin's Journey' that is 'the culminating point of the whole novel' (61). The deduction is logical, aesthetically justified, and totally new. Less striking, but equally important, are the analyses which Tynianov offers of the deforming effect on the verse of such linguistic devices as the use of an initial for a person. For example, in the line

Zavetnyi venzel' *O* da *E*.

[*The fatal monogram O and E.* (Three: XXXVII: 14)]

the letters, by assuming a metrical (and even rhyming) role, are 'unnovelistically' foregrounded.

It is difficult to speak of the 'influence' of the formalists on subsequent criticism – Tynianov's manuscript languished in limbo until the late 1960s, when parts of it appeared in Italian. Shklovskii's essay has been almost equally inaccessible save to the specialist in the Soviet Union. The true line of formalist criticism leads (at least for a considerable span of time) outside the confines of the Soviet Union. Roman Jakobson, in his 'Marginalia on *Eugene Onegin*,' published in Czech in 1937 (and recently translated into English), notes, apropos the characters in *Onegin*: 'Each of Pushkin's images is so elastically polysemantic and manifests such an amazing assimilatory capacity that it easily fits into the most varied contexts ... Either this kind of *oscillating characterization* evokes the notion of a unique, complex, unrepeatable individuality or, if the reader is accustomed to clear-cut typification, he gets the impression (let us cite several notable expressions of Pushkin's time) that in the novel "characters are lacking", "the hero is only a connecting link of descriptions", "the characterizations are pale", "Onegin is not depicted profoundly; Tat'iana does not have typical traits," etc.' (1937b, 54-5). Jakobson's observations (and the reactions of contemporary critics whom he quotes) bear out Tynianov's view that the verse plane is dominant, and that the characters therefore cannot be read simply as participants in a novel.

Of the other formalist writings on Pushkin, mention should be made of B. Tomashevskii's study 'The Rhythmics of the Iambic Tetrameter Based on Observations of the Verse of *Eugene Onegin*' (1918). This essay, which carries on from the symbolist interest in Pushkin's poetics, is a classical statistical analysis of the internal rhythmics of the iambic tetrameter line. It represents the first major scientifically based study of the poetics of *Onegin*. Although directed to some extent polemically at certain *idées reçues* (e.g., the presence of a caesura in the tetrameter), the study does give a firm statistical basis for generalization on the poetic organization of the line in *Onegin* and tends, parenthetically, to reinforce the 'poetry' side of the 'novel in verse' equation.

The other critical tendency of the post-October period that produced a lasting contribution on *Onegin* was the 'sociological' trend represented by the critic D.D. Blagoi, who devotes a lengthy chapter of his book *The Sociology of Pushkin's Art* (1929) to the work. In his study Blagoi examines the ideological content of *Onegin* in terms of Pushkin's class identity and his sociological perceptions. Blagoi stresses Pushkin's consciousness of his belonging to a class (the landed nobility) which was in decline (a concern which is demonstrated by the recurrent theme of the poet's ancient lineage). Blagoi sees the two main protagonists of the work – Onegin and Tat'iana – as representatives of two groups in the nobility. Onegin lives in the city, affects foreign fashions, wastes his fortune (as his father had), and has no interest in continuing his line (witness his rejection of marriage). His spleen is seen as the symptom of his sociological state. In Blagoi's phrase, 'Before our eyes psychology becomes sociology' as the poet uses class and economic features to characterize his hero.

If Onegin represents the decadence and decline of the nobility, then for Blagoi Tat'iana symbolizes the possibility of a renascence. Noting the fact that both Larin and Zaretskii choose to live in the country, and that their existence there is described in idyllic terms, Blagoi suggests that it is precisely in such a return to the land that Pushkin sees the sole salvation of the nobility. It is Tat'iana who represents in concrete terms that ancient nobility, rooted in the land, which is the best segment of the class: 'Tat'iana shows the possibility of a recuperation, a rejuvenation of a nobility which has returned to "its father's house," to the land, to its native roots – she is the symbol of the salvation of the class. The bringing together of Onegin and Tat'iana is the central moment in the plot' (146). The confrontation of Onegin and Tat'iana results, in Blagoi's view, in a victory for Tat'iana, who becomes the most important figure in the work and with whom 'the poet merges.'

Blagoi shows how the same problem recurs in work after work, the female figure gradually assuming the ascendancy; the shift in titles – 'The Prisoner of the Caucasus,' *Onegin*, 'The Peasant Noblewoman,' *The Captain's Daughter* – shows this. Blagoi sees a similar shift occurring from romanticism to realism and from poetry – specifically the *poema*, or long poem – to prose. The scheme which he proposes – combining the formalist concern with genre and the sociological question of the content and method – has become one of the most deeply rooted features of Pushkin criticism in Russian. It is a view which must be handled with a degree of circumspection: for example, how does one explain *The Bronze Horseman*, a late *poema* with a romantic male eponymous hero? The scheme is, one must recognize, a very attractive way of explaining what Blagoi describes as the 'semi-parodic form of *Eugene Onegin*' (168).

Blagoi's interpretation of *Onegin* is defective in many ways; it ignores the question of irony (e.g., in the depiction of Tat'iana, in Pushkin's attitude towards the 'rural idyll'), and it tends to 'read in' views that are Blagoi's rather than Pushkin's. For all that, it is interesting in that it investigates the possibility of a 'biographical imperative' which is operative at some level of the creative process in the choice of themes and images, and in that it poses the problem of the value system underlying the work. Blagoi was to modify his approach considerably in subsequent criticism, becoming a pillar of the Soviet literary establishment, and this early work is now viewed negatively in the Soviet Union.

THE STALIN PERIOD

The beginning of the 1930s was marked by profound social and ideological changes in the Soviet Union. The collectivization of agriculture, the transformation of industry under the five-year plans, and the concentration of absolute power in the hands of Stalin were reflected in the emergence of a new approach to literature by the Party which had at its core the desire for unity of thought and style. The first All-Union Congress of Writers of 1934, at which the doctrine of Socialist Realism was promulgated, left a profound mark on the development of Russian literature. The effect of this new (or old, if one sees it as the imposition

of the bases of Gor'kii's social realism of the turn of the century on
Soviet writing) literary doctrine on the criticism of Pushkin took some
time to appear, although the matter was of some urgency, since the
centenary of Pushkin's death (the most important *prazdnik* since 1899)
was approaching quickly, and it was essential from the Party's point
of view that Soviet critics develop a unanimous line to treat the event
in the appropriate manner.

The most important episode in the years leading up to the centenary
was the appearance, in 1934, of a triple volume of the series *Literary
Heritage* devoted to Pushkin. This collective volume contained much
previously unpublished material by and about Pushkin – letters, memoirs, etc. – as well as studies of different aspects of Pushkin's work and
biography (including an article by B. Tomashevskii on Chapter Ten of
Onegin). From the point of view of the critical interpretation of *Onegin*,
the most important part of the volume is the series of 'keynote' essays
in the first section, which is entitled 'Problems in the Study of Pushkin.'
Of interest in this section are the articles of a general character by
three critics, I. Vinogradov, I. Sergievskii, and D. Mirskii. The reader
is struck by the more or less complete unanimity of approach of these
three critics. They are united in rejecting the methods of the formalists
and also of Blagoi, and adopt a position that affirms the development
of realism in Pushkin's work. Most interestingly, all three speak of the
ideological 'capitulation' of Pushkin. For example, Sergievskii writes:
'It is in particular untrue to say that Pushkin capitulates to the feudal
régime only after the December uprising. Elements of disappointment,
distrust, and intellectual and psychological depression appear in him
even before his exile from Petersburg. A couple more years go by, and
Pushkin already openly criticizes the freedom-loving dreams of youth
and openly capitulates to the patriarchal way of life of the squirearchy:
this is precisely the meaning of *Eugene Onegin*' (120). The notion of
an ideological shift in Pushkin is made more explicit by Vinogradov:
'The opposition of the "Russian soul" and "foreign ideology" is clearly
represented for the first time in the images of Tat'iana and Onegin.
Tat'iana also is not immediately delineated from this side of her. At
first she is a provincial miss who speaks Russian badly. One cannot
perceive in her that bearer of a "Russian soul" and moral duty which
she will become in succeeding chapters' (78). Previous critics of the
'naive realism' school had tended to see the characters in the work as
wholes. The concept of a change in the portrayal of Tat'iana that is
stressed by these critics is therefore of importance.

It can scarcely be a coincidence that the same view is repeated (and

given flesh and blood) by Mirskii (who had recently returned to the
Soviet Union from England and was destined to die in a *gulag*). Mirskii
goes into the most detail on the image of Tat'iana. His remarks are
worth quoting at length because they represent the best expression of
the 'line' adopted by all three men:

> Extremely characteristic is the change in the image of Tat'iana
> in the course of *Eugene Onegin*. At the beginning Tat'iana is
> portrayed as an awakening personality opposed on the one
> hand to the philistine environment of the provincial squirearchy,
> and on the other to the mature Onegin. This Tat'iana is closely
> linked to the spring of the progressive gentry whose bard
> Pushkin was in those years. By the time of Chapter Eight,
> Pushkin does not need such a Tat'iana, and the fate of her
> character is now determined by the requirements of that ad-
> justment to the aristocracy surrounding Nicholas which was the
> first order of business for Pushkin. The Tat'iana of Chapter
> Eight is on the one hand the apotheosis of the grand lady, the
> highest expression of that aristocracy to which Pushkin had
> to adapt himself, and on the other a moral exemplar of the
> faithful wife for Natal'ia Nikolaevna who, being 'given' to
> Pushkin, related with the same lack of passion to him as
> Tat'iana did to her general, but whose future marital behaviour
> was an essential element in Pushkin's adjustment to the 'highest
> circles.' The hopes which Pushkin placed in her as the instru-
> ment of such an adjustment were sublimated in the lofty lyri-
> cism of Chapter Eight. (105-6)

Mirskii's view of Tat'iana has considerable merit: no doubt the existential concerns of Pushkin were highly influential in moulding Tat'iana's
character. One is disturbed, however, by the mechanistic way in which
the theory is applied. Surely the early Tat'iana and the proud Princess
N are intimately and organically related? Also, if Tat'iana's declaration
of marital fidelity is related (as I believe it is) to the question of Pushkin's marriage, then it is surely a superstitious self-assurance on the
part of a poet (who had formerly tended to take the part of the cuckolder)
rather than a moralistic homily to his intended.

Mirskii's and his colleagues' view presupposes an 'original conception' of *Onegin* by Pushkin that becomes modified by the different
social climate in which the poet finds himself after his return from
exile. The notion of this 'original conception' is a seductive one and

becomes a commonplace of subsequent Soviet criticism. That the related idea of Pushkin's 'capitulation' is developed in all three essays
suggests the degree of orchestration that was being imposed on Pushkin
criticism (as on other spheres of cultural life) with a view to achieving
a single unified line. The ironically minded observer might be tempted
to see in the image of Pushkin capitulating to an authoritarian régime
a parallel with the fate which Russian criticism was undergoing at
precisely the same time. In fact, the critical stance adopted by the
critics in the *Literary Heritage* volume was to prove only an episode
in the development of Soviet criticism. Their interpretation was too
doctrinaire and too condescending to prove acceptable as the official
view of Russia's national poet, the centenary of whose death was approaching. Firstly, the idea that Pushkin 'capitulated' to the régime of
Nicholas was at odds with the desire to see him as a progressive writer
whose development of a realist art would lead to the great writers of
nineteenth-century realism, the so-called 'critical realists,' and, beyond
them, to socialist realism. It was therefore necessary to lay more stress
on Pushkin's political engagement and his links with the Decembrists,
and to de-emphasize the biographical and social imperatives. Other
reasons would have to be found for the shift in the image of Tat'iana
and all the other changes which it exemplified.

On 17 December 1935 the Soviet government published its directive
on the creation of an All-Union Pushkin Committee, to be chaired by
Maksim Gor'kii, which would direct the celebration of the centenary
of Pushkin's death. The text of the decree characterized Pushkin as a
'great Russian poet, the creator of the Russian literary language and
the progenitor of the new Russian literature.'[22] The effect of this declaration of the position of the party was not immediately apparent as
it was not until the year 1941 that the first major expressions of the
new line appeared – two collective volumes entitled *Pushkin – Progenitor of the New Russian Literature* and *Pushkin: A Collection of
Articles*, with contributions by such critics as A.Tseitlin, D. Blagoi,
G. Pospelov, and G. Vinokur.

These volumes, and the collections and monographs which followed,
combine to form an orthodox, unified interpretation of Pushkin along
the lines of the party decree. One may generalize the features of this
interpretation as follows. Firstly, Pushkin is seen as a revolutionary,
even a Decembrist. Blagoi writes: 'Pushkin came to literature under
the sign of Decembrism. This initial content gave a great progressive-
ness, a vast progressive strength to all Pushkin's subsequent literary
activity. For a century the degree of his participation in the Decembrist

movement, his role in it has been, as a rule, underestimated for various reasons – censorship, the tendentiousness of biographers, the destruction or loss of the most important documents, beginning with the autobiographical notes of Pushkin himself' (5). The portrait was thus completely changed from that of an aristocrat who was never a Decembrist and who capitulated before Nicholas to that of a Decembrist, crypto-revolutionary poet.

Hand-in-hand with this rejection of 'vulgar sociology,' as it came to be known, was the view of Pushkin as 'national' poet (emphasizing his *narodnost'*). The same emphases obtained here as in earlier criticism of this type: Pushkin is considered to have transcended his own class limitations and to have created the bases for the national literature. The concept of *narodnost'* has as its necessary concomitant the idea of realism, in that the realistic portrayal of national types is, it is argued, what makes Pushkin *narodnyi* or national. The comment of G. Pospelov (in his article '*Eugene Onegin* as a Realist Novel') may be considered as a classical statement of the line: 'Realist poetry shows in the collision of typical heroes the laws of existence and, by the same token, reflects the more profound essential relationships in reality' (143). This remark is made in the context of Pospelov's discussion of how Pushkin 'overcomes' Byron and Byronic romanticism (*Don Juan*).

From this it can be seen that the line adopted by Soviet critics in response to the decree was essentially not new, but derived from the 'neo-Belinskian' criticism of the late nineteenth and early twentieth centuries. It was modified principally by the insistence on Pushkin's progressive (revolutionary) views. The poet's apparent capitulation was ascribed to the dissimulation of the poet in the face of strict censorship, a view that was lent some credence by the existence of such documents as the deciphered passages attributed to Chapter Ten.

As regards *Onegin* specifically, the new criticism tended to treat the work as a realistic novel, in the Belinskian manner, since in this way one could argue its importance for subsequent literature. The reference in the party decree to Pushkin as the founder of the Russian language legitimized discussion of Pushkin's language and style (see below), but the continuing swing against formalism made discussion of form, genre, and structure less acceptable, and generally critics limited themselves to appreciative remarks concerning the 'composition,' particularly in studies written for the mass audience. Pospelov, for example, argues that the digressions and authorial asides in *Onegin* are of less importance than in Byron's *Don Juan*, and implies that they are vestigial traces of the Byronic genre which Pushkin's realist art 'overcomes.'

The war years and subsequent economic hardships slowed the output of criticism, and it was not really until the 1950s that new writing begins to appear on *Onegin* in any quantity. What does start to be published finally is not essentially new, but rather rehashes of the 'neo-Belinskian' line set down by the decree and the collective volumes of 1941. The same few familiar names reappear again and again: B. Tomashevskii, D.D. Blagoi, author of *Pushkin's Craft*, G.A. Gukovskii, author of *Pushkin and the Problem of Realistic Style*, G. Makogonenko, and B.S. Meilakh.[23]

The most important problem in the interpretation of *Onegin* in the 1950s had to do with the character of Onegin. The debate in question revived the old problem of whether he was to be viewed as a positive or negative character, and, more specifically, whether he becomes, at the end of the work, a Decembrist. Belinskii, as we have seen, regarded him as a 'nice chap' (*dobryi malyi*) who had fallen victim to his environment. Pushkin, according to the memoirs of one M. Iuzefovich, is reported to have said that according to his 'initial conception' he intended Onegin to die in the Caucasus or become a Decembrist.[24] This information, and a judicious excerpting of Pushkin's cancelled drafts, leads to an extrapolation of Onegin's psychological development that runs roughly as follows. Onegin is horrified at the death of Lenskii. He travels through Russia, learning to love the Russian people and to detest the political system symbolized by the Arakcheev military settlements. When he returns to Petersburg he has been reborn. The new man, a democrat, and an appreciator of literature, falls in love with Tat'iana. She, however, rejects him, seeing only the earlier cold, cynical, and egoistic Onegin. He lays down his life in the Decembrist cause. This interpretation (as expounded by Gukovskii) has received widespread currency in the Soviet Union, but it has such obvious flaws, and does such violence to the established text, that dissenting opinions have been registered even by such orthodox Soviet critics as D.E. Tamarchenko, Iu.M. Nikishov, and B.S. Meilakh.[25]

Through the 1960s and 1970s the situation in orthodox Soviet criticism of *Onegin* has become increasingly unstable, as the group of critics who developed the unified line has aged, and as the line of criticism itself has become less and less productive. In a country where much importance is attached to the teaching of a single interpretation in schools and institutions of higher learning, the lack of a stable point of view appears not as a challenge and a stimulus to thought and discussion but rather as a source of alarm.

Although Pushkin criticism after 1937 was largely vitiated by the 'monolithic' acceptance of the neo-Belinskian line of the decree, it would be a mistake to assume that no meaningful work was being done in the field. In particular, the problems of Pushkin's language and poetics did offer an interesting area of research, and a number of works on the subject did appear during the Stalin period which add up to a very significant step forward, principally the work of V.V. Vinogradov – *Pushkin's Style* (1941) and *Pushkin's Language* (1935) – and G. Vinokur's long study, 'Word and Verse in *Eugene Onegin*' (in *Pushkin: A Collection of Articles*).

Vinogradov's study of Pushkin's language examines the hierarchy of language styles which Pushkin inherited from Russian literature of the eighteenth century and which coalesce in his work (just as the genres which accompany the styles combine to form hybrid genres). Vinogradov's study is refreshingly specific in a critical corpus which frequently exhibits a maddening tendency to generalize. For example, he notes 'in Onegin's speech (Four: XIII-XIV) ... there are many more reflections of the Russo-French style than in Tat'iana's letter even in its draft plan' (Vinogradov 1941, 229). His conclusion is that 'Pushkin portrays Tat'iana the future grand lady using a language which is more folkish [*narodnyi*], more pristinely Russian than that of Onegin' (230).

Vinogradov's volume on Pushkin's language is complemented by his later study of Pushkin's style. In this work Vinogradov traces in detail the development of Pushkin's style from the traditional literary styles of his 'spring' through the period of 'romantic daring' to the 'realistic correspondence of style to the depicted world of historical reality' (111-12). Vinogradov stresses in Pushkin the primacy of concern with 'new forms and combinations' – semantics, syntax, composition – rather than problems of morphology and lexicon, and his highly individual view of the word and its potential for complexity of meaning. Vinogradov's contribution specifically to the study of *Onegin* was to take the form of an analysis of Chapter One that is focused primarily on the problem of Onegin's relationship to the author. This essay, which was published in 1966, is disappointing. Its view of the problem had been superseded by this time (especially by Bakhtin, whom Vinogradov quotes). Vinogradov's main contribution to the study of Pushkin thus remains the two earlier volumes with their wealth of factual observations.

The seminal study by G. Vinokur of word and verse in *Onegin* may be reckoned one of the principal achievements of Soviet poetics in the Stalin period.[26] The study continues the line of research that we find in Tynianov's *Problem of Verse Language* (1924), which had been

concerned, among other things, with the question of the deforming
effect of the structure of verse on the semantic features of language.
Vinokur applies a similar methodology to the specifics of the verse in
Onegin. Central to Vinokur's study is the role of the stanzaic organization of *Onegin* on the inter- and intra-stanzaic structure of the language: problems of enjambement, both between the different stanzas
and between quatrain and quatrain (or couplet) within the stanza. Vinokur has a number of interesting and important observations, among
which one may specifically mention his discussion of the way the
stanzaic organization facilitates the form and structure of the work:
'Each new chapter, each new stanza, each new division of the stanza
offered the possibility of a new turn in the exposition of the theme, of
a shift from one thematic plane to another, of introducing new material
without prior preparation, etc., without risking turning the novel into
a heap of disjointed fragments and poetic trivia endowed with only a
separate significance' (172-3). As an example of sound scholarship based
on meticulous research and a sophisticated view of the structure of
Onegin, Vinokur's article surpassed anything published in the Stalin
period.

Mention must be made, however, of another important Soviet contribution to the study of the poetics of *Onegin*, written in 1940 but
not published until 1965. This is the essay by M.M. Bakhtin 'From the
Prehistory of the Novelistic Word,' part of which is devoted to the
novelistic structure of *Onegin*; it was this section that was printed, in
1965, in the periodical *Voprosy literatury*. The entire essay was printed
only in 1975 in a volume of essays on aesthetics by Bakhtin entitled
Problems in Literature and Aesthetics. Bakhtin's approach is based on
his theory, developed in the essay 'The Word in the Novel and in
Poetry,' of the novel as a polyphony of voices or 'words' corresponding
to the individual dramatis personae. On the subject of the lyrical digressions in *Onegin* Bakhtin writes: 'They are not lyrics, they are the
novelistic images of lyrics (and of a lyrical poet)' (414). Bakhtin's conclusion is that 'In *Eugene Onegin* hardly a word belongs to Pushkin
in that unequivocal sense in which it is the case in his lyrics or long
poems. The author (as creator of the novelistic whole) cannot be found
in any one of the language planes: he is located at the organizational
centre where the planes intersect' (415).

SOVIET STRUCTURAL POETICS

From about the early 1960s a renewed interest has emerged in the
Soviet Union in what has come to be called structural poetics. This

movement has its roots in the work of the Soviet formalists of the 1920s, and we may observe in the work which has appeared on *Onegin* the clear influence of Tynianov's and Bakhtin's essays which were, as we have seen, published only in the 1960s and 1970s. Although Tynianov's work, in particular, represents what Chudakov described in his introduction to it as a rejection of 'the traditional understanding of the character as the direct analogue of a real person,' of 'naive realism,' there has been very little in the way of polemics between structuralist poetics and the accepted realist interpretation of *Onegin*.[27] In this apparently peaceful coexistence we may register an increasing openness in Soviet literary affairs.

The main Soviet exponent of structural poetics to have written on *Onegin* is Iu.M. Lotman. In his 1966 essay 'The Artistic Structure of *Eugene Onegin*,' Lotman develops Tynianov's thesis of an opposition between poetry and prose into a perception of different structural styles which interplay to create the final text: 'This coordination of different stylistic planes makes the reader aware that each of them individually is important in creating irony. The dominant place of irony in the stylistic unity of *Eugene Onegin* is clear and has been pointed out by critics' (16). Lotman's discussion of the stylistic structure of the work leads him to an interesting conclusion: 'The sequence of semantic and stylistic shifts creates a point of view which is multiple and dispersed rather than focused, and which becomes the system of a superstructure which is perceived as the illusion of reality itself' (19-20). Lotman is essentially suggesting that the complexity of the text leads to realism (rather than to an estrangement on the part of the reader which would tend to invite disbelief). His goal is to synthesize the formalist approach with the traditional Soviet emphasis on realism. In this Lotman is following to a considerable extent Bakhtin, whose essay 'The Word in the Novel' strives precisely to 'overcome the division between an extreme "formalism" and an equally extreme "ideologism" in the study of the artistic word' (72). Bakhtin's work lays the foundation for the study of the different stylistic systems which Lotman analyses. Clearly, the Lotman/Bakhtin approach requires that the term 'realism' be redefined, at least with reference to *Onegin*.

The notion that the complexity of the text of *Onegin* leads ultimately to an illusion of reality is an underlying thesis in Lotman's writings on the subject. These are gathered together in a short book, *Pushkin's Novel in Verse 'Eugene Onegin'* (1976), which is a series of lectures given by him at the University of Tartu. In it material published in earlier articles is subsumed into a new text and systematically presented to cover a series of important problems posed by *Onegin*.[28]

Such problems are covered as the 'principle of contradictions,' point of view, intonation, the unity of text, and man in Pushkin's work. In a chapter on 'literature and literariness,' Lotman examines the way in which the literary allusions in the work serve to create an expectation in the reader which is then frustrated. A contrast is described between the expected conventional literary structure invoked by the allusions, and the textual reality. The actual principle of structure, Lotman suggests (following Tynianov), is that of accretion of new episodes and chapters, and the relationship of Onegin and Tat'iana as key characters to the paradigm of other figures or groups. Discussing the 'unity of text' Lotman points out (in an argument that shows his indebtedness to Bakhtin) the peculiar ambivalent nature of the *Onegin* text, especially as far as the non-authorial speech is concerned. He writes: 'the text of *Onegin* may be read as a polyphony – whereupon those features come into play which characterize the text as the contrapuntal interplay of various forms of non-authorial speech – and as an authorial monologue in which the ''non-authorial voices'' serve to indicate the extent of the diapason of the narrator's voice. The peculiarity of *Onegin* is that either approach is equally correct' (87). Lotman goes on to discuss the problem of the integrity of the characters, and is led to conclude that it is only the conditioning of the reader by conventional literature that maintains the characters as characters.

This view is subsequently developed further, when the problem of literature versus reality is discussed: 'the abundance of metastructural elements in the *Onegin* text does not let us forget that we have to do with a *literary* text: immersing ourselves in the immanent world of the novel, we do not receive the illusion of reality, since the author tells us not only about a particular sequence of events, but continually draws us into the discussion about how one might otherwise structure the narrative.' These remarks are then qualified by the observation that *Onegin* nevertheless has a tendency to 'tear itself from the purely literary sphere into the world of reality' (95). This Lotman attributes to the conditioning of the reader and the expectations absorbed from the novel tradition. This tendency on the part of the reader (which became the mechanism of its influence on the nineteenth-century Russian realist novel) goes, Lotman suggests, against the authorial intent. Although Lotman's book is brief, limited in scope, and has had little circulation, it discusses some essential problems and proposes novel solutions.

There is, however, at least one other critic working in the field of structural poetics whose work is of equal importance: S.G. Bocharov, whose two articles devoted to *Onegin* break new ground. In the first, entitled 'The Form of the Plan,' Bocharov, like Lotman, examines the structure of the text as it relates to reality. He finds that it is composed of at least two 'worlds' or 'novels' – the 'novel of the author' and the 'novel of the protagonists.' He asserts: '*Eugene Onegin* portrays the consciousness of the author, a universal sphere which unites the worlds of reality and the "second reality" of the novel' (1967, 217). It is in this way that Bocharov is able to describe the curious structure of *Onegin* in which the author is at the same time consciousness, narrator, and dramatis persona. Bocharov sees the reason for such a structure as the need to create distance in a work which treats 'unrealized contemporaneity.' He concludes: 'The novel of the protagonists is not equal to the novel of Pushkin, their limits do not coincide. The novel of Pushkin is "greater" (or "broader") than the novel of the protagonists: the image of the world "in the third person" is subsumed by the image of the author "in the first person." '

In the second essay, 'The Stylistic World of the Novel,' Bocharov develops Lotman's analysis of the prose/verse opposition in *Onegin*. Bocharov offers a motivation for the stylistic structure of the work by viewing it as the struggle with the Karamzinian periphrastic style, and analyses the meaning of Lenskii in these terms, concluding that 'the author of the novel constructs the image of a particular poetics from which he distances himself here in the novel' (1974, 56). Bocharov pushes this commonplace of *Onegin* criticism a step further by showing that the problem is one of the relationship of poetic style to life: 'Onegin finds in Lenskii's choice of Ol'ga a stylistic contradiction, a "misalliance." The misalliance is not in life, where Lenskii and Ol'ga are, apparently, suited to each other, but precisely in the integrated sphere of Lenskii's poetic consciousness and his empirical life, his everyday existence' (58). Tat'iana, by contrast, suits Onegin, or rather would suit him if he were a poet.

It is the interplay of different stylistic realities, e.g. Lenskii's and Onegin's descriptions of Ol'ga, that Bocharov sees the stylistic meaning of the novel, which he characterizes as 'translation.' He writes: ' "Translations" are the *creative* force of Pushkin's novel, the text and the world of which they are built, constructed of "translations," shifts from one stylistic language to another and, ultimately, from each and every "subjective" language into, as it were, the "objective" language of life itself. The structure of the world of the novel as a whole is thus described by the concept of "translation," and in certain places the word itself figures with particular significance'

(71). Bocharov uses this insight to inform his analysis of such problems as the 'multilingual' nature of the work, the influence of foreign literature on the characters (Onegin as a 'Muscovite in Harold's cloak'), and Tat'iana's search for the 'word' in her ponderings on Onegin's character. The search for the 'word' amidst a paradigm of stylistic choices is, as Bocharov points out, the 'discovery of reality.' It is this linking of the stylistic problem to the essential meaning of the novel which makes Bocharov's analysis important: 'We observe, reading the text, how the action of the novel advances amid many possibilities which, in the course of the narrative, are constantly sketched by the author around the unfolding plot' (93).

Another study of *Onegin* with a structuralist orientation that merits discussion is Iu.M. Chumakov's essay 'The Composition of the Artistic Text of *Eugene Onegin*.' Chumakov builds on Tynianov's notion that 'Onegin's Journey' is an integral part of the text. Chumakov notes that Pushkin twice published the text that we have, and he therefore assumes that the author wished the reader to consider it complete. Chumakov points to the contrapuntal effect of the Journey, e.g., Pushkin's day in Odessa contrasted with Onegin's day in Petersburg. Although Chumakov's belief that the contrast is created in order to criticize Onegin seems pushed to an extreme, his comment on the ending seems just: 'The true finale of the novel, glowing with rapture and joy, does not detract from the mournful, heart-rending finale of Chapter Eight, but rather interacts with it to create a complex, tragic yet bright, ambivalent note' (1970, 27). Chumakov's is the first criticism to give the Journey its proper weight and try to evaluate its effect.

The work of reevaluation of *Onegin* which has gone on in the Soviet Union in the past twenty years has been the product of some of the best literary scholarship in the Soviet Union. It has been characterized by its originality and a willingness to break with accepted views. In addition, it has led to a much finer (or more tenuous) definition of the 'realism' of *Onegin*. A culmination of the process of reevaluation is Lotman's *Commentary* on *Onegin* (1980), in which the insights of the structuralist scholars are disseminated to a wider audience for the first time.[29] It is to be expected that the next period of time will see the gradual permeation of the ideas of the Lotman school into wider circles of the Soviet educational system, which is still largely oriented towards the Marxist sociological approach.

EUGENE ONEGIN IN THE WEST

The study of Pushkin in the West has been woven out of two strands: the émigrés who have left Russia in succeeding waves, bringing with them a significant part of her intellectual life, and the home-grown Western scholar – frequently a student first and foremost of his own literature – who has been attracted primarily through his reading of the works of later and more accessible authors – Tolstoi, Chekhov, Dostoevskii, Gogol' – to the more difficult task of decoding Pushkin's elusive charm.[30]

The initial problem for the assimilation of *Onegin* in English has been one of accessibility. Although a number of translations have been made, of greater or lesser fidelity and charm, the problem does not reside precisely in the creation of an equivalent text in the target language, but in the fact that the importance and meaning of the Russian original is intimately bound up with the specifics of style and language. It is precisely the importance of the stylistic texture, the complex stanzaic form, and the nuances of the language that render the translation so difficult. Pushkin's early poetry, especially, was littered with attempts to imitate various foreign models, and he had before him the example of Zhukovskii, whose 'translations' of such writers as Gray and Schiller were rather poetic recreations of the original (with varying degrees of fidelity to the latter). He lived in an age when translators took considerable liberties with the text of the original and when the transplanting of a work of literature from one language to another could take the form of 'free' translation, rewriting, recognized imitation, through the pastiche to original work in which elements of the foreign model could be discerned. Against this background Nabokov's *Eugene Onegin* is a radical exercise in what may almost be called anti-translation, the appearance of which sparked a furious debate. Nabokov's version, which sacrificed all considerations of grace and charm to the requirements of accuracy of literal reproduction, is essentially, as K.J. Skovajsa has shown in his 1971 dissertation on the subject, designed to prove a point – that of the primacy of style over content in *Onegin*. The point is well taken, but it must be said that the difference between the aesthetic experience derived by the English reader from Nabokov's text and that derived by a Russian reader from the original is analogous to the difference between reading the score of a Beethoven symphony and hearing it played. Perhaps an additional hidden motive for the polemical nature of Nabokov's translation may be found in the reproachful impatience of the polyglot scholar and writer with those who, for reason of lack of past education or present energy, are unable to read the work in the original.

As it stands, Nabokov's translation is more important for the framework of notes and commentary (e.g., on the stanza of *Onegin*) than for the translation itself, although that will go down in the history of Russian studies in English as a cause célèbre and had the very salutary effect of attracting the attention of the English-speaking reader to the importance of the work. In particular, the notes and commentary provide massive evidence of the importance of Pushkin's background in French literature, in the allusions and reminiscences that form a considerable part of the substance of the work. Apart from this, the major contribution of Nabokov's commentary is the new reconstruction which he offers of the fragments known as Chapter Ten. This reconstruction has now been accepted by Soviet scholars. Nabokov's formidable erudition does not, however, add up to a critical portrait (if anything, it tends to create a scholarly smokescreen, the expression of Nabokov's own aversion to critics and critical exegesis). Nevertheless, traces of Nabokov's influence can be seen here and there in many subsequent writers on the subject. These influences are not always to the good, especially as they have led to the increasing use of what one might call the irrelevant novelistic aside.

Although a number of critics, such as D.S. Mirskii (in his English period) and Edmund Wilson, had previously written in English on *Onegin*, it was only in the 1960s that English-language criticism began, with the appearance of several monographic studies on Russian literature, to approach the topic in any depth.[31] Even then, some critics, such as A.F. Boyd, have little that is new to offer, preferring to stick to the well-worn topics of the untranslatability of *Onegin*, Onegin as the superfluous man, and Tat'iana as 'a Russian soul, quickened by contact with European culture' (Boyd 1972, 19). F.D. Reeve, in his 1966 book *The Russian Novel*, seems likewise to place *Onegin* in the traditional role of realistic precursor of subsequent Russian novelists (although it is, as Mirskii points out, really only the last scene between Tat'iana and Onegin that is influential in this regard).

A much more original analysis than these is provided by Richard Freeborn, who, in *The Rise of the Russian Novel from 'Onegin' to 'War and Peace'* (1973), follows up Shklovskii's remark on the 'play with the *fabula*' by pointing out the two 'disciplines' that ensure integrity of text: the formal features of verse and stanza, which give what he characterizes as a 'dance rhythm' to the text and which are in harmony with the 'musical-box mechanism' of the plot; and the role of the poet in the plot structure as 'biographer who was at one time his [Onegin's] close friend and who is concerned to describe the most important episode in his life' (14). Freeborn's remarks on the verisimilitude of the 'cameos of Russian life' are equally perspicacious and nuanced, as he points to the distance which is preserved in the readers' view of them. In general, Freeborn shows a precise understanding of the difference between *Onegin* and later Russian fiction. Like Mirskii, he sees in the last scene the kernel of the future. But here too his observations are precise, and he points to the moral statement by Tat'iana, which he sees as the ultimate value of the work: 'Tat'iana asserts ... the privacy of conscience, the singularity of all moral awareness and certitude, the discovery of the single, unique moral self which opposes and withstands the factitious morality of the mass, of society, or the general good' (37).

To date the most important piece of critical writing on *Onegin* in English is that by John Bayley in his book *Pushkin: A Comparative Commentary* (1971). Bayley's study is comparative not in the sense of investigating 'influences' but in that it creates as it were a map of European literature in which to situate Pushkin and offers some illuminating points of reference and juxtapositions. The analysis of *Onegin* is, fittingly, divided into two parts: in the first the work is discussed *qua* novel. Here Bayley's comparisons are especially revealing. He points out that it is the type of novel 'which keeps our attention fixed on its medium' (other such novels are *Tristram Shandy, Dead Souls, Don Juan, Finnegans Wake,* and *The Waves*) and notes the necessity of a complex stanza: 'The impression is one of constant and brilliant improvisation, problems and contingencies recurring in endless permutation, and being solved and disposed of with an ever renewed cunning, labour, and expertise.' On the question of the genre, Bayley places it as a novel of sentiment, comparable to Austen – 'The stylization of their art conveys the real as part of its *insouciance'* – and thus distanced from realistic fiction. Bayley brings an equal precision to his descriptions of the narrative voice ('The complex tone of the novel is kept in continuous balance between objectivity and confiding engagement') and of the role of what the Russian commentator would call *byt*, which he sees in a 'tragi-comic' relation with the literary aspect of the novel.

Having discussed the novel 'in naturalistic terms,' Bayley, sensitive to its dual nature, turns to Shklovskii's formula of the 'play with the *fabula*.' To Bayley, *Onegin* has an existence both as story and as parody. Shklovskii's formula is, as Bayley shows, ultimately inexact. To Bayley, the parodistic elements of the work are concentrated in the figure of

Onegin: it is Tat'iana who is related to life beyond the poem and who rescues it from simple artifice. Over Onegin Pushkin passes an aesthetic judgment which is, Bayley suggests, expressive of the poet's disdain for romanticism. As he shows, in the use of the poetic formulae of classical genres Pushkin is far from the dishevelled insouciance of romanticism – the romanticism of Onegin is encapsulated and ultimately rejected. Bayley's analysis of *Onegin* stands as one of the most sensitive and subtle. He takes account of previous critical attitudes and pushes them a step further. His remarks have also a completeness in the sense that, however brief, they suggest a reading of the totality of the work.

The remainder of Western criticism consists of brief studies of different aspects of the work – some of them important. Predominant among these are comparative studies of the 'traces' of different (Western) writers on *Onegin*: Goethe (*Werther*), Dante, Benjamin Constant, Chateaubriand, Byron.[32] There are a number of articles on structure and genre: by Ettore Lo Gatto (1955, 1958, 1962), whose formula of 'diario lyrico' has formed a useful, though one-sided, antidote to the novelistic interpretation; and by Jan M. Meijer (1968), who reexamines the problem of the digressions. Tat'iana's dream has also prompted three articles by Gregg (1970), Nesaule (1968), and Matlaw (1959). In sum, one may say that the body of critical work in English on *Onegin* has brought some new light to different aspects of the work, but that the task of creating a definitive critical line of seeing the work as a whole in all its complexity has, with the exception of Bayley's and Freeborn's contributions, barely begun.

If this is true of English-language criticism in the West, it is not for the Russian-language writing on *Onegin*, since the publication of an article by Leon Stilman, 'The Problems of Literary Genres and Traditions in Pushkin's *Eugene Onegin*.' Stilman's article was read at the 1958 International Congress of Slavists in Moscow. It was a polemic against the reigning orthodoxy of Soviet realism, and challenges the concept of typicality in *Onegin*. Stilman operates with the commonly held Western view of the 'suspension of disbelief,' pointing out: 'Realism assumes a contract between author and reader as to what will be assumed to be reality, and this contract, once concluded, is observed to the end. It is precisely this effort to create an illusion of reality which is lacking in *Onegin*' (330). Stilman's critique of the realist interpretation of *Onegin* was very timely, for it was precisely at this period that Soviet scholarship began to feel the inadequacy of that new orthodoxy. The paper is known and quoted in the Soviet literature, but has, undeservedly, not yet been translated into English. I should add that it has served to a considerable extent to inspire my own views on *Onegin* as expressed in this present study.

Drawing by Pushkin, apparently of Eugene Onegin. 1830

2

The Broken Column:
Genre, Structure, Form

> As for what I am doing, I am writing not a novel but a novel in verse
> – a devil of a difference. It's in the genre of Don Juan. There's no
> use even to think of publishing; I am writing the way I feel like writing.
> Our censorship is so arbitrary that it is impossible to determine the
> sphere of one's activity with it. It is better not to think of it – and if
> you're going to take something, take it, else why dirty your claws?
> (*Letters*, 141)

Pushkin's first reference to *Onegin*, in a letter to his friend and fellow
poet Viazemskii written in Odessa on 4 November 1823, has become
almost as famous as the work itself and is an indispensable starting
point for any discussion of genre. The passage is an excellent example
of Pushkin's epistolary style: chatty, witty, and colloquial to the point
of untranslatability, in it we find encapsulated some of the tones which
Pushkin the conversationalist must have had (although that air of negligence is deceptive: he frequently wrote drafts of his letters and worked
upon them as if on a poem). These letters, sent mostly through trav-
elling friends – and therefore not subject to perlustration or censorship
– were frequently read, not only by the addressee, but by a broad circle
of acquaintances, and copied for even wider circulation. They represented a free-content, and also free-form, underground literary genre.[1]
As regards *Onegin*, Pushkin contrives in a few lines to define the
problem of genre with extreme brevity, and to hint at a couple of other
problems which were – he might have guessed with his writer's instinct
– to exercise critics and scholars of *Onegin* from the moment of its
appearance: the influence of Byron, and the role of censorship (or self-
censorship, which is at this point denied) in the shaping of the work.

Despite the gay, even flippant tone of the letter, the point that Pushkin is making to Viazemskii is a serious one: a first corrective to any false expectations that might be aroused by the news of his work on the new piece, and a first attempt to educate the reader and critic in how to relate to the unusual genre. Since the choice of genre brought with it a set of predetermined expectations or desiderata, it was important to disrupt those expectations by modifying the genre 'novel' with the unconventional qualification 'in verse.' Since, as we have said, Pushkin could expect his letter to be read not only by Viazemskii but by those of his acquaintances whom Viazemskii knew (and to be carried by word of mouth further into the literary circles of the capitals), we have to do here with a significant (and not the last) attempt by Pushkin to educate his readership.

The point is reinforced in the text itself:

> Druz'ia moi, chto zh tolku v etom?
> Byt' mozhet, voleiu nebes,
> Ia perestanu byt' poetom,
> V menia vselitsia novyi bes,
> I, Febovy prezrev ugrozy,
> Unizhus' do smirennoi prozy;
> Togda roman na staryi lad
> Zaimet veselyi moi zakat.
> Ne muki tainye zlodeistva
> Ia grozno v nem izobrazhu,
> No prosto vam pereskazhu
> Predan'ia russkogo semeistva,
> Liubvi plenitel'nye sny,
> Da nravy nashei stariny.
>
> Pereskazhu prostye rechi
> Ottsa il' diadi starika,
> Detei uslovlennye vstrechi
> U starykh lip, u rucheika;
> Neschastnoi revnosti muchen'ia,
> Razluku, slezy primiren'ia,
> Possoriu vnov', i nakonets
> Ia povedu ikh pod venets ...
> Ia vspomniu rechi negi strastnoi,
> Slova toskuiushchei liubvi,
> Kotorye v minuvshi dni
> U nog liubovnitsy prekrasnoi

Mne prikhodili na iazyk,
Ot koikh ia teper' otvyk.

[*My friends, what is the sense in this? Perhaps, by the will of
the heavens, I will cease to be a poet, and a new fiend will
possess me; and, despising the threats of Phoebus, I will de-
scend to humble prose; then a novel in the old style will occupy
my merry sunset. In it I will not describe in threatening tones
the secret sufferings of the evil doer, but will simply relate
to you the traditions of the Russian family, the captivating
dreams of love, and the mores of our olden time. I will relate
the simple speeches of a father or aged uncle, the secret trysts
of the children by the old lime trees, by the brook; the sufferings of unhappy jealousy, separation, tears of reconciliation; I
will have them quarrel again, then finally I will bring them
to the altar ... I will recall the speeches of passionate delectation, the words of pining love, which in bygone days came
to my lips at the feet of a beautiful mistress, and of which I
have now lost the habit.* (Three: XIII-XIV)]

Although we may see some elements of this plan in *Onegin*, especially
the 'traditions of the Russian family' and the 'mores of our olden time,'
with this exception the plan of this humble novel in prose is in complete contrast with *Onegin*, especially the projected 'happy ending.' In
this little capsule, Pushkin gives us a sketch of the features of the
typical prose novel, amounting to a mini-parody, in order to define
Onegin better, although again negatively: here is what the present work
is not.

Such a method of negative definition (a method which he also uses
with regard to Onegin – he is *not* a portrait of the author) was imposed
upon Pushkin, who rightly foresaw that the genre of *Onegin* would
create difficulties for his readership. The poem was different from anything he had undertaken, or was to undertake, and it was a far cry from
the Decembrists' demand for a return to exalted forms and language.
Pushkin likewise distanced himself from them in his mocking echo
of Kiukhel'beker, chief theorist of this 'archaist' movement: 'Write
odes, gentlemen!' In particular, the far from admirable character of the
hero and the seemingly excessive attention given by the author to
mundane detail stuck in the throats of Ryleev and Bestuzhev.

As we have already seen, Pushkin tried to forestall such criticisms
in the Foreword to the initial edition of Chapter One. We find him, in

his correspondence to Ryleev and Bestuzhev and to his friend Raevskii, trying to do the same. The Foreword caused as many difficulties as it solved, since in it Pushkin described *Onegin* as a satire and invited comparison with Byron. In the correspondence he had to backtrack:

> You compare the first chapter with *Don Juan*. Nobody esteems *Don Juan* more than I do ... but there is nothing in common with *Onegin* in it. You talk of the Englishman Byron's satire and compare it with mine, and demand of me the very same thing! No, my dear fellow, you want too much. Where do I have *satire*? There is not even a hint of it in *Eugene Onegin*. My embankment would crumble if I were to touch satire. The very word *satirical* ought not to appear in the preface. 24 March 1825. (*Letters*, 209-10)

The Decembrists' demand for satire was natural, since the bases of their art reflected the didacticism of eighteenth-century classicism which they had disinterred.[2] Characters could be noble, and thus an object of emulation, or ignoble, and an object of satirical scorn. That Pushkin should portray an ignoble character yet not satirize him did not fit their canon.

The difficulties that Pushkin experienced in describing the genre of his new work were real because nothing like it had appeared in Russian (or foreign literature for that matter) with which it would bear exact comparison. The genre was unique and could but be summarized by the enigmatic formula contained in that initial reference – 'a novel in verse' – which became the subtitle of the work. In a sense Pushkin appears to be barely in control of his new creation at this point. As John Bayley writes: 'Like all great novels it seems to have grown rather than been made, and yet at the same time it is constructed like a perfect curve or parabola, with a totally satisfying logic of its own.'[3] Moreover, its development took place according to its own peculiar laws, which did not correspond to the taxonomy of contemporary literature. Pushkin appears at a loss for words. In this he was not alone; the genre of *Onegin* has exercised the thoughtful critic ever since. In this discussion, however, Pushkin's initial insight must be heeded: *Onegin* is *not* a novel. That is to say, the laws of its structure are not those which readers would expect from a novel. (True, the all-embracing quality that we have come to expect in a novel, a genre which has been able to assume the most surprising forms and absorb the most disparate elements, permits us to see in *Onegin* a novel in the modern

sense, and a brilliant one at that.) Pushkin himself offers us some hint
as to the underlying principle of *Onegin*. It is, characteristically, when
he is being himself and writing unguardedly to his friends that he puts
his finger on it: 'I am writing the way I feel like writing' (in Russian,
spustia rukava – literally, 'letting my sleeves down'). In a letter to
Del'vig, written 12 November 1823, he remarks, 'I am now writing a
new poem, in which I chatter [*zabaltyvaius'*] to the limit' (*Letters*,
143). The same root occurs in a subsequent letter on the theme to
Bestuzhev (May-June 1825): 'But a novel requires *chatter* [*boltovnia*]:
say everything out plainly' (*Letters*, 224). It is precisely the *chatter* –
perhaps better rendered by the French word *badinage* (or by Tynianov's
more precise and comprehensive term, 'verbal dynamics') – that defines
Onegin and is, as Tynianov has suggested, the organizing principle.[4]
The tone of voice of the narrator expresses the author-reader relationship, which is fundamental to the novel. Indeed, the characters 'author'
and 'reader' are the two enduring ones that have an existence outside
the confines of the 'novel.' In the last stanzas of Chapter Eight this
relationship dominates as the characters are dismissed. The tone of
'chatter' or 'banter' which expresses this relationship is that 'verbal
dynamics' which gives the work its structure. Interestingly, it has
much in common with the tone of Pushkin's letters, a tone which, as
we have seen, is highly colloquial and ironic.[5]

The author-reader relationship which is initiated by the dedication
(to Pletnev, Pushkin's publisher, a piece of information which was
suppressed in the *ultima editio*) and is foregrounded at various points
in the text – principally the chapter endings – is, as several researchers
have shown, a highly complex one. There is (as in all fiction) what
Hoisington (following Booth) calls an 'implied reader.'[6] This is the
reader that we strive to be – a mirror image of the author, sharing his
view of events and understanding every hidden allusion, every shade
of irony. Then there is a paradigm of other narratees, individuals who
are addressed or invoked at various points in the text, who are – as
Hoisington shows – treated with greater or lesser irony: Pushkin's
fellow poets (Baratynskii, Viazemskii, Kiukhel'beker, Tumanskii, Katenin), whose poetic tastes or talents differ from Pushkin's; the critics,
whom Pushkin takes to task in the footnotes (and in 8: XLIX); fashionable young men of the Onegin type (curiously, given the bizarre
narrative structure, Onegin himself could appear to be a reader, but is
not, a fact which may be indicative); and the fair sex. The latter group
were treated with the irony of a poet who was distancing himself from
the notion of the innocent young girl reader characterized by a line

from Piron, 'la mère en préscrira la lecture à sa fille,' which was originally intended as a footnote to the rough draft variant of Two: XII.
This doctrine, and the critics who demand its observance, are mocked
in footnotes 7, 20, 23, 32, and 36 ('Our critics, true admirers of the fair
sex, severely criticized the indecency of this verse'). It is a representative of the 'fair sex' readership who enters the confines of the novel
briefly (while remaining a reader) to pause at Lenskii's grave and wonder about the fate of the other protagonists (Six: XLI-XLII). Her sentiment contrasts with her preceding breakneck gallop through the fields
in a way which is, the (initiated) reader suspects, not without its charm
for Pushkin.

If a principal structural element is the banter that informs the tone
of the novel and arises, as we have suggested, from the author-reader
relationship, it should be noted that the ironic tone diminishes or is
suspended at certain moments. It is at these moments (to be discussed
in subsequent chapters) that we (i.e., author/initiated reader) come face
to face with facts and events which cannot be ironized and which
therefore constitute the nexus of the work, the kernel of meaning.

If we accept Pushkin's dictum that 'a novel requires banter' and agree
that this is the formative element in *Onegin*, then we must accept the
necessity of defining banter a little more closely. Implicit in the root
is the notion of the spoken word: colloquial speech is the dominant.
In *Onegin* reported speech is relatively rare, and limited to some half-
dozen dialogues between different characters: Onegin and Lenskii,
Tat'iana and her nurse, the Larins, mother and daughter, when they
arrive in Moscow, and Onegin and Prince N (Tat'iana's husband). (The
final scene is really a monologue by Tat'iana echoing Onegin's earlier
'sermon' to her of Chapter Four). This kind of reported speech is not
what Pushkin means by 'banter,' however; on the contrary, they are
opposites. Banter is the chatty, conversational mode in which the entire
text is delivered, in which an 'I' addresses a 'you' who may be specific
– Zizi Vul'f in 5: XXXII: 11 and Pletnev in the dedication – or, as we
have seen, a more generalized spectrum of narratees. The conversational mode in which *Onegin* is written is, at first sight at least, at
odds with Lo Gatto's description of *Onegin* as a *diario lyrico*, since a
diary is a reflective mode in which the author posits no audience but
himself.[7] In *Onegin*, by contrast, the audience is an omnipresent factor.

The conversational mode is expressed by the predominant speech
level, in which the author (or 'speaker') apostrophizes his reader (sometimes using the familiar *ty*, sometimes the formal – or plural – *vy*), in
which he inserts asides ('hm, hm,' 'by the way,' etc.), and above all by

the ironic tone which predominates. A characteristic expression of the conventional mode is the abundance of digressions, which are tangential or utterly remote from the plot line of the 'novel.' Equally typical are the frequent stylistic shifts, in which the author mimics the features of a specific style. The style mimicked may be a literary one, which gives the passage in question the force of a parody:

> *Poiu priiatelia mladogo*
> *I mnozhestvo ego prichud.*
> *Blagoslovi moi dolgii trud,*
> *O ty, epicheskaia muza!*
> *I vernyi posokh mne vruchiv,*
> *Ne dai bluzhdat' mne vkos' i vkriv'.*
> Dovol'no. S plech doloi obuza!

> [*'I sing a young friend and the multitude of his caprices. Bless my lengthy work, o thou, epic muse! And, placing the trusty staff in my hand, let me not wander from the straight and narrow.' Enough. There's a load off my shoulders!* (Seven: LV: 6-12)]

The passage reads as a 'Sternian' reference, since in *Tristram Shandy* a similar mock-epic introduction is introduced late in the course of the novel. A similar 'Sternian' effect is achieved by Lenskii's 'Poor Yorick' outburst over Larin's grave (Two: XXXVII: 6). Here the parodistic effect is more complex, since Lenskii clearly *means* it to be Hamletian, although the comparison of the solemn Larin to the joker is ridiculously misapplied and reveals Lenskii's pose.

An equally crucial example of parody is the elegy which Lenskii composes on the eve of his duel with Onegin:

> Kuda, kuda vy udalilis',
> Vesny moei zlatye dni?
> Chto den' griadushchii mne gotovit?
> Ego moi vzor naprasno lovit,
> V glubokoi mgle taitsia on.
> Net nuzhdy; prav sud'by zakon.
> Padu li ia, streloi pronzennyi,
> Il' mimo proletit ona,
> Vse blago: bdeniia i sna
> Prikhodit chas opredelennyi;

Blagosloven i den' zabot,
Blagosloven i t'my prikhod!

[*Whither, whither have you fled, golden days of my youth?
What does the coming day prepare for me? My eye seeks it in
vain; it is hidden in the deep gloom. There is no need; the
law of fate is just. Whether I fall, pierced by the arrow, or it
flies past, all is well: the appointed hour of waking and sleep
must come; blessed is the day of cares, blessed too is the
coming of darkness!* (Six: XXI: 3-14)]

Here the parody blends into an ironical capturing of the character's
'voice.' Strangely, however, through the parody a 'real' content is visible, namely Pushkin's frequently expressed fatalism, the sentiments
in Lenskii's elegy 'rhyming' with those in the last stanza of Chapter
Eight: LI: 9-14. The question of where parody ends and narration begins
is ultimately unresolvable. Is Tat'iana's letter, for instance, or the song
of the peasant maidens in the garden a parody? The answer is in the
ear of the reader, so delicately is the irony nuanced.

The panoply of styles which is a feature of *Onegin* – the parodies,
letters, songs, dialogues, and even the passages of quoted text – all is
subordinate to the intonation of a single narrative voice.[8] That is to
say, whether the narrator quotes what purports to be an autonomous
text – for example, Onegin's letter to Tat'iana, which Akhmatova demonstrates to be a pastiche of Benjamin Constant's *Adolphe* – or a passage from another author, in the text or notes or as an epigraph, the
choice of text, and its tangential position with respect to the narrative,
inevitably read as more or less ironic, from the blatant *lasciate ogni
speranza* to the subtly exaggerated air of excessive respect accorded
Gnedich's pedestrian idyll (in note 8), which stands, despite Pushkin's
description of it as 'charming,' in ironical contrast with the lightness
and impressionism of Pushkin's stanzas.[9]

Another important aspect of the banter and an element in the irony
is the presence of foreign words. As Bocharov has shown, they reflect
the fundamental role of the concept of translation in the stylistic structure of the poem (1974, 77, 89). Words may be given in the foreign
language (*comme il faut, vulgar*) or in Russian transliteration (*vasisdas,
Ay*), or they may be translated into a Russian 'calque' ('temno i vialo'
– *obscur et traînant;* see Nabokov, III, 31). The frequent attention that
Pushkin gives to these words, and to the relationship of Russian voc-
ables to foreign, ensures that this ironic situation is emphasized. For

Pushkin, who spoke and wrote French fluently and was steeped in French culture, French had an undeniable influence on the language, and he expressed his feelings on the subject (apropos Tat'iana's letter to Onegin):

> Nepravil'nyi, nebrezhnyi lepet,
> Netochnyi vygovor rechei
> Po prezhnemu serdechnyi trepet
> Proizvedut v grudi moei;
> Raskaiat'sia vo mne net sily,
> Mne gallitsizmy budut mily,
> Kak proshloi iunosti grekhi

> [*Incorrect, careless twitter, the imprecise pronunciation of speeches will, as before, produce a flutter of the heart in my breast; I do not have the strength to repent that gallicisms will be as dear to me as the sins of my spent youth* (Three: XXIX: 1-7)]

Pushkin elevates imperfection (of language, in this case) to the level of an idiosyncratic aesthetic ideal. In any case, the admixture of Gallicisms and insertion of foreign elements are essential to Pushkin's 'banter.'

Equally essential to the tone of the text are the literary allusions. In *Onegin* we do not simply have a narrator recounting some novelistic events to a reader. The author and the 'aware' reader are assumed to be highly literate. Again, as with foreign words and stylistic levels, there is a paradigm of literary allusions. There are, first, the quotations which are tangential to the text and the author of which is identified. Such are the mottoes and quotations from texts given in the footnotes. In *Onegin* Pushkin refrained from Scott's practice of inventing quotations for the occasion, with the sole exception of the epigraph to the entire novel ('Pétri de vanité ...'), which was, it seems clear, composed by the author.[10] Next to the identified and distinct quotations stand the quotations, sometimes slightly altered, which are embedded in the verse. These might be anonymous – 'Qu'écrirez-vous sur ces tablettes ...' (Four: XXVIII: 10) – or identified as to author – e.g., the quotation from Griboedov (note 38) – without any apparent irony (beyond a shade of pedantry). Next in line come the parodies and pastiches. Here again, we must distinguish those where the author is identified (note 34) from those where the allusion is hidden –

Poroi belianki chernookoi
Mladoi i svezhii potsalui

[*At times the young, fresh kiss of a dark-eyed white-skinned
girl* (Four: XXXVIII: 3-4)]

which, as Nabokov discovered, is a 'hidden quotation' from Chénier:

Le baiser jeune et frais d'une blanche aux yeux noirs.[11]

The number of such reminiscences is very large. From a specific
quotation, such as that cited, to the general stock of images and phrases
of the French pastoral tradition in poetry, the sentimental and romantic
novel, classical literature (e.g., Horace: Zaretskii planting cabbages),
the text of *Onegin* is a vast amalgam of literary allusion and reminis-
cence, all subsumed into the ironic *badinage* of the worldly and widely
read narrator. Numerous scholars have delighted in excavating this
burial ground of allusions and classifying every bone. Of these, the
scholiast-in-chief is Nabokov, whose formidable erudition and passion
for detail provide a fascinating commentary on Pushkin's reading (although even Nabokov misses certain echoes) and fix *Onegin* as a type
of literary text to be unsurpassed in this respect, at least until the
modernists.

Although Pushkin's emphasis on the necessity of banter is important
in defending the nature of *Onegin*, it does not stand alone in the organization of the poem. A novel that was composed of sheer banter
would tend to lose all limits and structure. It is therefore placed in a
creative tension with another unique element: the verse, or more precisely, the stanza. The question of the origin and form of the *Onegin*
stanza has been examined by several critics.[12] The fourteen-line sonnet-
like stanza with its unique rhyme-scheme (ababeecciddiff), whatever
its inspiration, imposes a severe discipline on the iambic tetrameter
line (which was already becoming trite under the weight of repetition
– a consideration which later induced Pushkin to move to the penta-
meter in 'The Little House in Kolomna'). The intricacy of the rhyme
pattern reflects the importance that Russian verse accords to rhyme
(blank verse having had only intermittent success in that language).
As Vinokur has pointed out, the stanza imposes regular divisions upon
the narrative (thus distancing the reader somewhat from the events
narrated), both inter-strophic divisions, and intra-strophic ones, especially after the eighth line (1941). These divisions have the advantage

for the author of providing 'natural breaks' for him to switch from story to digression, or from one stylistic level to another, so that the stylistic complexity of *Onegin* goes hand in hand with the *Onegin* stanza. The banter, the colloquial rhythms, the passages of dialogue, the lines of foreign-language text, the outrageous rhymes, all are subordinate to the precise discipline of this demanding form, which rarely tolerates even enjambment. The poet thus creates a challenge for himself – as Bayley has aptly pointed out – to fulfil again and again the demanding requirements of his self-imposed stanzaic structure, and yet maintain the facility and tone of colloquial banter.[13] That he manages to do so with apparent ease suggests the level of his art. The effect of the imposition of this complex form is to create another level of irony, the requirements of the rhyme scheme being fulfilled, occasionally, in bizarre or even outrageous ways; for example, with a foreign phrase or initials:

> Podumala chto skazhut liudi?
> I podpisala T.L.

> [*She wondered what people would say*
> *and signed: T.L. (PSS, VI, 320)*]

– lines from a draft in which T.L. (Tat'iana Larina) is pronounced according to the names formerly given the letters in the Russian alphabet: 'Tverdo, Liudi.' Another example is the macaronic rhyme:

> *Qu'écrirez-vous sur ces tablettes,*
> I podpis': *t. à v. Annette*

> [*'Qu'écrirez-vous sur ces tablettes'; And the signature: 't[oute]*
> *à v[ous]. Annette'* (Four: XXVIII: 10-11)]

It is important to note, however, that, as with language, Pushkin recoils from a rigorous perfection of form. The stanzaic text here is broken three times: by the intrusion of the two letters (in iambic tetrameter but not in stanzas) and by the song of the maidens. It stands, moreover, in contrast to the prose elements – mottoes, notes, and the introduction and comments in the Journey. Prose lurks like an ever-present threat, beyond the manicured gardens of the stanza, like the forests through which Tania roams after passing through the lune-shaped beds and alleys of the manorial park. The reader tends to forget that the letter, the epitaphs on the graves of Larin and Lenskii, and the dialogues and monologues are prose that has conformed, for the occasion, to the magic of the stanza. Pushkin's references to 'humble' or severe prose to which the years are driving him serve to emphasize the tension and elevate (as Tynianov and Lotman have suggested) 'prose versus verse' to a theme of the work (and one, again, which is adumbrated by the laconic subtitle 'a novel [= prose genre] in verse').[14]

The avoidance by Pushkin of formal perfection goes beyond the places where the text slips out of the *Onegin* stanza. In his discussion of the structure of *Onegin*, Nabokov remarks that 'its eight chapters form an elegant colonnade' (Nabokov, I, 16). This remark forms a curious lapsus on Nabokov's part. The latter defended the inviolability of the *editio optima* of 1837 as the text of the novel: 'It is ... the structure of the end product, and of the end product only, that has meaning for the student – or at least for this student – confronted by a master artist's word' (ibid.). Yet in the final text one of the 'columns' – Chapter Eight – had fallen down, to be hastily dragged to one side where it would remain as Onegin's Journey, while Chapter Nine was blatantly renumbered 'Eight.' There is a gap in that colonnade, which Pushkin himself had carefully constructed in all its symmetry and which was represented by the plan that he had prepared at Boldino in the fall of 1830 (giving titles to the chapters – cantos – and the place written):

ONEGIN

Part First	Foreword	
I canto	*Hypochondria*	Kishinev, Odessa
II canto	*The Poet*	Odessa 1824
III canto	*The Damsel*	Odessa, Mikh[ailovskoe]
Part Second		
IV canto	*The Countryside*	Mikh[ailovskoe] 1825
V canto	*The Name Day*	Mikh[ailovskoe] 1825-6
VI canto	*The Duel*	Mikh[ailovskoe] 1826
Part Third		
VII canto	*Moscow*	Mikh[ailovskoe] P[eters].B[urg] Malinn[iki]. 1827. [182]8
VIII canto	*The Wandering*	Mosc[ow]
IX canto	*The Grand Monde*	Bold[ino]

The reasons that motivated Pushkin to disrupt this classical symmetry may be guessed at.[15] The introduction that he places in front of the fragments of the *Journey* is characteristically – and playfully – evasive. The reasons, the poet claims, are important for him, but not for the public. It may be surmised that some (destroyed) portions of it contained material that was subversive. Katenin, in a letter to Annenkov, was of this opinion. Pushkin had confided to him that Onegin visited, in the original text, the Arakcheev military settlements, 'and here occurred remarks, judgements, expressions that were too violent for publication' (Nabokov, III, 257).

The remaining stanzas (extant in rough draft) could, however, conceivably have been placed in the position of the eighth chapter, with an indication of the missing stanzas. Such an arrangement would have preserved the 'elegant colonnade' (at least in a diminished form) and made, as Katenin suggested, a smoother transition to the Petersburg scenes of Chapter Eight (Nine). The 'pressure of censorship theory' does not, therefore, appear in itself to be of sufficient weight. More cogent would be the aesthetic argument – having suggested this image of perfect symmetry, Pushkin deliberately disrupts it. His breaking of the colonnade is another aspect of his eschewal of formal perfection: it is the defects, the slight disproportions, which make a fair face beautiful, and give it life, just as the solecisms and gallicisms give charm to Tat'iana's speech. By breaking the story line (placing the fragment of the Journey after the events of Chapter Eight, which it precedes in time), Pushkin signals that it is not formal perfection that is his goal, nor the chronology of the novelistic story-line that is paramount. The Journey forms a coda which has, in fact, an important poetic function. It returns us to the themes and the poetic world of Chapter One: Odessa, the romance of Italy, and a day in the life, not of Onegin, but another young rake – Pushkin. The symmetry becomes of a different type: instead of the 3:3:3 structure (or an early variant, 6:6, suggested by treating the end of Chapter Six as the end of the 'First Part'), the structure becomes rather 1:7:1.[16]

The principle of 'avoidance of formal perfection' or 'avoidance of symmetry' that is operative here is one that many scholars have failed to understand. The most egregious example, the émigré V.L. Burtsev, urged that the drafts be used to fill in all the missing stanzas and that the Journey be restored to its position as Chapter Eight. Burtsev (1934), asserting that the Boldino plan cited above was Pushkin's 'will,' demanded that the headings be added to the chapters, that the motto to Chapter One be moved to Eight (the Journey) and that the motto 'Pétri de vanité' be placed at the beginning of One. His entire essay is saturated with a strident dogmaticism and is a curious example of the intentional fallacy, but it is illustrative of the temptations to 'restore' that *Onegin* offers. The *Onegin* that we have, though its chapters do resemble Nabokov's elegant colonnade, is, like those infrequently visited manor-houses where Pushkin achieved much of his creative work, slightly ramshackle, with a fallen column, some shutters missing, and humble outbuildings appended. The less dogmatic reader should be prepared to see in this a rustic charm rather than a perfection lost.

Discussion in this chapter has centred upon questions that may appear peripheral in the light of the historically accepted view of *Onegin* as a novel. In fact the reverse is closer to the truth: the work is not defined by the term 'novel,' and that term forms only one part of Pushkin's definition. Pushkin's own perception of the piece is blurred: in speaking of it he uses the terms novel (*roman*) and poem (*poema*), chapter (*glava*) and canto (*pesn'*) interchangeably. Certainly, this ambiguity (Tynianov wrote of the 'principle of paradox' in *Onegin*) is a reflection of the tension between the prose genre (novel) and the verse which is a (perhaps even *the*) central theme of the work.

The question then arises of the extent to which we may speak of *Onegin* as a novel – how does the term 'novel' fit into the structure of the final work? Opinions on this subject are diverse. In the nineteenth century the most common approach was simply to ignore the limiting factors of the verse and treat *Onegin* as a realistic novel. Although this approach still has adherents (especially among a broader reading public) it has been severely discredited. For Shklovskii, the novel was a parody, the theme of the novel consisting in the manipulation of the action. For Lo Gatto, the work was a 'lyrical diary' in which the novelistic elements formed, presumably, a convenient frame on which the poet might hang his lyrical transports. The notion has been revived by L. Stilman, who, after his refutation of the 'realist' interpretation, goes on to discuss similarities between *Onegin* and Byron's *Don Juan*. He writes:

> This fairly obvious similarity lies in the 'form and manner'
> about which Belinskii spoke, in the poetic and stylistic struc-
> tures, which rest on completely different skeletons. If in *Don
> Juan* the skeleton is the ancient adventure novel and the bur-
> lesque epic, in *Onegin* an analogous role is played by the
> sentimental novel with motifs from the early romantic novel
> and the psychological novel of the beginning of the nineteenth
> century. (1958, 343)

Such references to the novel of *Onegin* as a 'framework' or a 'skeleton' or even as 'parody' are useful as a corrective to the traditional 'realistic novel' approach. But do they provide a satisfying description of the actual role of the novel? In the way they tend to reduce the importance of the novelistic events narrated, which do, after all, occupy the greater part of the reader's attention, it would seem that they are deficient.

It is certain that the author is describing, in *Onegin*, what appears to be a novel. There is a cast of characters – Onegin, Lenskii, Tat'iana, Ol'ga, Prince N, Zaretskii, the Larins, Tat'iana's nurse, Onegin's uncle, the housekeeper, M. Guillot, and many more – a surprisingly large list, especially for such a small work. There is, likewise, a list of novelistic events. A young man inherits an estate; a young girl falls in love with him. He rejects her. He has a fatal duel with her sister's intended. She goes to Moscow to be married off to a fat general. Some two years later she, now married, meets Onegin again. He falls in love with her. She rejects him.

Clearly there is, as part of the 'banter,' the stream of inspired commentary which forms the text of *Onegin*, the idea of a novel. It is, however, impossible to generalize about the narrator's attitude to (and hence the stylistic presentation of) both characters and events. It has been shown that the narrator is blatantly negligent (contemptuous even) of at least some of his characters. This is true of Ol'ga:

> Vsegda skromna, vsegda poslushna,
> Vsegda kak utro vesela,
> Kak zhizn' poeta prostodushna,
> Kak potsalui liubvi mila,
> Glaza kak nebo golubye,
> Ulybka, lokony l'nianye,
> Dvizhen'ia, golos, legkoi stan,
> Vse v Ol'ge ... no liuboi roman
> Voz'mite i naidete verno
> Ee portret ...

> [*Always modest, always obedient, always as merry as the morning, as simple-minded as the life of a poet, as darling as the kiss of love, with eyes as blue as the sky; her smile, her flaxen locks, her movements, voice, slender form, everything in Ol'ga ... but take any novel and you'll surely find her portrait.* (Two: XXIII: 1-10)]

Here the character 'Ol'ga' has, not the believable existence of a realistic portrayal (the 'illusion of reality'), but a purely conventional (*uslovnyi*) function, a theoretical existence as the parody of the muse of an elegiac poet.

The same is true of Onegin himself, at least the Onegin of the Onegin-Tat'iana romance. Chizhevskii quotes Jakobson's discussion of metonymy as a realistic device in *Onegin*, in particular the interior of Onegin's study, noting 'these surroundings, created by the hero himself, allow his essence to be discerned' (Chizhevskii 1968, 153-4). It is curious to note, however, that Tat'iana's conclusion, after acquainting herself with Onegin's intimate surroundings, is to ask herself: 'Might he not be, in fact, a parody?' (Seven: XXIV: 14). We receive no image of Onegin from the work (significantly, his externals are not described), and the intellectual bric-a-brac with which he is surrounded is typical of a young man of the period (as generations of critics have pointed out) rather than expressive of Onegin's individuality. Like Ol'ga, Onegin is a cipher, a question mark.

The characters in *Onegin* thus are scattered in a limbo which varies from parody through stylization to an approximation of psychological reality. The character whose psychological reality is most clearly sketched and whose thoughts and emotions we know in most detail is Tat'iana (so much so that the notion that the work should really be called *Tat'iana Larin* has become a critical commonplace). There is therefore a distinct note of iconoclasm in Shklovskii's question: 'Baldly stated, did "Pushkin" weep over Tat'iana, or was he joking?' (1923, 214). The critic's own opinion is given later: he believes the tone of the narrator's declarations of his love for Tat'iana is Sternian. Strictly, we may discern here a further complication – a paradigm of narrators, as suggested by Shklovskii's quotation marks: 'Pushkin' (character in novel) wept over Tat'iana, but Pushkin (writer) was joking. In my discussion of Tat'iana in chapter four I will analyse further the realization of her character. Whether she appears as realistic or not, it is certain that she had, as a poetic image, a certain charm for Pushkin that Shklovskii fails to take into account.

The discussion of the novel element in *Onegin* has to involve also the question of the completeness of the plot. The beginning, although it is abrupt – in medias res – as we encounter Onegin on the road to his uncle's estate, conforms to novelistic convention by offering a sketchy biography of the hero in the retrospective stanzas which constitute the larger part of Chapter One.[17] The ending is, however, of an unprecedented abruptness, which the author, far from mitigating, draws attention to:

Kto ne dochel Ee romana
I vdrug umel rasstat'sia s nim,
Kak ia s Oneginym moim.

[[*Blessed is he*] *who has not read its* [*life's*] *novel through to the end, and was able to part with it suddenly, as I do with my Onegin.* (Eight: LI: 12-14)]

The effect of this abrupt ending is to destroy any trace of the illusion of Onegin as a reality that has developed in the reader's mind, and to show us, as Stilman has it, the artificiality of the decorations.[18]

The fact remains that, despite the tone of artificiality and conventionality, bordering upon and frequently becoming parody, with which the narrator frequently treats the novel, the novel is an essential element in the composition, not merely as a 'skeleton' or 'framework,' but as a poetic construct through which issues are examined that are meaningful for poet and audience. The 'novel' which we have in *Onegin* is in ironical counterpoint to the expectations of the reader. As both Lotman (1976,90) and Bayley (1971, 265) have suggested, these expectations arise out of the reader's knowledge of the vast antecedent literature that Pushkin invokes in *Onegin*.

Indeed those expectations can be viewed as an autonomous construct (given life by the 'sensitive reader' who comes to muse at Lenskii's grave). The novel can be imagined as having a complete existence in the mind of the reader, whereas the author expresses an ambivalent, sometimes involved but more often negligent and cavalier, attitude towards it.

Although the narrator tends to undermine the illusory reality of the novel by his irony, and by the frequently conventional, parodistic descriptions of character and event, in another way he paradoxically attempts to heighten the sense of immediacy. This is achieved by intertwining the novel with elements of the reality of his own life. Pushkin the narrator is a friend of Onegin, and an admirer of Tat'iana. Other real personages, such as Viazemskii and Kaverin, pass through the invisible walls and participate in the novel in a minor way. Thus, though the author in one way stresses the artificiality and conventionality of his novel, in another way he endows it with a great deal of specificity and actuality. The events of the novel blend into a stylized (and shadowy) version of his own biography, a fact which has fascinated many readers.[19] (Studies have been made, for example, of the chronology of events in the novel, placing perhaps a little too much credence in Pushkin's tongue-in-cheek remark that 'in our novel the time is calculated according to the calendar.')[20]

Tantalizingly, the novel of *Onegin* exists and does not exist within the wide confines of the total work. It is, as the author is at pains to make us aware, a figment of his imagination, an imagined extension of his own world in which reality (or a stylized version of it) and fiction are interwoven in an elaborate conceit which has the plot features of a novel, but whose illusion is frequently disrupted and eventually destroyed by the author. Questions about, for example, the fate of the protagonists are simply not relevant, since the protagonists cease to exist as soon as they disappear from the text. Pushkin was aware of the impact of his *ex abrupto* finish. Although in terms of the sentimental novel, whose features he had borrowed, this was 'ungrammatical' – the required ending being death or marriage – in terms of *Onegin* the 'doh' to which the work returns at the end is not that dictated by the novelistic convention, but that of the narrator's life. Hence the great importance of the (apparently casual) last line of the Journey: 'And so, I lived then in Odessa ...,' echoing note 10 from Chapter One and evoking, through the prism of time (and with a tinge of nostalgia), the themes of Odessan exile of Pushkin.[21]

Earlier in the discussion on *badinage*, it was suggested that one of the most distinctive elements in the form of *Onegin* is the dominant position occupied by the narrator-audience mode. It was further suggested that the 'audience' was composed of a number of elements (Hoisington's 'hierarchy of narratees') – intimate friends and poets, critics, sensitive young ladies, etc. Equally important is the problem of the author in the narrative structure. Several critics (e.g., Hoisington 1976, Hielscher 1966) have emphasized that the author is analysable into several distinct figures. For the purposes of the present argument, three can be distinguished, although they overlap and at times merge. They are:

$Pushkin_1$	$Pushkin_2$	$Pushkin_3$
Actual historical figure	Narrator and lyric poet	Participant in the novel (friend of Onegin, admirer of Tat'iana)
Term: implied author –	author/narrator –	'Pushkin'

These distinctions are not, it should be emphasized, pursued rigorously throughout the novel. On the contrary, the ambiguity of the 'I' is part of the overall ambiguity of the work. There is, so to speak, a 'paradigm' of Pushkins, and at any one time it may be one or another which dominates. For example, all three Pushkins listed relate to a female (although in each case this relationship is – or appears to be – chaste).

True, the author includes some coy references to his affairs of the heart:

> A ta, s kotoroi obrazovan
> Tat'iany milyi Ideal ...
>
> [*And she, from whom I shaped my dear ideal Tat'iana ...* (Eight: LI: 6-7)]

In a parallel way, the poet-narrator who comments on the technical aspects of the text has a muse (described in Eight: I-VI) who is comically replaced at one point by his old nurse (in a disquisition on muses provoked by the Lenskii-Ol'ga relationship), and a paradigm of other equally comic listener-victims (Four: XXXV: 1-14).

'Pushkin,' the participant in the action, presents himself as a secret and sympathetic admirer of Tat'iana:

> No zdes' s pobedoiu pozdravim
> Tat'ianu miluiu moiu
>
> [*But here let us congratulate my dear Tat'iana on her victory* (Seven: LV: 1-2)]

or:

> Tat'iana, milaia Tat'iana!
> S toboi teper' ia slezy l'iu.
>
> [*Tat'iana, dear Tat'iana, I now pour out my tears with you.* (Three: XV: 1-2)]

It is possible to extrapolate, from such hints, a Pushkin-Tat'iana relationship.[22] But such a relationship is present in the text only as a potential. There is, indeed, a considerable amount of 'play' in it: 'Pushkin' the character sympathizes with Tat'iana, while Pushkin her creator manipulates her fate. It is the blurring of the different 'Pushkins,' as well as the overlay of Tat'iana on the various hypostases of 'muse' and shadowy existential referents, which makes *Onegin* such an extraordinarily complex text.

The facts of the real Pushkin's biography serve as the basis for a shadowy, stylized biography of the 'Pushkin' of the text. This biography, as I shall argue in chapter six, is in fact a 'second plot,' which runs in counterpoint to the novel plot and is ultimately more important. The hints and allusions to the Pushkin biography are scattered throughout the text, including the footnotes. They are mostly cryptic in character and therefore presuppose an initiated reader (as do Pushkin's letters). Nevertheless, the events that they recreate form an important narrative. We can trace in them Pushkin's life in St Petersburg to 1820, his visits to the country (Mikhailovskoe) during that time, his exile to the South – the Caucasus, Yalta, Bessarabia, Odessa – his subsequent sojourn in Mikhailovskoe, the Decembrist uprising, and his return to the Capitals.

The *badinage* that *Onegin* contains is therefore directed at a specific problem: to create an image of 'Pushkin,' complex in structure and composed of at least the three components that we have sketched, and to hint at a biography of that 'Pushkin,' which forms the second plot. The problem of 'Pushkin' is inseparable from another question that must be mentioned since it has an important bearing on the form and structure of *Onegin*: the so-called 'digressions.'[23] These are passages that are inserted into the novelistic narrative and deal with problems and themes outside the mainstream of the novelistic plot. Some are by way of introduction or conclusion to a chapter, while others are inserted directly into the midst of the story-line and have the effect of retarding the novelistic unfolding of events and distancing the reader from them. Although Pushkin uses it himself at one point, the term 'digressions' (*otstupleniia*) is not totally satisfactory, since there is a great variety of such features in the text: the generalization offered as a commentary on the novelistic plot; the authorial aside or parenthetical quip (be it on a personal matter – 'but harmful is the North to me' – or on a professional one – 'now the reader expects the rhyme "frosts-roses" '); the apostrophizing of a real person – e.g., the poets Baratynskii and Iazykov – or, of course, of the 'reader'; the discussion on, say, Russian weather – 'But our Northern summer / is a caricature of Southern writers' – which manages at the same time to be a generalization, a description of the fall Onegin spends on his estate, and, beyond all that, of Pushkin's sojourn at Mikhailovskoe; the lyrical flight – most notably, the interpolation on the charms of 'little feet,' which is simply inserted without apology or motivation into Chapter One and is the purest form of digression; and the introductions and conclusions to certain chapters which likewise have the function of distracting the reader from the novelistic plot-line. To these must be added the mottoes and footnotes, which add yet another discursive layer whose function is closely related to that of the digressions. In these, the voice may belong to any one of the three 'Pushkins.'

Of the three, the fictional 'Pushkin,' who is Onegin's friend and shares a similar outlook on life, is the least satisfactory. As Nabokov has pointed out, the content of the digressions in Chapters One to Three is a reflection of conventional Gallic cynicism (Nabokov, I, 19-20). One of the 'sources' of this is the aphorisms of Chateaubriand, one of which is quoted in note 15: 'Si j'avais la folie de croire encore au bonheur, je le chercherais dans l'habitude.' The effect of these digressions is to diminish the distinction between Pushkin and his hero. Where Pushkin is content to permit such 'blurring' in the case of the female characters, he is careful to stress the distinction between himself and Onegin:

> Vsegda ia rad zametit' raznost'
> Mezhdu Oneginym i mnoi,
> Chtoby nasmeshlivyi chitatel'
> Ili kakoi-nibud' izdatel'
> Zamyslovatoi klevety,
> Ne povtorial potom bezbozhno,
> Chto namaral ia svoi portret,
> Kak Bairon, gordosti poet.

> [*I am always glad to note the difference between Onegin and me, so that a mocking reader or some publisher of a malicious calumny, discerning my features here, should not then blasphemously say that I have scrawled my own portrait like Byron, the poet of pride.* (One: LVI: 8-11)]

There has been a tendency, especially among Soviet scholars, to read these lines too literally. Pushkin and Onegin have, indeed, much more in common than Pushkin would have us believe. These lines are to be read as a conventional disclaimer, derived in part, seemingly, from the preface to the second edition of Benjamin Constant's *Adolphe*: 'J'ai déjà protesté contre les allusions qu'une malignité qui aspire au mérite de la pénétration, par d'absurdes conjectures, a su y trouver.' (We should compare this with Sismondi: 'Je reconnais l'auteur à chaque page.') The fact that Constant's protest is not without a certain irony should not prevent us from seeing behind it the marking of a real problem: the distinction of author and hero. Lermontov was to refer once again to this 'old and sad joke' in his foreword to *A Hero of Our Time*. In fact, Onegin and 'Pushkin' are practically indistinguishable as far as their social opinions, attested in the digressions, are concerned. What divides them – crucially – is Onegin's inability to distinguish an iambus from a trochee.

If the digressions on social matters – friendship, relatives, women – are a little disquieting to read and tend to confuse the images of Onegin and 'Pushkin,' the digressions and footnotes on professional matters – choice of genre, foreign words, etc. – have the important, and useful, role of distancing the reader from the novel by drawing attention to its artifice. They create the image of an author involved in a running battle with critics and fellow poets on such questions as genre, foreign words in Russian, and style. It is here that the difference between creator and creation is felt most strongly (Pushkin even mocks Onegin who, falling in love with Tat'iana, 'almost became a poet' – 'Pinocchio becoming human'). Together with the mass of literary allusions, quotes, borrowings, pastiches, parodies, and echoes that saturate the text, this set of asides and digressions serves to create a work that is hyper-conscious of the literary process and could validly be read as a meditation on literary form and convention.

An additional measure of disruption of the novelistic pattern is provided by the 'omissions,' i.e. the places where omitted material is marked by stanza numbers in the final version. The omission of stanzas, far from being unique, is a commonplace of romantic poetry. Pushkin's use of the device may be seen to be prompted firstly and simply by the necessity to remove material that was too personal, too likely to cause offence, or simply unsatisfactory as poetry. For the omitted stanzas there exist fair-copy or draft variants with the exception of four. Over these there is a question mark: were they 'artificial' breaches in the narrative that were intended to have a specific poetic weight (Nabokov seems inclined to think so, at least with regard to Seven: XXXIX), or is it simply that the variants have been lost, and they have the same status as the other omissions? Whatever the case, the fact that variants exist is 'illicit' information and should not colour our view of the function (rather than the cause) of the omissions. In general we may say that they heighten the air of negligence and insouciance which permeates the poem, and add a layer of mystery as the reader is invited to conjecture about the 'reasons' for the omission – is it because of some gossipy detail of the poet's private life (evidently the case in Eight: II: 5-14), or because the poet deemed certain satirical descriptions of individuals too risqué (Eight: XXV: 9-14), or is there a political reference to be guessed at in certain omissions (prompted by the exigencies of censorship)? Such are the conjecturings which the omissions had the effect of provoking. They are, as Tynianov has it, fillable with 'any content' the reader may add, and increase the 'opening' of the novel, the confines of which are, thanks to the deformations which Pushkin imposes, far from clearly defined.[24]

In trying to define the nature of the genre of *Onegin* (and the form which gives it shape), one becomes aware of the similarities with Tat'iana's search for the 'word' to describe her demonic hero. The 'word' that fits Onegin most closely is 'parody.' In discussing the nature of parody Tynianov proposes a theory of 'two planes' – the plane of the text and a deeper plane, that of the remembered work which is the object of the parody (1929b, 416). In a similar way, the text of *Onegin* is the deformed parody of an underlying concept in the mind of the reader. Lotman and Bayley have each asked in different ways how it is that readers have perceived and continue to perceive *Onegin* realistically. Is it naiveté on the part of the reader, perversity, or a reflection of that underlying concept, the novel that the text parodies? The first half of Pushkin's original definition can be reduced thus: *ne roman* (not a novel) = *neroman* (a non-novel) = *antiroman* (the anti-novel) (Siniavskii's definition).[25] This anti-novel is the bright moon-like sliver that contains the dark shape of the novel in its arms, the circle which the reduced silvery shape we see only hints at. The examination of that novel, of its plot, its characters, its possible importance, is the substance of the chapter that follows.

3

Zhenia and Tania: The Novel Transformed

Vot tak, stoletiia podriad,
Vse vliubleny my nevpopad,
i stranstvuiut, ne sovpadaia,
dva serdtsa, sirykh dve lad'i,
iamb nenasytnyi uslazhdaia
velikoi gorech'iu liubvi.

[*So it is for centuries on end, we forever miss our mark in love, and two hearts wander without meeting, like two lonely barks, sweetening the insatiable iambus with the great bitterness of love.* (Bella Akhmadullina)]

There is a way of looking at a novel, in particular at the realistic novel, which assumes that the text we read describes directly only a part of the vast sum total of imagined events that it implies. Indeed, in that that sequence of imagined events dovetails into the real world, and in that even the tiniest action could be described in infinite detail, the 'all-telling' novel would be infinitely long; it would be a total description of reality, both the real and the imagined parts, in its chronological infinity. This premise serves to remind us that the selection of events to be described in a novelistic text is highly restricted and conventional, and that there are hierarchies of other events – real and imagined, expressed or understood – lying beyond the reach of the narrative. A similiar convention is the frame around a painting, which more or less arbitrarily limits the matter depicted while suggesting a world beyond. To apply this assumption to *Onegin*: we know that two days after Tat'iana's name-day (14 January 18??), Onegin pulls the trigger and his bullet kills Lenskii. This event is described 'first-hand' in the narrative, although a close scrutiny of the text would indicate that the narrator is highly selective in the detail which he chooses to mention. At a more remote level, but still relevant and still unambiguous, is the fact that Tat'iana is married to Prince N at the point at which we observe her in Chapter Eight. Even more remote are sets of facts that may or may not be understood. Thus, we are told that Onegin was born (to quote a banal example), but are we also to assume (as seems to be implied by the narrator's use of the past tense) that Onegin is dead at the time of the actual narration? The answer is unknowable. Outside the frame the characters have no existence. It is impossible to know if Onegin is dead, because his death takes place in the oblivion beyond the pale of the recorded events.

The premise sketched here is basic to the novel that is embedded in *Onegin*. The way a narrative actually treats the set of real and imagined events that it comprises determines what kind of novel will result. The treatment given by Malcolm Lowry, say, to the events in his novel *Under the Volcano* is very different from that given to the events in Turgenev's *Fathers and Sons* (although in the latter novel, too, the manipulation of the narrative is far from simple). It is, however, too simplistic to say that the greater the degree of manipulation of the narrative the greater the tendency to destroy the illusion of reality, to break the contract between the author and the narratee that sanctifies the suspension of disbelief. The human sensibility has been trained (by previous reading and conditioning – perhaps by the very structure of the human intelligence) to allow for all manner of distortions. The eye can understand and believe in the existence of an object whether it is seen with the naked eye, through a stained-glass window, on a black-and-white or coloured television screen, or in a stylized painting, although all these media have a greater or lesser degree of conventionality. Finding the exact point at which credibility is either maintained or destroyed (i.e., is in a fine balance) is a task that many artists have perceived to be crucial. The contradictory critical interpretations of *Onegin* – as parody or realistically perceived novel – indicate that Pushkin pitched his text at precisely such a point of balance between illusion and parody. Thus, although there are good reasons for the formalist critics to see in *Onegin* a Sternian 'anti-novel,' a parody of novelistic conventions, the novel or 'romance' exists within *Onegin* as a web of episodes and relationships that have a specific content and meaning and deserve to be examined in their own right. Such an analysis of *Onegin* as a novel that creates an illusion of reality, that is 'realistic,' though an enterprise that is distortive of the text as a whole, can in some ways be instructive. The following attempt to pursue this line of inquiry – though hypothetical and ultimately obliged to fail – is intended to illuminate the specific nature of the novelistic structure that is contained within *Onegin*.

It is typical of *Onegin* that the 'novel' – i.e., the sum total of the imagined events centred on Onegin and Tat'iana, Lenskii and Ol'ga – is subjected to a large number of transformations, of selections and distortions, before it becomes text. One egregious example of this tendency that is worth analysing is the visit to the Larins by Lenskii and Onegin at the beginning of Chapter Three, when Onegin and Tat'iana meet each other for the first time. We do not receive from the narrator a direct account of this episode, but rather see it reflected in the subsequent accounts of it, by Lenskii, Onegin, and Tat'iana. This is an elegant stratagem of Pushkin's, since the episode described subjectively by the participants in the event is ambiguous in a way that a direct account by an omniscient narrator could not be. As they return home after the visit, Onegin asks Lenskii which girl is Tat'iana. The question indicates either how little importance he attaches to the meeting and the young lady's identity, or (if the question is disingenuous, i.e., he does not want to reveal his interest) how much. The comment that he prefers her to Ol'ga (or would, if he were a poet) suggests that he saw more than he admits, and that his inquiry was indeed a far from casual one. It is instructive to compare the description by Lenskii of Tat'iana's outward appearance – 'the one who, melancholy and silent like Svetlana, entered and sat down by the window' (Three: V: 2-4) – with her own account in the letter to Onegin (where it is, on the contrary, Onegin who enters): 'Hardly had you come in, when in a trice I recognized you, became all weak, flushed, and in my thoughts said: That's him!' (Three: Letter: 44-6). Thus, Tat'iana's description of the event is diametrically opposed to Lenskii's. Later the narrator has Onegin recall 'both pallid hue and mournful appearance' (Four: XI: 6), but one wonders whether this is not a dim echo of Lenskii's remark in the recesses of Onegin's mind. Pursuing this 'realistic-psychological' chain of interpretation, we may remark that Onegin's confession that, if he had a desire to marry, he would choose Tat'iana suggests that he had observed her closely during the visit. There is a last echo of that initial meeting in Tat'iana's monologue in Eight, where she recalls 'those haunts where I saw you for the first time, Onegin' (Eight: XLVI: 10-11). The contradictions and vaguenesses with which the episode is reflected in the narrative are instructive. Far from constructing a realistic and precise psychologically convincing description of the event, the author's effort is directed at showing how the event is reflected in the sentiments of the different participants.[1] This is so far the case that at least one critic with expectations of verisimilitude has railed against the 'love at first sight' assumption in the episode. In terms of the realistic novel he would be right – but that would be another story.

The oblique description, by the different characters, of one of the most important episodes in the romance of Evgenii and Tat'iana is but one example of the transformations which that romance undergoes as Pushkin develops his text. Another is the common narrative device of the inversion. Thus, the poem begins in medias res with Onegin's thoughts as he speeds post-haste to his uncle's sick-bed. We then step back in time for the rest of One to review Onegin's education, a typical day in his life in the capital, and his friendship with Pushkin. Chronologically speaking, the chapter returns to its beginning as the two friends depart for their different destinations. We have to do here with a relatively conventional narrative inversion. Compared with this inversion is that which takes place as a result of the omission of the original Chapter Eight, which is placed at the end as the Fragments from Onegin's Journey. Here we have to do with an unconventional fictional device – the casual expression of the author's negligent attitude towards the events of the novel, offered as a sort of encore, an additional titbit of information for the curious, the 'Onegin fans,' or a simple recognition of the fact that parts of the Journey had already been published.

In at least one instance in the narrative there is an event of considerable importance that is totally undescribed: Tat'iana's marriage. Although this is adumbrated, in Tat'iana's forebodings about the trip to Moscow to the 'bride market' and also, it has been argued, in the first part of her dream, where the bear can be taken as the fearful husband of the arranged marriage before whom she flees, the event of the marriage itself is passed over entirely. We see Tat'iana make her conquest of 'that fat general' at the Moscow ball in Chapter Seven, and then we see her at the rout after Onegin's return to Petersburg in Eight. The laconicism of Pushkin's treatment of the event contrasts with the detailed realism with which Lev Tolstoi, say, describes the marriage of Levin and Kitty in *Anna Karenina*. That kind of detail is beyond the direct concern of the kind of novel Pushkin is writing, and the silence with which he treats the emotional aspect of Tat'iana's marriage is more effective in its delicacy than any detailed digging into her psychological state would be. If we accept the notion that the putative addressees of the poem are intimates of the narrator and therefore frequenters of Moscow and Petersburg society, then we may assume that they would be familiar with the 'external' social event of the wedding, which could therefore be skipped. The narrative is, by contrast, concerned with the intimate life of the heroine and hero, their sentiments and private agonies – events about which such a socially informed narratee would not know and at which he could not guess, given the aplomb with which Tat'iana comports herself in society, but to which the narrator has privileged access.

If we imagine the 'romance' of Onegin and Tat'iana occurring over a space of time, and that time, which the protagonists 'experience,' unrolling at a measured speed, then by contrast the text of the poem that relates this romance is highly selective and frequently highly compressive in its approach to the events of the romance. The narrative can be seen to be organized into three basic types of time unit: the general description of a period of time; the 'typical day'; and the specific day (which may be supposed to correspond to a specific date in history). Pushkin uses the second type very sparingly – on a total of only three occasions: the famous description of the typical day of Onegin in Petersburg in One (XV-XXXVI); the description of Onegin's day in the country in Four (only two stanzas long, XXXVI-XXXIX) with a modification (for the coming of winter, XLIV); and the description of Pushkin's typical day in Odessa (from 'Time was, the sunrise canon ...' – Onegin's Journey: XXIV: 1 in Nabokov's notation – to '... only the Black Sea sounds' – XXIX: 14). The text is mainly constructed of generalized periods of time, in which the days are a blur, interspersed with descriptions of 'specific days.' Since the time element is manipulated with great subtlety, the reader must be very aware in order to retain his precise bearings in the chronological landscape.

By his use of the three units in question the author is able to speed up or brake the narrative, so that novelistic time is occasionally reduced to slow motion – e.g., the night during which Tat'iana composes her letter to Onegin – and at other times so accelerated that a considerable length of time is squeezed into a few lines – e.g., the stanzas in Eight (XXXIV-XXXIX) in which Onegin shuts himself up in his cabinet to read. The 'typical day' device is a different way of covering a more or less large period of time without, however, losing the focus on detail. Strictly speaking, one should add to these three 'chronological building blocks' a fourth which is typical of *Onegin*: the blank or gap in the narration such as the marriage of Tat'iana already discussed. The latter device is really an invasion into the narrated time of the oblivion that surrounds the events in any novel 'beyond the frame.' To put it in cinematographic terms, it is as if we were watching a very erratic projector which speeds up and slows down a film with pieces missing and others spliced in the wrong order and yet other sections with simple numbers on them.

In the manipulation of chronological time, as in the selection of novelistic events for treatment, there is an underlying principle. The selection is partly that of the 'novel of sentiment,' which focuses, slow-motion, on such specifics as the tête-à-tête with Onegin in the garden and its subsequent sequel in Tat'iana's Petersburg house. The other principle that appears to be operative is the 'sociological vignette' – the typical day of Onegin in the city, or of Pushkin in Odessa, which serves to fix the character of two of the most important and contrasted dramatis personae.

The internal chronological structure of the novel is rendered more complex by the existence (and superimposition upon the novelistic line) of two other time scales: the authorial time, i.e., the point where the poet is putting pen to paper (to which he draws attention by asides – 'But the North is harmful for me' – and footnotes – 'Written in Odessa'; and the reader's time, which was originally slow (as the novel was published, chapter by chapter) but became speeded up when the work was published as a separate monograph. The reader's time scale is 'created' by the frequent apostrophizing of the reader by the poet, and by the introduction of the character of the 'reader' (Chapter Six: XLII).

In the penultimate stanza of Chapter Eight, Pushkin, bidding his characters farewell, writes:

> Promchalos' mnogo, mnogo dnei
> S tekh por, kak iunaia Tat'iana
> I s nei Onegin v smutnom sne
> Iavilisia vpervye mne –
> I dal' svobodnogo romana
> Ia skvoz' magicheskii kristal
> Eshche ne iasno razlichal.

> [*Many many days have passed since youthful Tat'iana and with her Onegin first appeared to me in a vague dream – and I perceived, as yet unclearly, the distant perspective of a free novel through my magic crystal.* (Eight: L: 8-14)]

There is considerable evidence, in the draft of the novel and in the text itself, that Pushkin developed his plot (*fabula*) while writing the work, and that the final result differs in a number of details from the concept with which he started out. Thus, the plan seems to have called for Onegin, finding himself in the country, to fall in love with a simple Russian girl. The references to Tat'iana's destruction at various points in the text suggest that she was to die (e.g., Three: XV: 1-5 and Six: III: 11-12). It is unknown what fate the writer had in store for Onegin. His late remark, reported by Iuzefovich, to the effect that Onegin was either to die in the Caucasus or become a Decembrist must be viewed with suspicion, since the work was well advanced before the Decembrist revolt took place. The ending of 'The Gypsies' ('Tsygany') and 'The Prisoner of the Caucasus' ('Kavkazskii plennik') may serve as indication of what was probably intended: that Onegin would be reduced to a state of mindless mortification by the destruction of the girl. The use of the past tense for the work, and the fact that 'Pushkin' feels free to write about the intimate life of his 'friend,' do indeed suggest that Onegin is dead. The process of development this 'unclearly perceived' situation was to go through was complex. Among other matters, the important change was that the girl split into two figures: Ol'ga and Tat'iana. Onegin fails to fall in love with the latter at first sight. Also, the figure of Lenskii undergoes considerable development, from a positively evaluated figure to a parodistic one. There is another 'contradiction' that remains in the final text, about whether Lenskii was to marry Ol'ga. Evidently this development was a relatively late addition. (Nabokov notes, for example, the contradiction that Lenskii is to get married some two to three days after Tat'iana's name-day party.)[2]

The shift of scene for the long poem, from the exotic setting of the southern poems to the Russian countryside and capitals, is one clear reason for the restructuring of the plot. Tat'iana's ultimate fate, to endure a marriage of convenience, is much more probable than that she should be destroyed for her love. Ol'ga's reaction to the death of her swain is even more (and ironically) realistic (in the non-literary sense). That Pushkin was not compelled to remove all the ambiguities wrought by his changes to the plot is evidence, not of any carelessness, but of the operative 'principle of contradiction':

> Protivorechii ochen' mnogo,
> No ikh ispravit' ne khochu
>
> [*There are very many contradictions, but I don't feel like correcting them* (One: LX: 6-7)]

Despite the past tense of the observation at the end of Chapter Eight, all is not clear with the novel even after its completion, and a number of problematical areas exist (which will be discussed). The action of the plot may be summarized as follows. (The events are chosen with a certain amount of arbitrariness.)

THE NOVELISTIC 'EVENTS' OR PLOT

We meet Onegin as a young man in his mid-twenties. He has wasted some six years in riotous living in Petersburg – principally in eating, drinking, seducing the wives of others, and duelling. In the course of his life in grand society, Onegin has lost his enthusiasm, has become bored, disenchanted, and cynical. It is in this state that he meets the narrator/poet. His father dies leaving nothing but debts, and then Onegin's uncle dies while the nephew is on the way to the estate leaving him a rich man. Onegin decides to stay on the newly inherited estate. He exchanges the burdensome corvée of the peasants for a light quit-rent, thereby making enemies of his conservative neighbours, but he acquires a friend, Vladimir Lenskii, a poet newly returned from Göttingen. With the latter he visits the Larins – the widowed mother and the daughters Ol'ga, betrothed to Lenskii, and Tat'iana. Tat'iana falls in love with Onegin and writes him a letter. He visits the Larins and patronizingly rejects her advances, pleading his inability to be a loving husband. The autumn passes. In January, on Tat'iana's name-day, there is a party to which Lenskii persuades Onegin to go, suggesting that it will be a quiet affair. It turns out to be too crowded and raucous for Onegin's taste: peeved, he pays court to Ol'ga and when Lenskii discovers that she has promised Onegin the last mazurka, Lenskii storms off to his house. In a huff he writes a note demanding satisfaction of Onegin. Although a visit to Ol'ga the next day convinces Lenskii that his fears about her fidelity are unfounded, Lenskii goes to his duel with Onegin in the morning and is killed by him. Shortly after, Onegin leaves and journeys around Russia (and perhaps abroad). Ol'ga marries a young hussar and Tat'iana is left alone on the estate with her mother. She visits the grave of Lenskii regularly and one day comes by chance to Onegin's house, where she asks permission to go in, and reads the novels in his study. From this she gains a better understanding of her hero. Her mother, anxious about her future, takes her to Moscow the following winter to find her a husband. There she is married to a prince (apparently a fat general who spies her at a ball). Onegin returns a couple of years later to Petersburg and falls in love with the transformed

Tat'iana – now Princess N – whom he meets there. He besieges her with letters, to no avail. He then closets himself off all winter with books. At the approach of spring he visits Tat'iana once more. She reproaches him for his desire to destroy her, informs him that she loves him still, but that she will remain faithful to her husband, who at that point enters and interrupts the conversation.

Such a brief (and highly selective) retelling of the chain of novelistic events, although based on the evidence in the text, is still speculative in at least one particular: is it the 'fat general' whom Tat'iana marries, or someone else? The little 'leaps of faith' necessary to reconstruct the novelistic events are also very much in evidence in the chronology that is usually applied to the sequence of the events. This chronology is summarized by Shaw as follows:

> He [Onegin] was born about 1796, ended his education and entered St. Petersburg society in 1812; met Pushkin in 1819-20, and both went their separate ways in early summer 1820, when Onegin was about 24. He met Lenskii and the Larins, including Tat'iana, in summer 1820; duelled with Lenskii (two days after St. Tat'iana's Day) in January 1821, in early summer 1821 at about 25 started in his travels, where he arrived at Bakhchisarai three years after Pushkin, and hence in 1823, from where he went to Odessa and was to see Pushkin there in 1823-24; he was in St. Petersburg for the season of 1824-25, where he met and fell in love with the now married Tat'iana, and had his meeting with her in April 1825. (1980, 41-2)

The 'leaps of faith' necessary to create such a chronology are numerous. Thus, one relies on the introduction to the first chapter (later eliminated when the novel was published in its entirety) for the information that we see Onegin in 1819. From this it follows that the meetings between Onegin and Pushkin took place in early May, before the poet's departure for the south – May 1820, which does not exactly fit with 'How frequently in the summer time ...' (One: XLVII). At least two critics (Gustafson and Marchenko-Narokov) have expressed dissatisfaction with the accepted chronology, Gustafson pointing out that the remark in footnote 17, 'We dare to declare that in our novel the time is calculated according to the calendar,' could well be read as ironic (1962, 18). An émigré critic, Marchenko-Narokov proposes a much more spread-out calendar, according to which the final scene takes place in 1828 (1967). He bases his criticism on questions of verisimilitude – i.e. the amount of time it would take Onegin to transfer his uncle's property to his own name, etc. Such concerns (as we have seen with Tat'iana's sudden love for Onegin) are hardly those of Pushkin. It is true, however, that the last chapter, especially, is overlaid with a tone suggestive of the years after Pushkin's return from exile (1826-30), when he brought his muse to the balls and routs of the capitals. In a sense, perhaps, the chapter exists in two time zones – the 'plot' one and the one in which it was written. Such an ambiguity could be seen as another example of the principle of paradox that runs through the novel.

The problem of the plot of *Onegin* is not yet exhausted, however. The role and relationship of the narrator to the plot remains to be discussed. Thus, the narrator tells us that he possesses a number of documents, which he cites in the text. These are Tat'iana's letters to Onegin, Lenskii's verse on the eve of the duel, and Onegin's letters to Tat'iana (only one of which is quoted). The image presented is that of the 'editor' of the epistolary novel who is publishing a correspondence that has fallen into his hands. The implication of the narrator in the events is increased by his admiration for Tat'iana – as if she were a person of his acquaintance. The 'plot' framework behind this narrator can only be imagined. Pushkin is a friend of Onegin. When the latter dies (in some unknown fashion), Pushkin finds the letter from Tat'iana among his papers. He is touched, and turns to Tat'iana for more information. She gives him Lenskii's poetry and (copies of?) Onegin's letters to her, and describes the details of the romance. This would be a possible interpretation of the facts. The epigraph 'Pétri de vanité ...' could well be interpreted as being taken from a 'letter' from Tat'iana to Pushkin, in which she describes the events in the novel and gives her own opinion of Onegin's character.[3]

If one can perceive the outlines of such a narrator-centred 'subplot,' derived from the tradition of the epistolary novel, then it is equally clear that the totality of the novel structure goes beyond this: there are details in the narration which an 'editor,' relying on documents and on the account from Tat'iana, could not know – e.g., the details of the conversation between Onegin and Lenskii in Four. The 'editor' model for the narrator is thus combined with the 'ubiquitous' and omniscient narrator later to become the conventional narrative mode in the realistic novel. The narration in *Onegin* is ambiguous: it oscillates between the two modes.

The action may be reduced from the outline sketched above to a simpler pattern of two 'triangles,' each with different circumstances and a somewhat different outcome. The first 'triangle' involves Lenskii, Onegin, and Ol'ga. The duel occurs because Onegin pays court to Ol'ga and deliberately provokes Lenskii. The duel, and Lenskii's death, are the logical conclusion of the triangle. Ol'ga's willingness to respond to Onegin's advances is ironically echoed when, after Lenskii's death, she marries a mustachioed hussar (in somewhat indecent haste). This first 'triangle' links in with the second: Onegin, Tat'iana, and Prince N. If Onegin had initially fallen in love with Tat'iana, and their relationship had been consummated, neither triangle would ever have existed. The marriage of Tat'iana to the Prince creates the conditions for the second triangle to become operative. The emotional relationship of Tat'iana and Onegin is rendered poignant by the fact that neither before nor after does Tat'iana or Onegin achieve fulfilment. Tat'iana's famous declaration of fidelity to her husband – 'but I've been given to another: and I shall be eternally faithful to him' – is only one of two obstacles in the way of the consummation of the Onegin-Tat'iana relationship. The other obstacle is the death of Lenskii. The latter, being on the verge of marriage to Ol'ga, is morally and virtually, if not technically, Tat'iana's brother (-in-law). Indeed he declares in his poem written on the eve of the duel, 'Ia suprug' – 'I am your spouse.' The result is to create a 'Romeo and Juliet' situation – Tat'iana, morally, cannot contemplate a relationship with Onegin because he is also the destroyer of Lenskii. Thus, beneath the 'fidelity' theme, the 'Romeo and Juliet' theme looms large. The crucial statement of this problem is in Six:

> Kogda b on znal, kakaia rana
> Moiei Tat'iany serdtse zhgla!
> Kogda by vedala Tat'iana,
> Kogda by znat' ona mogla,
> Chto zavtra Lenskii i Evgenii
> Zasporiat o mogil'noi seni;
> Akh, mozhet byt', ee liubov'
> Druzei soedinila b vnov'!
> No etoi strasti i sluchaino
> Eshche nikto ne otkryval.
> Onegin obo vsem molchal;
> Tat'iana iznyvala taino;
> Odna by niania znat' mogla,
> Da nedogadliva byla.

[*Had he but known what wound burned the heart of my Tat'iana! Had Tat'iana but been aware, had she known that tomorrow Lenskii and Evgenii would compete for the shelter of the grave; oh, perhaps her love could have united the friends once more! But no one had yet discovered this passion even by chance. Onegin was silent about everything; Tat'iana pined in secret; only her nurse could have known, but she was slow to catch on. (Six: XVIII: 1-14)*]

The stanza is, however, in such an ironic tone as to place in doubt the seriousness of the function of the 'Romeo and Juliet' situation that is here as a potential – with the conventional 'happy ending' conjured up, only to be rejected. The 'divided family / happy outcome' theme is thus reduced in importance and treated as a necessary device in the novel, and therefore subject to parody.

The sketches that have been presented of plot and chronology suggest – and herein lies a fundamental ambiguity – a completeness that does not exist. In plans of ruined cathedrals it is customary to sketch in the lines of broken arches, to show with dots the contours of roofs, towers, etc. In *Onegin*, the 'arches' never existed, the 'roofline' is pure fantasy. Rather than a ruined cathedral, a better analogy for *Onegin* would be a 'gothic folly' – a romantic ruin whose arches and roofs never existed, but are the suggested figment of the landscape artist's fantasy. Although Pushkin did have some classic premises in beginning his novel – hero and heroine, at least – the model given at the beginning of this chapter is the opposite of the truth: instead of working from 'romance' to 'text,' he worked – improvised – the text that gives an illusion of substance to the romance. The 'plot' or 'romance' sketch is, in fact, never clearly perceived in the magic crystal, even in the last stages of the work, and there remain as many questions unresolved as resolved. More important, the answers, like the roof of a bijou gothic ruin, do not exist. The 'assumed reality' offstage is, in fact, oblivion. This fact prevents the conclusions reached so far from having any more than a limited significance. The 'realistic model' simply does not adequately cover *Onegin* because it makes assumptions about the 'romance' that are not operative in the text. Ultimately, though it may present vignettes of Russian life and portraits of Russian characters, *Onegin* does not strive to meld fiction with reality, despite the fact of the 'friendship' of Onegin and Pushkin, which may be construed rather as a conceit, a cunning literary joke, than as an attempt to efface the borders between the fiction and a wider reality.

A major question (and one that is clearly incapable of resolution) is that of the 'ending' of the novel: is it complete, or is it broken off ex abrupto? Can a continuation be imagined?[4] The fact that Pushkin toyed with continuations suggests that although he might have been persuaded by his friends – and money considerations – that the novel was unfinished, in real aesthetic terms it proved impossible to continue. This critic's money, for what it is worth, is on the side of 'completeness.' I.M. Semenko has pointed out that the ending – where the hero is left dumbfounded and discomfited – has its parallels in numerous other of Pushkin's works (1957, 141). Such a fact permits one to believe that the novel had come, in Pushkin's terms, to its 'organic' end, although his contemporaries, who expected a novel to end with the hero's marriage or death, were not necessarily receptive to this. It is to the 'inconclusiveness' of Onegin's fate (in terms of the convention of the novel) that we may attribute the encouragement given Pushkin by friends to continue the work: 'You tell me: he is alive and not married. Thus the novel is not finished – this is treasure' (PSS, III, 1, 396). Ia. L. Levkovich notes: 'The advice of "friends" (or more precisely of those to whom the envoy was addressed) corresponds, not to the plans of Pushkin himself ... but to the then existing conventions of novelistic endings: the happy one, in which the author settled the fate of hero and heroine by marrying them, and the unhappy one, in which the hero perishes' (1974, 266). The 'zero presence' of marriage or death for Onegin in the narrative is itself significant. It signals to the reader that he has to do with an unconventional novel. The device of 'incompleteness' is thus part of the tendency to mystification which is essential to the treatment of the narrative. The reader is, as it were, invited to imagine his own version of Onegin's fate. The ending is thus another version of the device of the 'omitted stanza,' which may, as Tynianov put it, have 'any content.'

It is typical for Onegin that the answer to the question posed – in this case the subsequent fate of Onegin – lies not in some anecdotal remark by Pushkin to a contemporary, not in any arcane interpretation of the text, its variants and unpublished drafts, but in an understanding of the genre of the work itself. Since the work permits a variety of interpretations, then all must be granted equal validity – or invalidity: the ambiguity is the message. Critics have also pointed out the independence of the actions of the characters from their author – Pushkin's reported surprise that Tat'iana should suddenly get married. Belief in an 'initial plan' which Pushkin was frustrated from carrying out by censorial or other consideration borders on the intentional fallacy and contradicts the notion of the independence of work of art from its author's will.

A like question concerns the problem of tragedy and comedy. Some assert that *Onegin* is a comedy (e.g., Hoisington) while others emphasize the 'tragedy' of Chapter Eight (*tragizm*). Since the terms 'comedy' and 'tragedy' are borrowed from drama, it is worth comparing the 'plot,' the 'fabula,' with the traditional dramatic situation. We know from the literature (e.g., Northrop Frye) that the traditional comic situation is composed of a simple triangle. Thus, a young couple fall in love. The fulfilment of their love is hindered by circumstances. In its most traditional form, the hindrance is an older man who is a rival for the physical possession of the girl. He may be the girl's father or an aged suitor, or even an ancient, impotent husband. In comedy the hindrance is overcome, not without moments in which a tragic outcome appears inevitable, the young lovers are united at the end, the differences are reconciled, and there is a 'celebration' or 'feast.'[5] In tragedy (e.g., *Romeo and Juliet*), the circumstances prove stronger. The young couple is first united for a brief moment of love and happiness, but then outside circumstances (in *Romeo and Juliet* the death of Juliet's cousin at Romeo's hands, in *Faust* Part One the death of Valentin at Faust's hands) prove too strong and the couple are destroyed.

An example of the 'comic' situation in Pushkin is *Ruslan and Liudmila*. Here, after many adventures, Ruslan is reunited with Liudmila, who had been snatched from their marriage-bed by the wizard Chernomor. In *Onegin* the comic situation is modified in ways which are significant. The two lovers – Evgenii and Tat'iana – are separated at first by the character of Evgenii – his 'chondria' (*khandra*), his inability to respond to Tat'iana's advances. It is only later that 'external' (as opposed to 'psychological') obstructions become operative. These are, firstly, the death of Lenskii (as discussed above) and, secondly, the arranged marriage to a man who is older than Tat'iana and, apparently, a little older than Evgenii. The opposition love : arranged marriage is, as Richard Gregg has shown in his study of Tat'iana's dream (1970), an important one. It is discussed with reference to Tat'iana's mother and also the nurse. These obstacles are, however, not in themselves decisive. The ultimate obstacle is Tat'iana's refusal to indulge in an affair which would compromise her husband and of which she is morally incapable. Thus, the external obstacles, though present, have a strongly emphasized psychological content.

The comparison with drama shows that in *Onegin* the cast of characters is not united at the end, there is no feast. The menacing step of

Tat'iana's husband is the sign that outside circumstances, the world, but also morality, have triumphed in the final, crucial encounter.[6] But yet, we cannot say that the dénouement corresponds to that found traditionally in tragedies. The lovers are not united, their love is not requited only to have them torn apart. It remains, at best, a wistful, unfulfilled potential – 'happiness was so possible, so close,' says Tat'iana to Onegin. Although Belinskii was indignant that Tat'iana should not have yielded to Onegin's advances and engaged in an affair with him, her reproaches to him indicate clearly the course such a relationship would have taken:

> Chto zh nyne
> Menia presleduete vy?
> Zachem u vas ia na primete?
> Ne potomu l', chto v vysshem svete
> Teper' iavliat'sia ia dolzhna;
> Chto ia bogata i znatna,
> Chto muzh v srazhen'iakh izuvechen,
> Chto nas za to laskaet dvor?
> Ne potomu l', chto moi pozor
> Teper' by vsemi byl zamechen,
> I mog by v obshchestve prinest'
> Vam soblaznitel'nuiu chest'?

> [*Why do you pursue me now? Why do you have your sights on me? Is it not because I must now appear in high society; because I am rich and of the highest rank; because my husband was maimed in battles; because as a result we are well-received at court? Is it not because my shame would now be seen by all, and could bring you a tempting fame in society?* (Eight: XLIV: 3-14)]

It would, despite the best wishes of the participants, have assumed the usual course of an affair in the *grand monde*, culminating, possibly, in the death of her husband in a duel. It is a commonplace to point out that there are, in Tat'iana's dilemma in Chapter Eight, the seeds of the plot of *Anna Karenina*, the beautiful woman, married without love, who says yes to her seducer. One might add that Lermontov, in his *Maskarad*, offers another alternative to the dilemma: supposing Onegin had married Tat'iana; would their marriage have been a happy one, or would it have been torn apart on the rocks of passion and jealousy? By its potential for such various lines of development, the plot of *Onegin* reveals its richness.

The emotional experience delivered to the reader of *Onegin* is neither the fulfilment of desires found in the comedy nor the wrenching, cathartic loss found in tragedy. If the tone of the piece as a whole is ironic, then the tone of the final scenes of the romance is rather nostalgic, ironical, slightly ritualistic in the way Tat'iana metes out her punishment to Onegin, as he had done to her in his monologue. Nostalgia, wistfulness, pathos underlie a work in which the message is sad, not tragic, and the treatment ironic, not comic. In the following chapter I shall examine this question in more detail in discussing the fate of Tat'iana, and in my conclusions I shall look at the problem of the tone of the work.

Questions of tragedy and comedy have to do with the difficult problem of the interpretation of the events in Chapter Eight. The laconicism and Delphic nature of the text have given rise to a variety of interpretations. Some critics (believing that the ending is muffled because discretion before the censor made Pushkin unable to express his true meaning) have made use of cancelled drafts and of the existence of the fragments of the so-called Chapter Ten to 'reconstruct' a Decembrist future for Onegin. According to this argument, Onegin's 'reformation' is symbolized in his love for Tat'iana and his becoming (after the finale) a Decembrist. There is little in the final text that would support such a view. It should be axiomatic that any interpretation proposed of the novelistic events of Chapter Eight must be based upon the actual text, not on that *Onegin* which Pushkin might or might not have written and published under other circumstances. The attempt to make Onegin into a Decembrist is, however, a tacit admission of the fact that he is very far from the idealistic Decembrist youth, a fact for which Ryleev and Bestuzhev reproached Pushkin. When he, in addition, insisted that Onegin, the spleen-stricken parasite, was not a satirical portrait either, they must have been further mystified. The 'Onegin as Decembrist' reading serves only to show the unsatisfactoriness of any interpretation which goes beyond the existing text.

The contradictory interpretations of the finale – whether of Gukovskii (whose 'Decembrist' theory is sketched above), or of Nabokov (who saw in the finale a drama of misunderstanding), or (most egregious of all) of Belinskii, may be resumed in the following contradictory positions:

1. Onegin is reformed / is not reformed
2. Onegin loves / does not love Tat'iana

3. Tat'iana understands / does not understand Onegin
4. The rejection of Onegin is caused:
a) by Tat'iana's submission to social convention
b) by Tat'iana's failure to recognize Onegin's love
c) by Tat'iana's moral sense

The question remains: is it possible to construct a valid interpretation of the finale, one which would take account of the text only and which would be preferable to any other? In general, contemporary researchers on *Onegin* have tended to avoid coming to a conclusion or expressing that conclusion. Since the interpretation of the finale has, since Belinskii, tended to have an ideological content, it is not surprising that many have preferred to leave the topic undiscussed. The following argument is offered, not in the hope that it will end all the controversy, but because the question must be addressed.

If Onegin is a different character in Eight, then it is because there has been a shift in the manner of his depiction. It is this shift in the approach to Onegin that leads Bayley to write: 'Onegin's silence and his absence tell us much more about him than his words do – it is typical of his precariously balanced creation that his actions reveal him clearly while his speech or writing ... blur his image' (1971,250). I should say parenthetically that Bayley's remark illustrates the difficulty that we encounter in reading *Onegin* as a realistic novel. It is this problem which leads Tynianov to write:

> The largest semantic unit of the prose novel is the character –
> a unification under one external sign of heterogeneous
> dynamic elements; the external sign acquires in verse a different
> shading from that in prose. Hence, the character of a verse
> novel is not the character of the same novel transferred to prose.
> When we characterize it as the largest semantic unit, we
> cannot forget the peculiar deformation it has undergone when
> integrated into the verse. *Onegin* was just such a verse novel,
> and all the characters of this novel were subjected to such a
> deformation. (1975 in 1977, 56)

This observation of Tynianov's about the deformation of the sign we denote as 'character' in the verse novel coincides with Jakobson's remark on the 'polysemy' of the characters in *Onegin* (1937b, 54-5). In the early chapters the description is largely what Jakobson called 'metonymic': that is to say, Onegin's character was described by externals – the objects in his study, the books he read, and also his actions. His words and his thoughts are used to a much lesser degree to convey his character. This fact is attributable to the 'sociological portrait' of Onegin which we receive in One and the methods which it implies. In Eight we receive more glimpses of Onegin's internal world. This is done by a shift towards the method used to describe Tat'iana, which had from the beginning involved the description of her conscious and even her subconscious (through the dream). We may say that in Eight, for the first time, the character 'Onegin' has a content.

This content may be expressed by two elements: love for Tat'iana – always there in potential, since his first encounter with her – and remorse for Lenskii's death, which is also 'pre-programmed' in Onegin's original justification for accepting the challenge. The reciprocal nature of these two elements is evident in a crucial stanza:

> I postepenno v usyplen'e
> I chuvstv i dum vpadaet on,
> A pered nim Voobrazhen'e
> Svoi pestryi mechet faraon.
> To vidit on: na talom snege
> Kak-budto spiashchii na nochlege,
> Nedvizhim iunosha lezhit,
> I slyshit golos: chto zh? ubit.
> To vidit on vragov zabvennykh,
> Klevetnikov, i trusov zlykh,
> I roi izmennits molodykh,
> I krug tovarishchei prezrennykh,
> To sel'skii dom – i u okna
> Sidit *ona* ... i vse ona!

> [*And gradually he falls into a trance of feelings and thoughts, and imagination deals its multi-coloured faro before his eyes. Now he sees: a youth lies motionless on the melting snow as if sleeping at a bivouac, and he hears a voice: 'Well! – he's dead.' Now he sees forgotten enemies, slanderers, and malicious cowards, and a swarm of young traitresses; now – a country house, and by the window she is sitting – always she!* (Eight: XXXVII: 1-14)]

Tania is not only or not simply the source of the change in Onegin – she is his *fatum*, the tangible expression of the weight of his conscience, his nemesis. The irony is that love – which, we learn in One, he has always been willing to feign in order to seduce – now has become real. What he formerly did mechanically he now does with conviction. Tat'iana is the instrument of his punishment, and the deep irony of her reproaches to him, quoted above, is evident. She knows that Onegin loves her, but she knows that such a love could never find fulfilment, that they are both trapped in the web of attitudes and positions imposed by society, which would reduce an affair to the usual pattern of intrigue and gossip. In a sense, Tat'iana's words have a double motivation – as the heroine of the romance she is speaking to the hero, but also as a punisher she is avenging the humiliation of other women by Onegin, and Lenskii's death. The psychological level is coordinated with a deeper plot structure in which she is the instrument of fate.

Are we to see in Tat'iana's rejection of a liaison with Onegin an expression of her acquiescence in the rules of society? Belinskii believes so, and would have her rather reject the 'double standard' and make a stand for romantic love: 'Eternal fidelity! – To *whom* and in *what*? Faithfulness to relationships which constitute a profanation of feelings and feminine purity, because relationships not sanctified by love are highly immoral.' In fact, to have a liaison would be fashionable in the society in which Tat'iana lives. (It was, after all, a society in which the emperor's mistress had a recognized social function.) The antagonism of Pushkin to that society is expressed in his heroine's rejection of Onegin's love, since an affair would have shown her conformity to social fashion (even if in reality faithfulness was more the rule than the exception). Tat'iana rejects both society's and Belinskii's rules: she is 'faithful' to her husband, but she 'loves' Onegin. That love is encapsulated, internalized as an unrealized and impossible dream, a potential which she cherishes as she does her memories of the fields and woods of her childhood. If Tat'iana acquiesces in anything, then it is in 'fate' – that fate which brought them together in the garden (Eight: XLII: 12) but which for her is now decided (Eight: XLVII: 2-3) by her marriage. It was that same fate which Onegin tempted by his rejection of Tat'iana and his provocation of Lenskii. It is that same fate which his newly awakened love for Tat'iana has become.

The morality of Tat'iana is of a special kind, since it is expressed precisely in her acquiescence in fate. It is here that we see the difference between the mature Tat'iana – 'Princess N' – and the earlier Tania. The writing of the letter to Onegin is a 'tempting of fate,' an act of boldness which brings Tat'iana not fulfilment (as she might have expected from her reading of Western novels) but chastisement. In particular, she is taught a lesson which it is proper to learn in youth, but which Onegin learns only from her: that the vision of romantic love in which two souls are united, found in the Western tradition dating back to the Renaissance, is a chimera. Whether one accepts the programmatic role of *Onegin* in setting the Russian literary tradition, or whether one sees the ending of *Onegin* as simply one of the first expressions of this fact, it is clear that the great works of nineteenth-century Russian literature almost without exception involve (those that treat the problem) a rejection of romantic love. In Pushkin's time the example of Griboedov's *Woe from Wit* is obvious. The epigraph from Bella Akhmadullina at the head of this chapter is another expression of this truth – that fate and love are at odds and that it is always fate that wins.

The discussion above serves, at the very least, to indicate that the 'novel' proper does have an important existence within the large work. However stylized and even parodistic the characters may seem at certain moments, their actions add up to a set of significant events that demand examination. It is a feature of *Onegin* that the novel is at one moment stylized and parodistic, and that it may then swerve towards seriousness. Bearing in mind at every point Tynianov's observation on the deformation of the novel and of the sign 'character,' I will next examine the main characters of *Onegin* and try to establish their meaning.

4

Tat'iana:
Diana's Disciple

... I am afeard,
Being in night, all this is but a dream,
Too flattering-sweet to be substantial.
            (*Romeo and Juliet*, II.2)

'Ah! madame ... quel fantôme de devoir opposez-vous à mon bonheur?'
(*La Princesse de Clèves*, 172)

Although Pushkin chose to call his work *Eugene Onegin*, and although
the first chapter of it is devoted almost entirely to the eponymous hero,
the reader becomes much closer, in the course of reading the novel, to
Onegin's female counterpart Tat'iana. Indeed, it is Tat'iana who makes
the transition from composite of literary traits to realized psychological
portrait much more fully than any other character (with the exception
of Pushkin himself). It is therefore not surprising that some critics have
even suggested that the work should really have been called 'Tat'iana
Larina,' since she dominates the action from Chapter Two onwards,
and by the tone of the narrative is clearly perceived to enjoy the sympathy of the narrator, who declares himself to be her secret admirer.
The reason for Tat'iana's dominance in the novelistic structure is simply the fact that it is Tat'iana whose innermost thoughts the reader is
privy to. She is perceived 'from the inside,' whereas all the other characters are viewed largely externally. It is only in Chapter Eight that
the poet gives us a glimpse of the thoughts and emotional 'interior' of
Onegin, and then his tone of sympathy for his character is much less
overt than it is for Tat'iana.

Pushkin was by no means alone in his admiration of Tat'iana. It is
perhaps no exaggeration to describe her as the most important character

in Russian literature, for she was to have a decisive impact on the shaping of subsequent heroines of Russian realism, in particular those of Turgenev and Tolstoi. Above all, those writers learned from Pushkin a sensitivity to the inner life of their characters which they might not otherwise have acquired. Richard Freeborn writes: 'What Tat'iana asserts – and what other heroes and heroines of the Russian novel will assert – is the privacy of conscience, the singularity of all moral awareness and certitude, the discovery of the single, unique moral self which opposes and withstands the factitious morality of the mass, of society, of humanity or the general good' (1973, 37). Freeborn's is a classically succinct summation of one aspect of Tat'iana's character – or one way of viewing it. It is revealed, as Freeborn shows, in one or two scenes of extraordinary clarity.

The character of Tat'iana is, however, much more complex than it appears in Freeborn's statement, as can be seen if we contrast it with the Russian critic Belinskii's commentary on the last meeting between Tat'iana and Onegin and her decision to 'remain eternally faithful' to her husband:

> There is the true pride of feminine virtue! 'But I have been given to another' – precisely, 'given,' not 'have given myself'! Eternal fidelity – to whom and in what? Faithfulness to relationships which constitute a profanation of feelings and feminine purity, because relationships not sanctified by love are highly immoral. ... But in Russia it all goes together somehow – poetry and life, love and the arranged marriage, the life of the heart, and the strict fulfilment of external obligations which are inwardly violated every hour. ... The life of woman is principally concentrated in the life of the heart; to love means to live for that life; and sacrifice is another word for love. (1843-6, 498-9)

Belinskii's position is a 'romantic' one – love and marriage must go together. Tat'iana's relationship with her husband is therefore seen as immoral, and provokes Belinskii's indignation. The Russian critic thus takes a view diametrically opposed to Freeborn. He sees in Tat'iana's marriage and her conformity to the morality of the day the pressure of society on the individual, who is forced to obey the dictates of the mass rather than listen to his own heart. One is inclined to side with Freeborn, since there are, as we shall see, certain other considerations – moral, as Freeborn says, but also practical and realistic ones – which militate against Tat'iana's initiating a liaison with Onegin. In a way, by conforming not only to the letter but also to the spirit of the social links she has contracted, Tat'iana paradoxically asserts her own individual strength of character in a world of hypocrisy in which the letter was customarily observed, but the spirit violated. The point is lost on Belinskii, who 'reads' Tat'iana's faithfulness as signifying her consent to a reactionary social order. Nevertheless, he admirably describes those contradictions in Russian life – the outward mask and the inner emotion. Somehow, as he says, it all goes together – perceiving the contrast between duty and freedom which is endemic in Russian literature and which is at the base of Tat'iana's (and perhaps her creator's) character. Tat'iana's solution to this dichotomy is passivity and personal suffering.

To account for the whole of Tat'iana's character, we clearly have to account for the paradoxes in it which can give rise to such contradictory interpretations as those of Freeborn and Belinskii. My own thesis, which will form the basis of the argument in the rest of this chapter, is that Tat'iana is a composite of two different, opposing character types, which I will designate, to some extent arbitrarily, as the 'Juliet' and 'Clèves' types. While it is the 'Juliet' type which dominates in the first part of the novel (approximately Chapters Two to Six), that type becomes interiorized – turned into the life of the heart, to use Belinskii's terminology – and replaced, at least on the outside, by the other.

This notion of the dual nature of Tat'iana is, by the way, suggested by Pushkin himself, who insists on the change in Tat'iana in Chapter Eight, and reinforces it by a jump of several years in the chronology:

> Kak izmenilasia Tat'iana!
> Kak tverdo v rol' svoiu voshla!
> Kak utesnitel'nogo sana
> Priemy skoro priniala!
>
> [How Tat'iana had changed! How firmly she had assumed her role! How quickly she had accepted the habits of her restrictive rank! (Eight: XXVIII: 1-4)]

As I have already suggested, the characters in Onegin begin life as amalgams of literary allusions or 'quotations,' often paradoxical in their juxtaposition. The author stresses this by the wealth of these references, both overt and covert. This is so to such an extent that some of the 'characters' (e.g., Ol'ga) remain catalogues of literary traits and borrowed features, and risk never becoming believable characters in the sense in which the realistic novel understands them. Although this is not the case with Tat'iana, it is nevertheless necessary to examine certain allusions which Pushkin invokes in connection with her, and use them to illuminate her meaning. In the following discussion I do not intend to be exhaustive, but rather seek to analyse certain basic references which I believe illustrate her 'dual' nature.

The 'first' or 'Juliet' Tat'iana is that dreamy, abstracted figure whom the reader (and Onegin) encounters in Chapter Two, and who, like Romeo, likes to greet the dawn.[1] We may call her both 'romantic' and romantic. That is to say, she is both influenced by her reading of romantic literature ('romantic'), and has traits of the romantic heroine. It is the latter traits which interest us specifically in her, and it is to these that we must now turn. They are derived, I would argue, from two principal sources – Shakespeare, with whom Pushkin had become familiar in his southern exile in French translations, and the romantic ballad, which had been transmitted to Russian literature principally by Pushkin's mentor Zhukovskii.

I have elsewhere argued the case for literary echoes in *Onegin* of Shakespeare's *Midsummer-Night's Dream*, and do not intend to repeat the arguments in detail here (Clayton 1975). The case for allusions to *Romeo and Juliet* has been less fully examined in the literature, although it is a commonplace to compare the relationship of Tat'iana and her nurse in Four with that of Juliet and her nurse. The resemblance that I wish to pursue here is to be found less in specific detail than in the general atmosphere of night-time and enchantment which pervades both *Romeo and Juliet* (especially II.2) and Chapter Three of *Onegin*. In Shakespeare's play, much of the imagery centres on the darkness of night (contrasted with day) and the night-time luminaries, as in Romeo's speech:

> But soft! what light through yonder window breaks?
> It is the East, and Juliet is the sun!
> Arise, fair sun and kill the envious moon ...
> (*Romeo and Juliet*, II.2.44-6)

Night-time is the time of love. It is presided over by the moon, the symbol of Diana (and, by neo-Platonic extension, of the Virgin), goddess of chastity. Romeo's reference to the killing of the moon is thus a veiled hint at the loss of Juliet's maidenhead (the penetration and bloodshed of which parallel his running through of Tybalt with his sword).

Night is thus not only a time for love, but also for dark deeds, including death, so that love and death are inextricably entwined. It is this truth that is worked out in Shakespeare's play, as the 'ill-starred' (another reference to night) love leads to Juliet's sleeping with the dead:

> Chain me with roaring bears,
> Or hide me nightly in a charnel house,
> O'ercovered quite with dead men's rattling bones,
> With reeky shanks and yellow chapless skulls,
> Or bid me go into a new-made grave
> And hide me with a dead man in his tomb ...
>
> (IV.1.80-5)

Apart from death and love, night connotes dreams and the deception which they wreak – Romeo's 'the flattering truth of sleep' (V.1.1) – and the stirrings of the subconscious.

The complex imagery of night-time, enchantment, dreams, and the relatedness of love and death in *Romeo and Juliet* is beyond the scope of this study. The imagery is akin to that in *Midsummer-Night's Dream*, save that there love is related, not to the tragic motif of death, but to the comic 'Circean' theme of the transformation of men into animals by lust (Clayton 1975, endnote 9). Both elements – the Circean and the mortal – are present in *Onegin*. There the word 'circe' is used to describe the 'fashionable coquettes' whose activities adorn their husbands with antlers (of cuckoldry) and who transform their lovers into beasts.[2] The death theme is present in the threat that Onegin represents for Lenskii and even for Tat'iana, a threat that is enacted in Tat'iana's dream, and then partially in the reality of the novel as Lenskii is killed by Onegin in the duel. Tat'iana's escape from death at Onegin's hands is the crucial difference between *Onegin* and *Romeo and Juliet*.

The *Romeo and Juliet* echoes in *Onegin*, though present, are somewhat muted, I believe, because they are transmitted through an intermediary source, which is indicated by Pushkin himself in the epigraph to Chapter Five. In Shakespeare's play there are two particularly important features of the imagery which suggest the link to the other source. The first of these is the necessity for the two lovers to consummate their relationship under the cover of night, and the attendant fear of the dawn, which threatens to reveal their love (cf. the famous 'aubade,' III.5). The second, not unrelated feature is the equation of Romeo with death itself, stressed by the numerous references in the play to Juliet sleeping with the dead.

It is my contention that the pre-Romantics appropriated Shakespeare's darkling, nocturnal, and deathly world such as we find in *Romeo and Juliet* and melded it with popular vampire myths to create the balladic theme of the midnight bridegroom that was so influential on Russian poetry in the nineteenth century. The source for the Russian versions of the ballad was Bürger's *Lenore* (1773). This was translated by Zhukovskii several times: as *Liudmila* (1808), a periphrastic version, and in a more accurate transposition as *Lenora* (1831) (Nabokov, III, 152-3). It was also translated as *Ol'ga* (1815) by Katenin. Although Pushkin was certainly familiar with all these versions, the most important version of the Lenore tale was Zhukovskii's *Svetlana* (1812), in which the process of the 'Russianization' of the ballad was brought to its conclusion.

Although the different versions of the ballad give different emphases, the motifs present in them can be listed, so that it is possible to see the individual divagations from the common stock, and especially to see how closely related to them is *Romeo and Juliet*:

1. The lovers are divided by war or feud.
2. The heroine questions the faithfulness of her beloved.
3. She boldly defies the conventions of the world.
4. The lover comes to her at night.
5. He carries her off to a church and a night-time marriage.
6. He experiences increasing anxiety at the approach of the dawn (usually signalled by the cock crowing).
7. He is discovered to be dead.
8. The tragic outcome is a punishment for the hubris of the heroine's rebellion against the existing world-order.

Romeo and Juliet can be readily seen to be an elaboration of these basic motifs, but with a 'real-world' solution of the 'dead bridegroom' motif. This is achieved by the intrigue of the 'poison,' its unforeseen miscarriage, and by the references to Romeo as 'dead' – first as metaphor, later as unconscious prophecy, as we see in the following passage from Capulet's speech to Paris:

> O son, the night before thy wedding day
> Hath death lain with thy wife. There she lies,
> Flower as she was, deflowered by him.
> Death is my son-in-law.
>
> (IV.5.35-8)

In contrast to the 'real-world' motivation of Shakespeare's ending, Bürger's is pure fantasy – the groom is dead all along, and he carries off Lenore to the grave on his steed. Typically for German romanticism, Bürger's ballad starts in a 'real,' believable world, and finishes in an incredible, fantasy one. If the comparison of endings is revelatory, so too is Romeo's fear of the dawn – the references to the graying light in the east, the song of the lark, and the cock betraying not only the lover's fear of discovery but the demonic nocturnal visitor's need to return to the other world. The resemblances are so striking that one is tempted to posit medieval, balladic sources as a substratum for the Renaissance facade of the Shakespeare play.

It was Zhukovskii's embroidering of the *Lenore* text in *Svetlana* that proved most inspiring to Pushkin. Zhukovskii, unhappy with the Bürger ending in a fantasy world, finds a different solution to the problem of the ending of the tale: the nocturnal visit is a *dream* which Svetlana experiences as she waits at midnight in front of a mirror in which she expects to see, according to ancient custom, the image of her husband. Svetlana's awakening from the dream provides a path back to the real world from the fantasy world of night and death in which Bürger had left his heroine, and preserves the strict boundaries between those two worlds, which German romanticism had tended to erase. Although Shakespeare had likewise respected these boundaries, banishing the notion of sleeping with death to the realm of metaphor, he too had left his heroine in the clutches of death. By contrast with both the preceding texts, we find that Zhukovskii's poem has a 'happy ending' – the day-time wedding of Svetlana and her beloved, who returns to her safe and sound across the distances. Lenore's blasphemy and its unfortunate consequences, and Juliet's defiance of the feuds and hatreds of the real world, contrast with the platitudinous world in which all is for the best that we find conjured up in Zhukovskii's moral:

> Luchshei drug nam v zhizni sei
>   Vera v providen'e.
> Blag zizhditelia zakon:
> Zdes' neschast'e – lzhivyi son;
>   Schast'e – probuzhden'e.

[*The best friend for us in this life is a belief in providence. Blessed is the creator's law: here unhappiness is a false dream; happiness is awakening.*]

Zhukovskii here recoils from the criticism of the world and of providence present in *Lenore* and in *Romeo*. The change of ending shows clearly his inacceptance of the romantics' rejection of the world order and flight into fantasy and demonstrates why Zhukovskii's romanticism is really a bijou-gothic decoration on a sentimental structure.

It is the lines immediately following those quoted above which Pushkin uses as the epigraph to Chapter Five:

> O, ne znai sikh strashnykh snov
> Ty, moia Svetlana!

> [*O my Svetlana, may you not know these terrible dreams!*]

This is one of the many ways that Pushkin signals to the reader that his heroine, at least as she appears in that chapter, is to be read as a sort of pastiche of Zhukovskii's. The resemblance, which would in any case be clear to any Russian reader of the time, is apparent in such matters as the similarity of their names, which rhyme; the fact that, like Svetlana, Tat'iana indulges in midnight soothsaying; like her, she experiences a 'horrible dream' in which her beloved figures, but which has a different content; and like her wakens to reality.[3] That Pushkin was fascinated by Zhukovskii's *Svetlana*, with its numerous original touches – the mid-winter blizzard setting of the dream, the raven, the candles, etc. – is attested to by the frequent recurrence of motifs from it in Pushkin's work, e.g., 'The Blizzard,' 'The Devils,' *The Captain's Daughter*, and elsewhere (Clayton 1980a).

There is one crucial difference between Zhukovskii's Svetlana and Pushkin's Tat'iana, which illustrates not only literary divergences between the two Russian poets, but philosophical ones too. When the former poet's heroine awakes, it is to be married to the man she loves, i.e., he and her 'nocturnal visitor,' the man she sees in her dream, are one and the same person. In Zhukovskii there is no tragic rift between day and night. In Bürger's version, there is, again, only one lover, but he is dead, and carries Lenore off to her death as well. If Zhukovskii's poem has a comic happy ending, Bürger's is pathetic. Again there is no dysfunction between day and night – the latter triumphs, just as the former did in Zhukovskii's poem. In *Romeo* and in *Onegin*, the night-time lover (Romeo, Onegin) and the day-time suitor (Paris, fat general) are different. Juliet marries her nocturnal lover and dies (tragedy). Tat'iana marries her day-time suitor and lives (realism).

The four different plot patterns could be represented graphically, as in the scheme at the top of page 123. What is important about this scheme is that it shows, firstly, that *Onegin* has to be seen in the matrix of plot possibilities, and that it fulfils the 'fourth alternative'

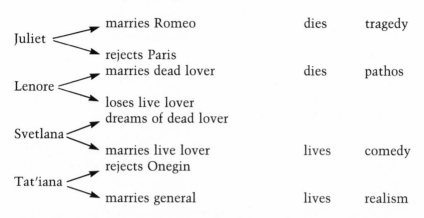

Juliet	marries Romeo	dies	tragedy
	rejects Paris		
Lenore	marries dead lover	dies	pathos
	loses live lover		
Svetlana	dreams of dead lover		
	marries live lover	lives	comedy
Tat'iana	rejects Onegin		
	marries general	lives	realism

within them, and, secondly, that Pushkin's solution to the problem of the plot ending, far from replicating that of Zhukovskii's poem, distances itself from it. Tat'iana, although presented as a pastiche of Svetlana, is in fact a critique of Zhukovskii's heroine and of the false conclusion that 'happiness is awakening.' Like Shakespeare, Pushkin knows too well the sweetness of the dreams of love to believe that awakening from them is happiness. In her last speech Tat'iana tells Onegin: 'Happiness was so possible, so close.' Unlike Shakespeare, Pushkin shows that the unattainability of happiness need not lead to death, but simply to resignation. Pushkin's world, like Shakespeare's, is a tragic one (in that the irreconcilability of night and day is expressed by the fates of the lovers), but Pushkin's resolution, avoiding Zhukovskii's comedy and Shakespeare's tragedy, is realism – in Pushkin's world, Juliet marries Paris, accepts the inevitability of unhappiness, and is reconciled to it.

Whatever the differences that divide the texts that we have compared here (and I am willing to concede that the comparisons given may appear daring), there is one crucial similarity between the heroines which leads me to speak of the 'Juliet' type with reference to Tat'iana. This is the fact that in all four cases we find a heroine who is willing to seek out boldly her 'nocturnal lover' and risk her happiness with him. In Juliet's case, it is her willingness to say 'ay,' to consent to the marriage with Romeo, which distinguishes her and seals her fate. For Lenore, the coming of the bridegroom is the fulfilment of her death-wish:

Lisch aus, mein Licht, auf ewig aus!
Stirb hin, stirb hin in Nacht und Graus!

Ohn ihn mag ich auf Erden,
Mag dort nicht selig werden. (Lenore, 1613-14)

Svetlana's 'seeking-out' of her lover takes the form of her midnight
vigil (a much less life-or-death enterprise than those of her literary
sisters, illustrating, again, Zhukovskii's 'salonization' of the Lenore
myth). In Onegin, Tat'iana's exploit takes the form of the soothsaying
that precedes the dream, and of one of the most famous features of the
novel – the letter which she writes to Onegin offering herself to him.

It is here necessary to cite a part of the letter in order to examine
the precise terms in which Tat'iana addresses Onegin:

Drugoi! ... Net, nikomu na svete
Ne otdala by serdtse ia!
To v vyshnem suzhdeno sovete ...
To volia neba: ia tvoia;
Vsia zhizn' moia byla zalogom
Svidan'ia vernogo s toboi;
Ia znaiu, ty mne poslan bogom,
Do groba ty khranitel' moi ...
Ty v snoviden'iakh mne iavlialsia,
Nezrimyi, ty mne byl uzh mil,
Tvoi chudnyi vzgliad menia tomil,
V dushe tvoi golos razdavalsia
Davno ... net, eto byl ne son!
Ty chut' voshel, ia vmig uznala,
Vsia obomlela, zapylala
I v mysliakh molvila: vot on!
Ne pravda l'? ia tebia slykhala:
Ty govoril so mnoi v tishi,
Kogda ia bednym pomogala,
Ili molitvoi uslazhdala
Tosku volnuemoi dushi?
I v eto samoe mgnoven'e
Ne ty li, miloe viden'e,
V prozrachnoi temnote mel'knul,
Priniknul tikho k izgolov'iu?
Ne ty l', s otradoi i liubov'iu,
Slova nadezhdy mne shepnul?
Kto ty, moi angel li khranitel',
Ili kovarnyi iskusitel':
Moi somnen'ia razreshi.

Byt' mozhet, eto vse pustoe,
Obman neopytnoi dushi!
I suzhdeno sovsem inoe ...
No tak i byt'! Sud'bu moiu
Otnyne ia tebe vruchaiu,
Pered toboiu slezy l'iu,
Tvoei zashchity umoliaiu ...
Voobrazi: ia zdes' odna,
Nikto menia ne ponimaet,
Rassudok moi iznemogaet,
I molcha gibnut' ia dolzhna.
Ia zhdu tebia: edinym vzorom
Nadezhdy serdtsa ozhivi,
Il' son tiazhelyi perervi,
Uvy, zasluzhennym ukorom!

[*Another! ... No, I would not give my heart to any other in
the world! It has been decreed in the loftiest council ... It is
the will of heaven: I am yours; all my life was a gage for the
true meeting with you. I know that you have been sent to
me by God, to the grave you are my guardian angel ... You
appeared to me in my dreams, unseen, you were already
dear to me, your wondrous glance tormented me, I have long
heard your voice in my heart ... no, it was not a dream!
Hardly had you come in, when I in a trice recognized you,
became all weak, flushed, and in my thoughts said: that's him!
Is it not true? Did I not hear you, did you not speak to me
in the hush, when I helped the poor or sweetened with a prayer
the woe of an impassioned heart? And did you not, dear
vision, appear in the translucent gloom, quietly lean down to
my bed? Did you not, with joy and love, whisper words of
hope to me? Who are you, my guardian angel or a cunning
tempter: resolve my doubts. Perhaps all this is vapid, the illusion of an inexperienced soul! And something quite different
has been decreed ... But so be it! Henceforth I place my fate
in your hands, I pour out my tears before you, I implore your
defence ... Imagine, I am here alone, no one understands me,
my reason is exhausted, and I must perish in silence. I am
waiting for you: with a single glance revive the hopes of my
heart, or interrupt this oppressive dream with a deserved –
alas! – reproach.* (PSS: VI: 66-7)]

In perusing Tat'iana's letter, the reader is struck by a number of important features. Firstly, the letter does not have a 'real' addressee. The Onegin to whom she directs the letter is unknown, a phantom. (In the same way the Romeo whom Juliet falls in love with is a shadow, and indeed the midnight bridegrooms of the ballads are all insubstantial, ghostly figures.) Tat'iana's letter is thus a missive into the void. Tat'iana is not even sure that she has seen a real person: 'Perhaps all this is vapid, the illusion of an inexperienced soul!' Secondly (and this is related to the first point), Tat'iana does not know if she is awake, or if the whole matter is a dream: 'You appeared to me in my dreams ... dear vision ... interrupt this oppressive dream ...' The last sentence is particularly important, since it confirms again that Tat'iana does not even know if she is asleep or awake (the words *tiazhelyi son* – 'oppressive dream' – may also mean 'deep sleep'). (Compare Bürger: 'Schläfst, Liebchen, oder wachst du?')

In short, the letter is a description of the 'first' Tat'iana – an enchanted sleeper, dreaming the oppressive dreams of adolescence. Not for nothing does Monsieur Triquet address to her the lines: 'Réveillez-vous, belle endormie,' for she is indeed a 'sleeping beauty.'

A third aspect of the lines quoted above which deserves comment is the emphasis on fate: Tat'iana's surrender to Onegin is, she tells him, 'the will of heaven.' The role of destiny in the life of the heroine who surrenders to her midnight lover is so striking that I have included it in the list of motifs given above. The 'fate' theme in *Romeo and Juliet*, for example, is well attested to in the critical literature.[4] In *Lenore*, it is the heroine's belief that God has turned against her that provokes her to blasphemy. In the case of Svetlana, the notion of fate is made brilliantly tangible in the form of the soothsaying. It is, of course, 'fate' which decides who will be the object of a girl's love (and whether he will love her). Fate is the root cause of the ties that bind each heroine and produce the various results in the life of each. Distinctive in the case of Tat'iana (as opposed, for example, to Lenore) is her acquiescence in her fate: 'Henceforth I place my fate in your hands.' Her passivity in the face of destiny contrasts not only with Lenore but also with Juliet, who is far from passive in her attempts to manipulate her fate. In this perspective, Tat'iana's letter is an act of supreme daring, her one thrust against her milieu, placing her in the company of the other literary heroines with whom we have compared her.

The other, principal 'moment' in *Onegin* that links Tat'iana with Svetlana and Juliet is, of course, Tat'iana's dream. This episode is saturated with folkloristic material, literary reminiscences, and original 'Pushkinian' motifs. The balladistic content is made clear by Lotman in his discussion of the folklore of Russian fortune-telling:

> First of all one must point out that fortune-telling 'by dream' is a dangerous activity typical of Yuletide fortune-telling – during which the fortune-teller enters into contact with the evil one. When undertaking such fortune-telling, girls take off their crosses and belts (the belt being the ancient pagan symbol of the protective circle). ... fortune-telling by dream takes place in an atmosphere of fear typical of all ritual contact with the evil one. The evil world is the reverse of the everyday one, and, since the marriage ritual to a large extent copies in a mirror-like, inverted fashion the burial ceremony, in enchanted fortune-telling the bridegroom is frequently replaced with a dead man or the devil. Such an interweaving of folkloristic elements in the figure of the Yuletide 'fated one' (husband) became in Tat'iana's consciousness consonant with the 'demonic' image of Onegin the vampire and Melmoth created by the action of the Romantic 'fictions' of the 'Britannic muse.' (Lotman 1980, 266-7; see also 270-4)

The difference between the dream of Svetlana and that of Tat'iana is that the latter sees, not one husband, but two: the 'desired' one – Onegin – who takes a demonic form, and the 'fated' one – the husband of an arranged marriage, represented symbolically by the bear from which she runs.[5] Neither is dead, but Onegin may be 'read' as the evil one, and certainly assumes such an aspect in the dream, where he is the master of the 'witches' sabbath.'

In introducing this discussion of the literary quotations associated with Tat'iana and hinting at the meaning of her character, I pointed out that literary allusions are generally, in *Onegin* (and perhaps also in the whole of Pushkin's oeuvre), combined in a startling, even paradoxical way. Thus, though I have stressed the very real parallels between *Onegin* and the balladic plot structure, there are other elements of the plot which do not fit. Onegin, for example, although Tat'iana expects him to play the role of demonic nocturnal lover, carrying her off to a midnight wedding (as in 'The Blizzard'), declines the 'role,' so that this plot structure is frustrated (and realized only in her dream), being 'deformed' by being welded to other plot structures with other expectations. Each 'role' (with the plot expectations it evokes) is in ironic juxtaposition to some other, unrelated element in a amalgam of 'quotations' from literature.

To this point the discussion has centred on what I have called the 'first Tat'iana' – the young romantic provincial girl who assumes the 'role' of the romantic heroine. To her, as I have suggested, we must oppose 'another Tat'iana' – again an unexpected juxtaposition of roles quoted from different literatures. The second Tat'iana might be called 'Princess N,' since the most important fact about her is that she is married to a man whose name the author judges it unnecessary for us to know (or too significant for him to lift the 'veil of secrecy'). She is the beautiful wife of a fat general, the queen of Petersburg society, and the person with whom Onegin falls in love. With this second Tat'iana, who is condemned to share the same character as the first, comes a new set of literary allusions. These have their source, not in Shakespeare and the Romantic balladic tradition, but in the French prose novel. There is, for example, more than a trace in Tat'iana of the Countess of Tournevel as she defends her chastity against the onslaughts of the Viscount of Valmont in Choderlos de Laclos's *Les Liaisons dangéreuses*. There is, indeed, much about *Onegin* which shows that it is written in the idiom of the French novel – the intimacy of the narrative, the character of Onegin himself, which owes much to the heroes of French fiction, the thematic importance of seduction and adultery, and the vestigial traces of the epistolary tradition.[6]

In particular, however, *Onegin* deserves to be discussed in relation to one French novel that has had very little attention in Pushkin studies, although it offers some very interesting parallels with Pushkin's novel in verse, namely *La Princesse de Clèves* (1678), by Madame de Lafayette. In this novel we find a beautiful young woman who is married to the Prince de Clèves, a man whom she respects but does not love. Pushkin does not give us the details of Tat'iana's marriage, save in a few laconic words she addresses to Onegin:

> Neostorozhno,
> Byt' mozhet, postupila ia:
> Menia s slezami zaklinanii
> Molila mat'; dlia bednoi Tani
> Vse byli zhrebii ravny ...
> Ia vyshla zamuzh.

> [*Perhaps I acted carelessly: my mother begged me with tears of supplication; all fates were equal for poor Tania ... I married.* (Eight: XLVII: 3-8)]

Pushkin does not need to add any detail to this laconic description of the *mariage de convenance*, since his readers would already be familiar with such matters from their reading of French novels:

> Dès le lendemain, ce prince fit parler à Mme de Chartres; elle reçut la proposition qu'on lui faisait et ne craignit point de donner à sa fille un mari qu'elle ne put aimer en lui donnant le prince de Clèves. Les articles furent conclus; on parla au roi, et ce mariage fut su de tout le monde. (*La Princesse de Clèves*, 50)

After her marriage, Mme de Clèves is pursued by, and falls in love with, the handsome M. de Nemours in a way that reminds us of Onegin's pursuit of Princess N. M. de Nemours's nocturnal penetrations of his quarry's garden at Coulommiers have more than a slight echo of the night-time lover motif. However, the crucial resemblance to *Onegin* comes at the end of the novel. With M. de Clèves dead, the way is now apparently clear for M. de Nemours and Mme de Clèves to consummate their love. In a final interview between them that is surely a precursor of the Tat'iana/Onegin scene in Chapter Eight, the Princesse de Clèves sets out the moral reason that motivates her to reject him:

> Il n'est que trop véritable que vous êtes cause de la mort de M. de Clèves; les soupçons que lui a donnés votre conduite inconsidérée lui ont coûté la vie, comme si vous la lui aviez ôtée de vos propres mains. Voyez ce que je devrais faire, si vous en étiez venus ensemble à ces extrémités, et que le même malheur en fut arrivé. Je sais bien que ce n'est pas la même chose à l'égard du monde; mais au mien il n'y a aucune différence, puisque je sais que c'est par vous qu'il est mort et que c'est à cause de moi. (172)

These moral considerations are similar to those in *Romeo and Juliet*, in which Juliet's love for Romeo is rendered tragic by the fact of Tybalt's death at Romeo's hands, and in *Onegin*, in which Tat'iana's 'brother' Lenskii is killed by Onegin in the duel. In each case someone close to the heroine is killed by the hero. Tat'iana has too much delicacy to bring up this point in the final conversation with Onegin, although it is one of the most powerful reproaches she could have made. It is, however, adumbrated at other points in the novel.[7]

To the principal moral objection to her marriage to M. de Nemours, the Princesse adds another, pragmatic or realistic one:

> Mais les hommes conservent-ils de la passion dans ces engagements éternels? Dois-je espérer un miracle en ma faveur et puis-je me mettre en état de voir certainement finir cette passion dont je ferais toute ma félicité? M. de Clèves était peut-être l'unique homme du monde capable de conserver de l'amour dans le mariage. Ma destinée n'a pas voulu que j'aie pu profiter de ce bonheur; peut-être aussi que sa passion n'avait subsisté que parce qu'il n'en aurait pas trouvé en moi. (173)

The Princesse brings in the paradoxical fact that love and a prolonged relationship, such as marriage, are two incompatible things – the realization of one destroys the other. Tat'iana, too, in rather similar terms, sees the dangers of a renewed relationship with Onegin, although her view is modified because of her marriage and the consequent results of an adulterous relationship:

> Chto zh nyne
> Menia presleduete vy?
> Ne potomu l', chto moi pozor
> Teper' by vsemi byl zamechen,
> I mog by v obshchestve prinest'
> Vam soblasnitel'nuiu chest'?

> [Why do you pursue me now? ... Is it not because my shame would be noticed by all and could bring you a tempting honour in society? (Eight: XLIV: 3-4, 11-14)]

It is because of the unrealizable nature of their love, and because they wish to preserve that love intact, that both heroines reject the advances of the men they love and to whom they even confess their feelings.

Tat'iana, then, makes the transition in the novel from young girl seeking out happiness in love to mature woman rejecting the possibility of that happiness – from Juliet to the Princesse de Clèves. It would not, however, be correct to see the two literary characters which I have proposed as emblems of the two states in Tat'iana's development as opposites. Rather, they are two sides of the same coin, or two developmental possibilities out of one situation. Again, it is fate which is to blame for the particular predicament in which each heroine finds herself at the end:

— Pourquoi faut-il, s'écria-t-elle, que je vous puisse accuser de
la mort de M. de Clèves? Que n'ai-je commencé à vous con-
naître depuis que je suis libre, ou pourquoi ne vous ai-je pas
connu devant que d'être engagée? Pourquoi la destinée nous
sépare-t-elle par un obstacle si invincible? (175)

Again, the different reactions of our four heroines towards fate are
nuanced. In Tat'iana's case, as in that of the Princesse, the attitude in
the face of the vagaries of life is acceptance of what cannot be changed
and willingness to suffer. It is this resignation that is the source of
their moral superiority over the other two heroines, Lenore and Juliet,
who are destroyed for their impatience. Both Tat'iana and the Princesse
grow, change, and become better people in the course of the novelistic
events to which they are subjected.

At this point it is appropriate to consider the relationship of Tat'iana
to another crucial character in the structure of the novel, namely her
sister Ol'ga, since it is clear that their roles are complementary and
that Ol'ga's main function is to serve as a conventional foil for her
remarkable sister. The 'conventionality' (uslovnost') of Ol'ga's character is stressed by the author, who seems not at all concerned to imbue
her with the characteristics of real life:

Vsegda skromna, vsegda poslushna,
Vsegda kak utro vesela,
Kak zhizn' poeta prostodushna,
Kak potsalui liubvi mila,
Glaza kak nebo golubye,
Ulybka, lokony l'nianye,
Dvizhen'ia, golos, legkoi stan,
Vse v Ol'ge ... No liuboi roman
Voz'mite i naidete verno
Ee portret

[Always modest, always obedient, always as merry as the
morning, as simple-minded as the life of a poet, as darling as
the kiss of love, with eyes as blue as the sky; her smile, her
flaxen locks, her movements, voice, slender form, everything
in Ol'ga ... but take any novel and you'll surely find her
portrait. (Two: XXIII: 1-10)]

Ol'ga, the poet seems to be telling us, is not a character but a cliché,
and the innocent reader is at first inclined to accept this apparent

judgment and pass on, as does the author himself, and look at Tat'iana. There is, however, a hint in the description which should give the attentive reader pause: Ol'ga, we read, is as simple *as the life of a poet*. This is an evident ironic barb, since we suspect that the life of a poet like Lenskii may be very simple, but the life of a poet like Pushkin can be very complicated indeed. The apparent conglomeration of clichés that serves to describe Ol'ga thus contains a hint at hidden depths which we would do well to heed.

That Ol'ga is not what she appears to be, especially to her enamoured Lenskii, is further stressed by the ironic tone which the author adopts when describing the young poet's love for her:

> Akh, on liubil, kak v nashi leta
> Uzhe ne liubiat; kak odna
> Bezumnaia dusha poeta
> Eshche liubit' osuzhdena

> [*Alack, he loved as in our years no one loves any longer; as only the foolish soul of the poet is any longer fated to love* (Two: XX: 1-4)]

The inference is clear: Lenskii's love, like his verse, is purely conventional, and does not perceive the object of the poet's desire as she really is. In other words, Pushkin is mocking the whole convention of a real person as the muse to whom a poet dedicates his verse:

> I vpriam, blazhen liubovnik skromnyi,
> Chitaiushchii mechty svoi
> Predmetu pesen i liubvi,
> Krasavitse priiatno-tomnoi!
> Blazhen ... khot', mozhet byt', ona
> Sovsem inym razvlechena.

> [*And indeed, blessed is the modest swain who reads his dreamings to the object of his poems and his love, a pleasantly langourous beauty! Blessed ... although perhaps she has something totally different in mind.* (Four: XXXIV: 9-14)]

Such hints that Ol'ga is not the chaste, pure-minded young virgin of Lenskii's imaginings (he leaves out of a novel he is reading her several pages which might prove embarrassing) culminate in an easily perceivable phallic quibble which serves to mock the muse convention:

Ne madrigaly Lenskoi pishet
V al'bome Ol'gi molodoi;
Ego pero liubov'iu dyshet,
Ne khladno bleshchet ostrotoi

[*It is not madrigals which Lenskii writes in the album of young
Ol'ga; his pen breathes love, and does not coldly sparkle with
wit* (Four: XXXI: 1-4)]

Pushkin leaves us in the dark about the true state of Ol'ga's amours.
The reader is led to wonder, however, at the blush that covers Ol'ga's
face when she runs into Tat'iana's room after the night-time sooth-
saying 'more crimson than the Northern dawn' (Five: XXI: 11). Like
Tat'iana, Ol'ga has been expecting to see her bridegroom in her dream.[8]
There is, likewise, fire in her eyes when she is married to the uhlan:

Moi bednyi Lenskoi! iznyvaia,
Ne dolgo plakala ona.
Uvy! nevesta molodaia
Svoei pechali neverna.
Drugoi uvlek ee vniman'e,
Drugoi uspel ee stradan'e
Liubovnoi lest'iu usypit',
Ulan umel ee plenit',
Ulan liubim ee dushoiu ...
I vot uzh s nim pred altarem
Ona stydlivo pod ventsom
Stoit s ponikshei golovoiu,
S ognem v potuplennykh ochakh,
S ulybkoi legkoi na ustakh.

[*My poor Lenskii! Pining, she did not weep long. Alas! the
young bride is unfaithful to her sadness. Another has attracted
her attention, another was able to quell her suffering with
the flattery of love, an uhlan was able to captivate her, an
uhlan is loved by her soul ... and there she stands with him
already before the altar, her head bowed chastely beneath
the wreath, with fire in her downcast eyes and a light smile
on her lips.* (Seven: X: 1-14)]

The reader is left to speculate on these hints, since there is no 'truth'
outside the lightly sketched detail of Ol'ga's 'character.' She does not

exist, and thus no hypothesis has more or less validity than any other, given the 'stylized' (uslovnyi) nature of Pushkin's text, the ambiguity of which permits a variety of interpretations.

I have already suggested that Tat'iana is associated in the poem with Diana, goddess of chastity and the hunt, and that this association is reinforced by the frequent mention of the moon in association with Tat'iana (the moon being, as I have said, the emblem of Diana and, in baroque parallels between Hellenic and Christian myth, of the Virgin). The similes that are applied to Tat'iana are most often those of the wild fauna of the forest, a deer or a tremulous hare hiding from the hunter, a fact which reinforces the Dianan aura around her. For Ol'ga, the corresponding image is that of a flower – visited by every passing moth or bee, or nibbled at by the worm (Clayton 1975, 56-9). The classical figure with which Ol'ga seems to be associated is not Diana, but Helen of Troy, the beautiful adulteress, as is suggested by the following lines from Chapter Five, dropped from the final version:

No Tania (prisiagnu) milei
Eleny pakostnoi tvoei

Nikto i sporit' tut ne stanet
Khot' za Elenu Menelai
100 let eshche ne perestanet
Kaznit' Frigiiskoi bednyi krai,
Khot' v krug pochtennogo Priama
Sobran'e starikov Pergama
Ee zavidia, vnov' reshit:
Prav Menelai, i prav Parid.
Chto zh do srazhenii, to nemnogo
Ia poproshu vas podozhdat'
Izvol'te dalee chitat'
Nachala ne sudite strogo –
Srazhen'e budet.

[But Tania (I swear) is more charming than your disgusting Helen. No one will even argue with this, even though because of Helen Menelaus will not stop for a hundred years yet to punish the poor Phrygian land, even though around the re-spected Priam the council of elders of Pergamon, seeing her, will decide again: Menelaus is right, and Paris is right. As for battles, I will beg you to wait just a little: please read on:

do not judge too strictly at the beginning; there'll be a battle.
[Five: XXVII: 13-14; XXVIII: 1-13; *PSS*, VI, 609)]

The 'battle' that ensues is, of course, that between Onegin and Lenskii, and Ol'ga is the 'adulteress' who is the *casus belli*, just as Helen is in the *Iliad*. The comparison of the squalid duel to the mighty battles of the ancient epic is a typical burlesque technique (the old-fashioned nature of which probably induced Pushkin to delete these rather awkward lines). They serve to fix Ol'ga in our minds as a 'Helen,' an adulteress who is the total antithesis of the Diana/Virgin figure of Tat'iana (although it should be noted that a possible reason for their omission in the final text is that they could make the character of Ol'ga too explicit). With this in mind we can appreciate the irony of Onegin's comparison of Ol'ga to a Van Dyck Madonna:

> Ia vybral by druguiu,
> Kogda b ia byl kak ty poet.
> V chertakh u Ol'gi zhizni net.
> Toch'-v-toch' v Vandikovoi Madone:
> Krugla, krasna litsom ona,
> Kak eta glupaia luna
> Na etom glupom nebosklone.

[*I would choose the other if I were a poet like you. There is no life in Ol'ga's features. Exactly as in a Van Dyck Madonna: she's round and red in the face like that stupid moon on that stupid horizon.* (Three: V: 6-12)]

Onegin's mockery of Ol'ga echoes that of Pushkin: Ol'ga is a mass of clichés: a blonde, blue-eyed, ruddy-complexioned Helen masquerading as a Madonna.

Ol'ga's role is thus to be a foil, a counterpoint to Tat'iana – the petty flirt or adulteress whose peccadilloes serve to underline Tat'iana's constancy and purity. Ol'ga is even, at the ball at least, the rival of Tat'iana for Onegin's attentions. That she is successful to some degree is less the result of her beauty than the expression of the fact that Onegin is not a poet, and therefore, it is suggested, incapable of love.[9] Since it is precisely love which Tat'iana is offering, he is more likely to choose a dalliance with her sister, whose changeable affections indicate no lasting consequences (except, of course, Lenskii's death, which none could foresee).

Beyond the point-counterpoint relationship of Tat'iana and Ol'ga, we can discern in the other female characters, however lightly drawn, a distinct ordering by Pushkin in terms of their fidelity. In her 'Russianness' and her constancy, Tat'iana is, as the author-narrator puts it, his 'faithful ideal' (Eight: L: 2). She is, however, not the only figure whom he evaluates positively: Tat'iana's nurse is projected in an equally positive light; indeed, there is some parallel to be discerned between their different fates. She represents the traditional Russian virtues of obedience, and, significantly, sees the word 'love' as a devilish, alien concept, so that she is moved to cross Tat'iana when the latter uses it as if she had been possessed by an unclean spirit. 'Love' – the idea of the selection by the individual of his/her sexual mate – was an important manifestation of imported manners and contrasted with the traditional institution of the arranged marriage. As a revolt against authority, it had connotations of the evil or devilish. Thus the obedience to parental will which Tat'iana shows in Seven and Eight, and her respect for her husband and her marriage vows thereafter, can be read as the manifestation of her rejection of the foreign. Although noble society insisted on the virginity (or at least the good reputation) of the bride, it tolerated, and even expected, extra-marital affairs (on the model of the French novel). Hence, Tat'iana's refusal of an affair was uncharacteristic, a sign of her 'Russianness' (and presumably of the influence of the old nurse).[10]

To some extent Tat'iana's mother can possibly be included in the group of women whom Pushkin evaluates positively: she is forced to give up 'Grandison' for Dmitrii Larin. She is, as it were, a parody of her daughter: carried away by literary stereotypes, then accepting of her fate (perhaps only because her wise husband has carted her off to the country), but still described with much irony – her French fashions, her domination of the household.

Ol'ga, by contrast, is in the other camp, as we have seen. She shades into the mass of coquettes who inhabit the balls and the 'routs' of society and who threaten their husbands with the horns of cuckoldry and death in the duel. Pushkin reserves the terms *izmennitsa* and *tsirtseia* for such females. The second word is Homeric, and suggests the turning of men into animals through sexual passion. The monsters who inhabit Tat'iana's dream are precisely such victims of the 'circes' of society.[11] The presence of such women in the text, and the suggestion that such behaviour is the norm, leads us to appreciate Tat'iana's worth and difference even more.

Pushkin's predilection for Tat'iana is an expression of his distaste for these society traitresses. His descriptions of society life and mores are filled with considerable venom, e.g., the satirical portraits of the *habitués* of the rout in Chapter Eight. Tat'iana – the pale chaste heroine who wanders the woods beneath the rays of Diana and passes unscathed through the horrors of society – is the fulfilment of the poet's search in womankind for a woman who is both ideal and faithful.

Drawing by Pushkin on a rough draft of Tat'iana's letter. 1824

5

Onegin:
The Fallen Angel

In a recent article on the author-narrator in *Onegin* and his relationship to the other principal male characters, Onegin and Lenskii, J. Thomas Shaw formulates the basic postulates which must guide any discussion of their role in the work. These can be resumed as the paradigmatic nature of these three figures, their differing roles symbolizing different stages in the search of man, or at least of Pushkin the individual, for maturity, and the function of poetry as a definition of maturity and human excellence:

> Actually, the entire novel suggests the importance of being poetic. Perhaps the basic underlying question of the novel is not simply the stages of development, but how a poet (or the poetic in man) can develop to maturity and remain, or once more become, poetic. From this point of view, both chief male characters of the fictional story fail to measure up, in that each insufficiently manifests the genuinely poetic. (1981, 35)

By 'poetic,' of course, Shaw means a particular attitude to the world and to experience which is manifested in the poet and his poetry and enables him to survive and achieve serenity where others fail. In this chapter I propose to examine the principal male characters, especially Onegin, in the light of these insights and challenge some of the traditional notions about them, notions which have persisted down to our time.

As we have seen in the first chapter, traditional nineteenth-century criticism insisted on Onegin's 'typicality,' a position which was reflected in orthodox Soviet writings. This position is the manifestation of the 'realist' or, as I would like to call it in this chapter, the 'mimetic' interpretation of *Onegin*, and was the result of a reading of the work through the prism of later, realist writings. Initially, perhaps, the interpretation of Onegin as a 'typical' representative of his age was established through the readers' expectations, evoked through the presentation and form of Chapter One: since a 'typical' day of Onegin is described, and since the genre adopted is that of the sociological portrait with its details of everyday existence, then surely Onegin must be the 'typical' young man of his time, who is seen to be a young 'dandy' with affected manners. This defective logic was reinforced by the apparent fitting of *Onegin* into a series or set of titles: Karamzin's *Rytsar' nashego vremeni* (*A Knight of Our Times*), Lermontov's *Geroi nashego vremeni* (*A Hero of Our Time*), and so on, through a 'creative misreading' of *Onegin*, to the Rudins and Lavretskiis, the Oblomovs and the Bazarovs of nineteenth-century Russian realism, each of which tried in some way to realize this goal of 'typicality.'

The notion of 'type' very quickly begins to break down when subjected to closer scrutiny – is it, to put it simply, the lowest common denominator or the highest common factor of the generation? Is a typical character ordinary, the statistical average, or is he exaggerated, a caricature possessing the 'typical' qualities of the age to an extreme degree? Even if we have accepted the latter proposition, we have simply moved the question a step back, for now it must be asked what the 'typical' qualities are, and how they are determined. Even a cursory glance at such figures as Oblomov and Bazarov suggests that, whatever their authors and audience thought they were, they are interesting not because they resemble their contemporaries but because they are different. It is some extreme facet of their make-up – Oblomov's laziness, Bazarov's nihilism – which makes them command the reader's attention, not their 'typicality.'

It is perhaps not news that the sterile debate about the realistic 'type' was, and is, a chasing after shadows. What I intend to dispute in the following pages is the notion that Onegin was a normal young man who was somehow representative of his age (which is what I take the word 'type' to mean). Even the foreword that was placed before Chapter One when it was first printed, if read carefully, does not bear out such an assumption: 'The first chapter is in a way a whole. It contains the description of the life of a young man in Petersburg society at the end of 1819' (*PSS*, VI, 638). Pushkin's statement is laconic, yet specific: we are to read the description of the life of a certain young man at a certain place at a certain time. The conclusions are left for the reader to draw for himself. No notion of typicality is imposed.

This is not surprising, since if we examine Onegin closely we find that, far from being the representative of his age, he is a very unusual individual, and that he is defined, not in terms of what he is, but rather in terms of what he is not, or more precisely, in terms of the activities that he avoids. Onegin has to be seen, that is to say, against the background of his age, an age that ascribed very clear roles to individuals. Lotman, in his article on theatricality and theatre in early nineteenth-century Russia, notes the pervasiveness of these roles:

> Gentry life at the end of the eighteenth and the beginning of the nineteenth centuries was built not only on the basis of a hierarchy of conduct, created in turn by the hierarchical nature of post-Petrine governmental structure, organized by the table of ranks, but also as a set of possible alternatives ('service/retirement,' 'life in the capital/life on one's estate,' 'Petersburg/Moscow,' 'military service/civil service,' 'the Guards/the army,' etc.) each of which presupposed a particular type of behaviour. (1973, 45-6)

A number of the alternatives that Lotman lists are incidentally operative in *Onegin* (e.g., 'Petersburg/Moscow'), but it is my intention to focus on one or two which are particularly significant in the work.

In the notional world of *Onegin*, a particularly important choice is that between service and non-service. All three principals, Onegin, Lenskii, and Pushkin, have essentially chosen the path of non-service. In the case of Pushkin, true, the poet was 'officially' a functionary in the Ministry (Collegium) of Foreign Affairs. In fact this was purely a matter of form and does not play any role in the work. As Lotman points out, however, the fact that Onegin had never served (in particular, had never served *in the army*) was highly significant: 'The military field was such a natural one for a nobleman, that the absence of this feature in a biography had to have a special explanation. ... Onegin, as has been said, never wore the military uniform, which distinguished him among his coevals who had been 16-17 in 1812. But the fact that he had never served anywhere at all and had none, not even the lowest rank, made Onegin decidedly a white crow among his contemporaries' (1980, 48-9). Lotman's point is that, although service (either military or civil) to the state was no longer absolutely obligatory, as it had been under Peter the Great, it was the normal path for the vast majority of Onegin's contemporaries. The reference to 1812 is very important, for, if we are to believe the chronology of *Onegin* as it has been sketched by numerous Pushkinists, Onegin entered the *grand monde*, and with it embarked on his life of seduction and high living, precisely at the point when those born around 1795, like Tolstoi's Petia Rostov, rushed out to enlist in the military in response to the motherland's dire need.[1] Onegin's non-service is thus not simply a chance feature of his biography but a highly significant trait which underlines Onegin's egoism and indifference to Russia, and it is made even more heinous by his cult of Napoleon, manifested by the presence of the French emperor's statuette in his study (discovered by Tat'iana in Chapter Seven). (In this context it should be noted that both Pushkin and Lenskii were too young to serve in the Napoleonic wars, and that their non-service is caused by their decision to undertake the life of a poet.)

The second kind of choice that Onegin appears to have made is in the category 'Decembrist/non-Decembrist.' The Decembrist movement (as it became known after its tragic dénouement on the Senate Square in Petersburg on 14 December 1825) was an underground movement of young officers who became inflamed with revolutionary ideas while serving in Europe during the Napoleonic wars and formed secret societies dedicated to the overthrow of the Tsarist régime and the abolition of serfdom in Russia. Pushkin himself was on the fringes of the movement, but was saved, paradoxically enough, from the dire consequences of involvement in the events of December by the fact that he was in exile on his family's estate of Mikhailovskoe for earlier misdeeds.

Pushkin could not, of course, write openly about the movement in *Onegin* for reasons of censorship (and to avoid implicating himself and others – he was already in enough trouble). The debate therefore about Decembrism in *Onegin* turns on various cryptographic references and evidence in drafts (including the famous 'Chapter Ten') and elsewhere. We have, for example, the reminiscences of Mikhail Iuzefovich discussed in chapter three: 'he [Pushkin] explained to us in considerable detail everything that had been in his first scheme, according to which, by the way, Onegin was either to die in the Caucasus, or to end up among the Decembrists.'[2] As I have already pointed out, such 'evidence' is, at best, highly tenuous, especially since *Onegin* was conceived, and a good portion of it was written, before the Decembrist uprising took place. In any case, the ending of *Onegin* gives no especial credence to such speculations about the continuation of the novel. On the contrary, the ex abrupto ending makes them 'illegal.'

The other important piece of evidence that might argue in favour of Onegin's being a Decembrist is the fact that, when he inherits his uncle's estate, he replaces the work obligations (corvée) of the serfs by a 'lenient quitrent' (Two: IV). This action is, however, far from unequivocal. It is of a piece with his ostentatious indifference to money in Chapter One (in which he abandons the remnants of his father's estate to the deceased's creditors [One: LI]). It also reflects his mouthing, in society, of fashionable theories of Western political economy:

> Za to chital Adama Smita,
> I byl glubokoi ekonom,
> To est', umel sudit' o tom,
> Kak gosudarstvo bogateet,
> I chem zhivet, i pochemu
> Ne nuzhno zoloto emu,
> Kogda *prostoi produkt* imeet.
> Otets poniat' ego ne mog
> I zemli otdaval v zalog.

> [*But he did read Adam Smith and was a profound economist,
> that is he could discuss how the state gets rich, and on what
> it lives, and why it does not need gold when it has the 'simple
> product.' His father could not understand him, and
> mortgaged his lands.* (One: VII: 6-14)]

Onegin's understanding of economics implies not a profound critique of Russian society but a justification for his life-style: like the state, Onegin does not need gold, but simply lives on credit (the state by printing money, Onegin through the indulgence of the good tradesmen of Petersburg). Onegin's father needs no high-falutin' foreign theories in order to justify his squandering of his inheritance by mortgaging it. Like father, like son. The irony of the 'economics' aspect of Chapter One is that Onegin is right: he is saved from any unpleasant shortage of liquidity by the providential death of his uncle, who receives as thanks only the thoughts expressed by Onegin in the very first stanza of the novel.

There is, needless to say, very little in the way of Decembrism to be wrung out of Onegin's thoughts on political economy. Far from being an idealistic revolutionary concerned with the fate of his country, Onegin is, like his father, a thoughtless spendthrift who squanders his patrimony and whose 'new order' on the estate he has inherited from his uncle reflects not a humanitarian concern for the serf but a lack of regard for his own financial interests, which he is willing to sacrifice to a whim, or at best to the desire to be in fashion. The reaction of the serfs is characteristic: 'the slave blessed his fate' – implying that the actions of the young lord are as incomprehensible to him as the turns of destiny, and that no thanks are required for such an act of folly. Pushkin, it seems to me, is ironical about rather than approving of Onegin's gesture, which is made, he suggests, out of boredom and is another manifestation of his insouciant nature.

Perhaps the most convincing argument about Onegin's 'un-Decembrist' nature is the reaction of the Decembrist writers themselves (principally Ryleev and Bestuzhev), who were dismayed at the Onegin whom they saw in Chapter One.[3] In the writings of the Decembrists themselves there had been a return to classical genres (ode, tragedy, etc.) and an adoption of folkloristic ones (e.g., the Ukrainian *dumy*). The purpose of Decembrist literature was a didactic one: to inculcate civic virtue and heroism by the example of great heroes of the past – of the antique world and Russia. In *Onegin* Pushkin pours scorn on the exhortation of Vil'gel'm Kiukhel'beker, a Lyceum schoolmate and now representative of the neo-classicist branch of Decembrist writing, to write odes, advice which Pushkin was happy to ignore (see Four: XXXII-XXXIII). Instead of finding in *Onegin* a virtuous, idealistic, and self-sacrificing hero to be emulated, the Decembrists were shocked by the frivolity, selfishness, and cynicism of Onegin's life-style. Lotman, writing about the tendency of young Russians of the time to be drawn to the 'norms of antique heroism,' notes 'this "Roman" poetry of poverty, which lent a theatrical grandeur to material need, was subsequently characteristic of many Decembrists' (1973, 39). It is therefore straining credulity to see in Onegin an attempt, either overt or covert, to portray a Decembrist. Neither his life-style of indolence, debauchery, and self-indulgence, nor his cynical and egoistic opinions nor his boredom and spleen correspond to the codes of behaviour and the literary norms which 'read' as Decembrist. His act of munificence – freeing his serfs from their corvée – is the arbitrary act of an 'eccentric' (*chudak* – which is what his neighbours call him) who is uncaring of his own fate and fortune and who feels no urge to preserve his patrimony for posterity.

Onegin, then, far from being a 'type,' is outside all the accepted career/behaviour codes – a non-military, non-functionary non-Decembrist. For the purposes of the novel, however, there is a fourth 'negative' which we have to add, and one which, in the context of *Onegin*, is of paramount importance. He is not a poet:

Vysokoi strasti ne imeia
Dlia zvukov zhizni ne shchadit',

Ne mog on iamba ot khoreia,
Kak my ni bilis', otlichit'.

[*Not having that exalted passion to not spare his life for the
sake of sounds, he could not distinguish an iambus from a
choree, however hard we tried.* (One: VII: 1-4)]

The detail is important since the other two principal characters – Lenskii and Pushkin – are poets, and because, as Shaw asserts in the passage
cited above, the notion of 'being a poet' has important existential connotations in the work. What we are talking about here, however, is
less these than the simple question of a function, a career, a role that
gives one a place in society and gives meaning to one's existence.

Poetry was not, of course, the kind of career that brought fortune. If
one adopted the role of 'gentleman poet' of the Karamzinian kind which
Lenskii, for example, favours, then it hardly even promised fame (see
the two 'future lives' that Pushkin sketches out for Lenskii – had he
not been shot by Onegin – in Six: XXXVI-XXXIX). Much of the meaning
of Pushkin's own life can be seen in the conscious (and unprecedented)
choice that he made to adopt poetry as an acceptable career *and source
of income* for a gentleman; in short, to drop the cloak of amateurism.
In a sense Pushkin in doing so 'transgressed the codes' of acceptable
behaviour for a nobleman-poet established by Vasilii L'vovich Pushkin
his uncle, I.I. Dmitriev, and other poets of the Karamzinian group.
Lenskii, it appears, would, unlike Pushkin, have adhered to the traditional mould.

Onegin as 'non-poet' has, however, another dimension that should
be mentioned, namely the fact that he cannot tell an iambus (– /) from
a choree (/ –). The reason is apparently that Onegin is largely a French-
speaker who has read only French poetry and for whom the notion of
stress as a significant feature in metre is foreign and incomprehensible.
It is made clear to the reader that the correspondence between Tat'iana
and Onegin is likewise in French (Three: XXVI), as, given the norms
of social behaviour of the time, would be the conversations as well,
especially since Tat'iana 'knew Russian badly, did not read our journals, and expressed herself with difficulty in her native language' (Three:
XXVI: 5-8).[4] It was, indeed, quite practical even for a young nobleman
of the time to function knowing hardly any Russian (as did A.N. Raevskii, a friend of Pushkin's whom some chose to see as the 'prototype'
on whom Pushkin modelled his hero). We are told that Onegin com-
municates to his neighbours without putting the polite enclitic -*s* when

replying *da* and *net*. One suspects that these monosyllables constitute the largest part of his conversation, so that if Lenskii, despite his Russian elegies, is described by his neighbours as 'half-Russian' (Two: XII: 5), then it would be legitimate to call Onegin 'non-Russian.'

Onegin, then, is a catalogue of negatives, a 'dangerous eccentric' who appears as the personification of the 'spirit of denial' (*Geist der Verneinung*) that inspired Pushkin's poem 'Demon' ('The Demon'). The relationship between this poem and the image of Onegin in *Onegin* is explored by Shaw in his article, and I do not intend to go over the same ground again. One should, however, mention the extent to which Pushkin seeks to reinforce this impression through the use of such terms as 'my demon,' which are summed up in the author's comment in Chapter Eight:

> Sozdan'e ada il' nebes,
> Sei angel, sei nadmennyi bes,
> Chto zh on?

> [*Creation of hell or heaven, this angel, this arrogant demon, what is he?* (Seven: XXIV: 7-9)]

Although the Soviet critic I. Medvedeva has asserted that Pushkin gradually removes the 'demonic' features from Onegin so that he becomes more and more realistic in the course of the novel, one can find little to support such an interpretation in the text.[5] Indeed, as late as Chapter Eight, we find the following speculation:

> Chem nyne iavitsia? Mel'motom,
> Kosmopolitom, patriotom,
> Garol'dom, kvakerom, khanzhoi,
> Il' maskoi shchegol'net inoi,
> Il' prosto budet dobryi maloi,
> Kak vy da ia, kak tselyi svet?

> [*What will he now appear as? Melmoth, a cosmopolite, a patriot, a Harold, a Quaker, a hypocrite, or will he sport some other mask, or will he simply be a nice chap, like you and me, like the whole world?* (Eight: VIII: 5-10)]

The appearance of an individual in a thousand guises was, of course, the sign of the devil. Interestingly, both this passage and the one quoted

before it are preceded by the description of Onegin as a *chudak* ('crank').
The suggestion is that this is one of Pushkin's code-words for the devil.
(His neighbours in the country, we recall, had likewise described him
as a 'most dangerous crank.') The word, though derived from *chudnyi*
('odd'), is related to *chudo* ('marvel'), which in turn has connotations
of the supernatural. It is therefore not unjust to conclude that Pushkin
wishes us to see some slight overtones of at least a mock-devilry in
his hero.

If we accept Shaw's interpretation, the fundamental meaning of *Onegin* is thus not a realistic one – a portrayal of a social type – but a
symbolic one, a transposition into the codes of the social-portrait genre
of a philosophical principle which had troubled Pushkin, and to which
he had returned obsessively again and again, trying to give it concrete
form in various ways.

It has frequently been pointed out that Pushkin, unlike Byron, differentiates between his hero, Onegin, and himself.[6] That is to say,
unlike Byron's heroes, Onegin is not a projection of the author into
the text. This view is acceptable only with certain modifications. The
principal method which is used to achieve distance is, of course, the
figure of the author-narrator who acts in the text as a differentiated
character. Pushkin goes out of his way to stress the point by his own
intervention in a digression:

> Vsegda ia rad zametit' raznost'
> Mezhdu Oneginym i mnoi,
> Chtoby nasmeshlivyi chitatel'
> Ili kakoi-nibud' izdatel'
> Zamyslovatoi klevety,
> Slichaia zdes' moi cherty,
> Ne povtorial potom bezbozhno,
> Chto namaral ia svoi portret,
> Kak Bairon, gordosti poet,
> Kak budto nam uzh nevozmozhno
> Pisat' poemy o drugom,
> Kak tol'ko o sebe samom.

> [*I am always glad to note the difference between Onegin and
> me, so that a mocking reader or some publisher of a mali-
> cious calumny, discerning my features here, should not then
> blasphemously say that I have scrawled my own portrait
> like Byron, the poet of pride, as if it were impossible for us to*

write poems about anything else but ourselves. (One: LVI: 3-14)]

These are, however, the words of the stylized Pushkin-narrator, and should be viewed circumspectly because of their importance in the 'battle with the critics' function which I have mentioned elsewhere. Onegin's biography, though it is different from Pushkin's, has a number of points of contact with it (his life in the country, for example, is clearly modelled after Pushkin's in Mikhailovskoe).[7] As has been recently been noted by L.I. Vol'pert, in Pushkin we observe a principle by which literary 'play' mingles with life, or biography, so that the presence of Pushkin as a character (together with Katenin and Viazemskii) alongside the 'fictional' Onegin, Tat'iana, and Lenskii was by no means paradoxical, but rather another manifestation of this rich interpenetration of real life and literature which is characteristic of Pushkin (1980, 8). This tendency gives rise to the speculation that has bedevilled Pushkin studies to find the 'prototypes' of Onegin, Tat'iana, etc. If there is a basis to such research, then it surely lies in the fact that Pushkin attributed to real-life individuals at different points in time the 'role' of these characters *who already existed in his imagination*: literature, in other words, imposed itself on real life for Pushkin, not vice versa, as many have supposed.[8] This interpenetration of literature and real life is the most remarkable feature of *Onegin*. It permits us to see Onegin not as the poet, nor as his projection into literature, but as the parody or dramatization of a philosophical and aesthetic principle. The fact that Onegin had deep roots in the matrix of ideological relationships means that Pushkin can make the concrete manifestation of this principle – the description of Onegin's actions, dress, day, reading, etc. – a composite of whatever traits he likes, taken from literature (*Childe Harold, Don Juan, Beppo, Adolphe*, etc.) or from life (Napoleon, Byron, A.N. Raevskii, Pushkin himself).

The creation of Onegin as the personification of negation, the realization of his own 'spirit of denial' with its obvious parallels to Goethe's Mephisto, is supported by a vast amount of detail and especially by literary allusions which serve as a 'source-book' of foreign literary models.[9] Pushkin uses these as a shorthand to define the demonic nature of Onegin (and identify him with the anti-hero of the post-sentimental novel). Since Jakobson and Chizhevskii it has been assumed that the use of detail in *Onegin* (e.g., the description of his cabinet in Seven) is metonymic, that it serves as a *pars pro toto* to describe Onegin as a character (Chizhevskii 1971, 153-4). This would be true if the description of Onegin (or Tat'iana for that matter) were mimetic or reflexionist, reflecting a particular 'reality' (type). However, in *Onegin*, I would contend, the reverse is true: Onegin is not a depiction of a type, but a parody of one, a mocking projection into life of an idea of which Napoleon, Melmoth, and such characters, are other manifestations. Onegin, in other words, is placed in a paradigmatic (and ironic) relationship with other figures, both historical and literary, who all constitute, as it were, hypostases of this 'spirit of denial.' (The use of detail in *Onegin* should be compared with, say, the use of the lip of the 'little Princess' in *War and Peace*, which is truly metonymic.)

As Shaw shows, the most important of the roles which Onegin eschews is that of poet – or rather, his being a non-poet is his most important feature. Onegin is the incarnation of that negative, cynical force which destroys those positive values that are poetry's theme. In the context of *Onegin*, there are two values that are central. They are expressed specifically in the poetry of Lenskii, and are the object of Onegin's scorn: namely the values of 'love' and 'friendship.' Lenskii is the personification of the sentimental, elegiac poetry which was the continuation of the Karamzinian tradition and which Pushkin himself wrote in his early period.[10] This poetry was characterized by a restricted, 'purified' vocabulary, periphrastic phraseology, and a restricted number of 'conventional' themes: those mentioned above (love and friendship) and the passage of time (together with impending death). It was a poetry of the salon, which aimed at good taste and avoided any depth of emotion or unusual expression that might give offence. Already in *Ruslan and Liudmila* Pushkin had broken out of the confines of this poetic, which had too much of the emptiness of a formalized routine and was too remote from the realities of life and language.[11]

In *Onegin* we find the author-narrator conducting a running battle against one of the most important aspects of the Karamzinian (sentimental) poetry, namely the notion of a chaste, innocent heroine who must be protected from anything indecent or risqué – a notion summed up in the quotation from Piron: 'La mère en préscrira la lecture à sa fille.' The weapons that Pushkin uses against this 'ideal reader' are manifold. He uses the footnotes as an ironical commentary on the remarks of critics who have criticized *Onegin* from this point of view – for example, footnote 36: 'Our critics, true admirers of the fair sex, severely criticized the indecency of this verse' (*PSS*, VI, 194). The verse in question – 'The girls skip in anticipation' (Five: XXVIII: 9) – was offensive only in its use of vocabulary, which transgressed the boundaries of Karamzinian good taste. This footnote is, as it were, a false

scent, part of the game that Pushkin plays with his critics in the footnotes, mostly by the use of bawdy quibbles to which the footnotes
draw laconic attention (e.g., footnotes 12, 20, and 21).[12]

Despite, then, Pushkin's disclaimer quoted above, it seems fair to
say that up to Chapter Four there is little or no distinction between
the voice of the author-narrator in the digressions on love and friendship and that of Onegin. This is nowhere clearer than in the stanzas
VII and VIII with which Chapter Four begins (I to VI are omitted) and
which express disgust with the falseness and dissimulation of the 'game
of love.' These stanzas 'read' as authorial digression until the beginning
of stanza IX, when we read: 'Precisely thus thought my Evgenii' (a lame
echo of One: II: 1: 'Thus thought a young rake'). A similar, 'cynical'
commentary is provided on the subject of friendship:

> No druzhby net i toi mezh nami.
> Vse predrassudki istrebia,
> My pochitaem vsekh nuliami,
> A edinitsami – sebia.
> My vse gliadim v Napoleony;
> Dvunogikh tvarei milliony
> Dlia nas orudie odno,
> Nam chuvstvo diko i smeshno.

> [*But there is not even that friendship among us. Destroying
> all prejudices, we consider everyone zeroes, and ourselves –
> ones. We all aspire to be Napoleons; the millions of two-
> legged creatures are for us a mere tool; sentiment is strange
> and laughable to us.* (Two: XIV: 1-8)]

The inclusiveness of the 'we' in this passage points to the identification
of Pushkin and Onegin in these sentiments, which are, as it were,
'common property' of them both. (The stanza quoted echoes in turn
the stanza One: XLVI: 1-14, which provides the initial basis for the
communality of interest between the author-narrator and the hero.)
The fact that Pushkin and his hero are seen to hold identical opinions
in these digressions on the nature of love and friendship, and that they
both express their contempt for the poetry of Lenskii, which is the
vehicle for these sentiments, permits us to see Onegin not as the reflection of the author in the text but as the expression of a part of the
author, of his opinions. He is, as it were, one side in the dialectical
opposition in Pushkin's own philosophical make-up.

What is important to recognize in Onegin is his dual nature. He has his roots in the concept of the 'spirit of denial' expressed in Pushkin's lyrical poetry, but he is projected into a novelistic situation, with the demands for realistic human detail which that genre demands. (In this, it should be noted, he reflects the hybrid form – poem/novel – of *Onegin* itself.) This is shown in the lines following the passage quoted above, in which the poet contradicts the view of a totally cynical Evgenii:

> Khot' on liudei konechno znal,
> I voobshche ikh preziral, –
> No (pravil net bez iskliuchenii)
> Inykh on ochen' otlichal,
> I vchuzhe chuvstvo uvazhal.

> [*Although he of course knew people and in general despised them, yet (there are no rules without exceptions) some people he very much sought out and he respected sentiment in others.* (Two: XIV: 10-14)]

The figure of Onegin, then, is delicately poised between the symbolic cynical demon and the human being, friend of Pushkin and Lenskii, and oscillates between these two modes.

How are we to account for this opposition? Lotman, in his commentary on *Onegin*, discusses duelling as a strict code which deprived the participants of their free will and reduced them to automatons: 'This ability of the duel to enmesh people, deprive them of their own will and turn them into playthings and automatons is very important' (1980, 102-3). He concludes this observation by referring the reader to the article by Roman Jakobson on Pushkin's 'sculptural myth.' The comment by Lotman is a brilliant extension of Jakobson's argument – on Pushkin's fascination with the static image of the sculpture, and the 'forced immobility' which it suggests – into the discussion of *Onegin* (Jakobson 1937a, 39). We may extrapolate Lotman's observation (which is not amplified) as follows. Put in 'realist' terms, Onegin is an individual who is 'locked into' codes of behaviour which make him behave like an automaton and which deprive him of the ability to express his free will and be a human being. Such 'codes' or roles are numerous: lover, seducer, cynic, landowner, duellist. Thus, although Onegin is a friend of Lenskii's, he cannot resist the impulse to flirt with Ol'ga, nor can he step outside the codes of behaviour which lead him *automatically* to the duel, the impossibility of compromise, and Lenskii's death.[13]

Most interestingly, the human-being/sculpture alternation which Jakobson pointed to and which is so important in such works as 'The Bronze Horseman' ('Mednyi vsadnik') and 'The Stone Guest' ('Kamennyi gost'' – Pushkin's version of the Don Juan theme) is present in *Onegin* in the figure of Napoleon, who lurks as a presence in the work (e.g., in the lines on egoism quoted above, and in the description of Moscow in Chapter Seven), and who is, as I have suggested above, another 'hypostasis' of the 'spirit of denial' which Onegin represents. Napoleon appears, in Onegin's study, metamorphosed into a little statuette:

> I stolbik s kukloiu chugunnoi
> Pod shliapoi s pasmurnym chelom,
> S rukami szhatymi krestom.

> [and a little column with an iron doll, with cloudy brow beneath a hat, its arms folded. (Seven: XIX: 12-14)]

Napoleon has received his punishment, and has been turned from human being into immobile figure. Most important, it is as a figure transfixed, immobile 'as if struck by lightning,' that we leave Onegin at the end of the novel (Eight: XLVIII: 2). Like Napoleon, he has been reduced to a state of 'enforced immobility.'

The presentation of Onegin is thus a dialectical one: as value-destroyer versus the value-bearers, versus poets. The dialectic, I would argue, is inherent in Pushkin's aesthetics. Onegin's physical destruction of Lenskii, on this symbolic plane, is the destruction of the value 'friendship.' It also implies the destruction or rejection of inadequate poetry: of poetry which has not penetrated to the root of life, which has not freed itself from the automatism that is in turn a denial of the will of the individual and hence of humanity. (For Lenskii the elegiac poet is as much a mask, a role-player, as is Onegin.) In the sense that only the best and most real can stand up to his negation, Onegin's cynicism, it can be argued, is useful, and even a necessary evil, like a corrosive acid that will eat away all but the most noble metals. In the sense that Onegin is an aspect of Pushkin's aesthetic thought, he is the force that leads Pushkin from Karamzinian versification to Pushkinian poetry.

Onegin is the most extensive of a series of portraits which have a common root in the formula 'demon falls in love with angel.'[14] Perhaps the most perfect expression of this formula is to be found in the lyric 'Angel' ('The Angel'):

V dveriakh edema angel nezhnyi
Glavoi poniksheiu siial,
A demon mrachnyi i miatezhnyi
Nad adskoi bezdnoiu letal.

Dukh otritsan'ia, dukh somnen'ia
Na dukha chistogo vziral
I zhar nevol'nyi umilen'ia
Vpervye smutno poznaval.

'Prosti, on rek, tebia ia videl,
I ty nedarom mne siial:
Ne vse ia v nebe nenavidel,
Ne vse ia v mire preziral'.

[*At the gates of Eden an angel shone with bowed head, while
a demon, gloomy and rebellious, flew above the abyss of hell.
The spirit of denial, the spirit of doubt beheld the pure spirit
and he experienced vaguely for the first time an involuntary
flush of tenderness. 'Forgive me, spake he, I saw you, and you
did not shine towards me for nothing. I have not hated everything in heaven, I have not despised everything on earth.'*
(PSS, III, 59)]

As we have seen, the transposition of this formula to the novelistic
genre entailed the addition of humanizing traits (e.g., the friendship
with Lenskii discussed above) and produced the oscillation between
the human and the symbolic/mask/parody. It is important to note that,
whether expressed in symbolic/lyrical or novelistic terms, the formula
shows that the nemesis of the demon is to be found in love for a pure
and innocent creature. It is a case of irresistible force versus immovable
object. Love, Pushkin tells us in Chapter Eight, is synonymous with
poetry, for it is precisely at the moment when Onegin feels his love
for Tat'iana most deeply that he comes closest to poetry:

I postepenno v usyplen'e
I chuvstv i dum vpadaet on,
A pered nim Voobrazhen'e
Svoi pestryi mechet faraon.
To vidit on: na talom snege
Kak-budto spiashchii na nochlege
Nedvizhim iunosha lezhit,

I slyshit golos: chto zh? ubit.
To vidit on vragov zabvennykh,
Klevetnikov, i trusov zlykh,
I roi izmennits molodykh,
I krug tovarishchei prezrennykh,
To sel'skii dom – i u okna
Sidit *ona* ... i vse ona! ...

On tak privyk teriat'sia v etom,
Chto chut' s uma ne svorotil,
Ili ne sdelalsia poetom.
Priznat'sia: to-to b odolzhil!
A tochno: siloi magnetizma
Stikhov rossiiskikh mekhanizma
Edva v to vremia ne postig
Moi bestolkovyi uchenik.
Kak pokhodil on na poeta,
Kogda v uglu sidel odin,
A pered nim pylal kamin,
I on murlykal: *Benedetta*
Il' *Idol mio* i ronial
V ogon' to tufliu, to zhurnal.

[*And gradually he falls into a trance of feelings and thoughts, and imagination deals its multicoloured faro before his eyes. Now he sees: a youth lies motionless on the melting snow as if sleeping at a bivouac, and he hears a voice: 'Well! – he's dead.' Now he sees forgotten enemies, slanderers and malicious cowards, and a swarm of young traitresses, and a circle of despised comrades; now – a country house, and by the window she is sitting – always she! ... He became so used to losing himself in this, that he almost went off his head or almost became a poet. Let's admit – that would have done us a favour! and truly, by hypnosis my unruly pupil almost understood at that time the mechanism of Russian verse. How he resembled a poet when he sat alone in the corner, and the fireplace glowed in front of him, and he purred: 'Benedetta' or 'Idol mio' and dropped either a slipper or a newspaper in the fire.* (Eight: XXXVII: 1- XXXVIII: 14)]]

These two stanzas are, arguably, the most remarkable in *Onegin*. They contain the crux of the argument: it is by poetry (which is seen and evoked in all its manifestations: muse – Tat'iana – friendship, love, guilt, remorse, but also the incantatory power of the verse itself) that the demon can be exorcised, and Onegin be turned from petty devil into human being. Far from Pushkin resembling his hero, it is the hero who must try to learn the role of the poet. But most important in the passage, surely, is the 'almost.' The jocular tone of the second verse reduces Onegin to his proper dimensions: he will never be a poet, will never have happiness, never be united with the object of his love. The life and the success of the poet are, as it were, defined by contrast. The spirit of denial which Onegin represents is thus stymied by the confrontation with love lost and friendship destroyed. The intensity of feeling is equal to poetry or madness (a fine note of irony from Pushkin) and represents the (at least temporary) triumph of the human side of Onegin over the demonic. Onegin, interestingly, even includes Russian poets on his reading list: 'He read some of ours, *not rejecting anything*' (my italics; Eight: XXXV: 7). The suggestion is that that Gallomane has for the first time come to appreciate what it is to be Russian.

Ultimately, however, for Pushkin the 'enamoured demon' syndrome was unresolvable: the operative word in the passage quoted above is 'almost': despite it all, the demon remains demon, angel angel, eternally fated to remain apart. The final scene of the novel, which follows these lines, has the air of inevitability about it. The reproaches which Tat'iana scatters on Onegin are left unanswered, and Onegin stands petrified with confusion as her husband approaches in a pastiche of the ending of the Don Juan myth: the suitor – Onegin – is turned to stone, while the threatening figure of the husband comes to life. It is in the ultimate unresolvability of the syndrome that we must seek the reason for the abrupt ending in Eight: there is simply no more to be said. Onegin has received his punishment for his deficient humanity, his scorning of love, his desecration of friendship, his inability to be poetic. The rest is silence.

An intriguing aspect of Shaw's argument concerns the notion of chances missed: 'Along with the theme of maturing in *Onegin* runs a central theme of a time for doing and a time for being. The stages of the author-narrator's development are suggested as the "natural" ones of the novel – youthful enchantment to 20 or so, then a period of disenchantment to 23 or 24, but a mature reenchantment by that time' (1980, 34). Shaw's formula seeks to define precise existential correlatives for what is worked out by Pushkin in symbolic terms. His argument – that the position of Pushkin in the poem is one of 'mature reenchantment' with life – rests perhaps a little too much on the use of the past tense in the poem 'Demon,' which suggests, according to Shaw, that the battle with the demons of denial was over for good as far as Pushkin was concerned. Rather, I would suggest, the 'demon versus goodness' situation continues to occur in Pushkin's work after this point, suggesting that each 'exorcism,' as I have chosen to call it, was only temporary, to be fought out anew in each succeeding work. One can see in Shaw's argument interesting parallels to the Soviet view that Pushkin 'overcame' romanticism in the period of exile, specifically in *Onegin*, which is contrasted with the so-called 'southern poems' as Pushkin's 'path to realism.' In fact, Pushkin returned to romantic themes in different forms throughout his creative life, so that such an argument is flawed (and depends on an overly narrow definition of romanticism).

Despite these criticisms, it seems undeniable that Shaw has a point in stressing the question of timeliness as a central aspect of *Onegin*. As I argued above, Onegin is a non-person as far as his function in Russian society is concerned: he has no career, no recognizable role, only a series of masks. On this 'career' plane he is contrasted with both the principal male protagonists: Lenskii and Pushkin. Lenskii, we recall, had chosen the path of amateur poet, Pushkin that of the professional. That the question of career was an important concern for Pushkin is suggested by the fact that Chapter One was originally published with the 'Conversation of a Poet and a Bookseller' – a poem that sets out, in dialogue form, the problems and frustrations of writing for inspiration work which is then to be sold for money. Pushkin felt only too keenly the contradictions between the mercantile pursuit of publishing for profit and the notion of the dignity of the nobleman. *Onegin* is thus concerned, on one level, with the question of how one is to live one's life. Pushkin, it is clear, was very conscious of the exigencies of time, the necessity of making a successful career at something, and the pitfalls that lurked for the unwary.

As we have seen, the three principal male characters in the novel all have 'eccentric,' exceptional lives. Pushkin is a professional poet, Onegin a non-person, and Lenskii an amateur poet who has eschewed any kind of service. In the case of Onegin, there is another character who scarcely figures in the text of the poem at all, and yet is in direct contrast with him. This is the husband of Tat'iana, whom we know only as Prince N. The mentions of him are exceedingly scant, yet incredibly important. We first encounter him in Chapter Seven in Tat'iana's remark: 'Who? That fat general?' (Seven: LIV: 14). He then recurs in Chapter Eight, when we learn that the general is an old-time friend of Onegin's and uses with him the familiar form 'ty' (Eight: XVII-XVIII). We further learn from Tat'iana that her husband was 'maimed in the battles' and that 'we are well-received at court' (Eight: XLIV: 9-10).

Although these details seem sketchy, there is a lot of essential information which is conveyed and which creates a picture of a figure who is a complete contrast to Onegin. Thus, we see that Tat'iana's husband is a contemporary of Onegin's, and that, while Onegin was entering society, Prince N was embarking on a splendid military career. The fact that he is a general does not necessarily mean that he is an old man. On the contrary, the top four levels of the 'table of ranks' carried the appellation 'general,' and Pushkin, in a letter to his brother of 21 July 1822, wrote: 'Are you in the service? It is time, I swear it is time. Do not take me as example. If you let the time slip by, you will regret it afterwards – in the Russian service you absolutely must be a colonel at 26, if you ever want to amount to anything.'[15] The rank of colonel, we note, is a 'general's rank,' which is to say that someone of Onegin's age at the end of the novel, or the age of Prince N, should have attained that rank in the service in order to have a successful career. Prince N has achieved that distinction, Onegin has not. The sketchy portrait of Prince N is made more explicit by a stanza in which Pushkin describes the characteristics of a successful careerist. Although the stanza is generalized, I believe that we can assume it applies to Prince N:

> Blazhen, kto smolodu byl molod,
> Blazhen, kto vo-vremia sozrel,
> Kto postepenno zhizni kholod
> S letami vyterpet' umel;
> Kto strannym snam ne predavalsia,
> Kto cherni svetskoi ne chuzhdalsia,
> Kto v dvadtsat' let byl frant il' khvat,
> A v tridtsat' vygodno zhenat;
> Kto v piat'desiat osvobodilsia
> Ot chastnykh i drugikh dolgov,
> Kto slavy, deneg i chinov
> Spokoino v ochered' dobilsia,
> O kom tverdili tselyi vek:
> N.N. prekrasnyi chelovek.

> [Blessed is he who was young in his youth, blessed who

matured at the right time, who gradually learned with the
years to suffer the coldness of life; who did not give himself
up to strange dreams, who did not shun the rabble of
society, who at twenty was a fop or a blade, and at thirty is
advantageously married; who by fifty has freed himself from
private and other debts, who has calmly attained in turn fame,
fortune and rank, about whom they have said for a whole
epoch: N.N. is a fine man. [Eight: X: 1-14)]

To be sure, the identification of this idealized figure with Tat'iana's husband is not made absolutely explicit; the use of the letter 'N' seems a possible pointer, although it was a common enough device in Pushkin. The stanza picks up on other moments in the poem when the 'beatus qui / heureux qui' formula is used, always with irony, if not sarcasm. It is evident that here is a picture of what the author-narrator will never be. The notion of 'timeliness' that Shaw has invoked is thus a complex one: N.N. is precisely a person who has been able to fit his career to the necessities of the different ages of man. He has followed the ideal career that Pushkin seems to have in mind for his brother in the letter. The image is evidently not without its attractiveness for Pushkin, who had enough self-esteem to wish he too could share in the spoils of a successful career: wealth, a position in the court and society, and the hand of a beautiful woman (even if she did not love him).

The image of a successful careerist which is sketched in the lines quoted and in the character of Prince N stands in equally stark contrast, I would suggest, with the figures of Lenskii and Onegin. As noted above, Pushkin, after the death of Lenskii, describes, in two stanzas, the two possible fates that one might imagine for him (Six: XXXVII-XXXIX). They represent a study in contrasts: the one, which is by the ironic tone of the narrative marked as less likely, is the path of fame achieved through poetry; the second, which is again marked by the tone as the likely one, is an 'ordinary fate': Lenskii abandons poetry, marries, and settles down to a humdrum existence as a 'happily married man.' Indispensable concomitants of this existence, as far as Pushkin is concerned, are the dressing-gown, an excessive appetite, cuckoldry, and a death in bed surrounded by 'snivelling wenches and medicoes.' Lenskii's 'future' echoes those of two other individuals: Tat'iana's father, Dmitrii Larin, whose 'life and times' are described in Two: XXXIV and XXXVI. Only the question of cuckoldry is described differently in the case of Larin, unless we are to believe that the stress on 'faithful'

(*vernoiu*) in Two: XXXVI: 7 is ironic and that the very different appearances and natures of Tat'iana and Ol'ga are not a genetic quirk –
although one is tempted to think that Pushkin inserted the mention
of 'Grandison''s son (Seven: XLI: 14) as a tantalizing glimpse of Tat'iana's
half-brother (in Nabokov this would certainly be the case). The other
individual whose fate resembles that of Larin and Lenskii is the husband of Pelageia Nikolavna:

> U Pelagei Nikolavny
> Vse tot zhe drug mos'e Finmush,
> I tot zhe shpits, i tot zhe muzh;
> A on, vse kluba chlen ispravnyi,
> Vse tak zhe smiren, tak zhe glukh,
> I tak zhe est i p'et za dvukh.

> [*Pelageia Nikolavna still has the same friend Monsieur Fine-
> mouche, the same spitz dog, and the same husband; he, still
> a stalwart member of his club, is still as docile, still as deaf,
> and still eats and drinks [enough] for two.* (Seven: XLV: 9-14)]

The sequence – Finemouche, dog, husband – indicates the esteem in
which Pushkin believes the husband is generally held. We see, too,
that the healthy appetite of a husband is, for Pushkin, a sign of cuckoldry – he is eating for himself *and* Finemouche. The portrayals of the
decaying, complacent husband which we find in *Onegin* serve, among
other things, to heighten the exceptional quality of Tat'iana: she is
that rarity, a constant wife who does not take a lover and is loyal to
her husband (even, apparently, obedient to him, and an asset in his
social life). When the wife is faithful, it is the husband who can be
assumed to be the philanderer. Such is the fate which Onegin foresees
for any union between himself and Tat'iana when they first meet in
the country (Four: XIV-XVI). The only exception to the general rule is
the marriage of Tat'iana and Prince N, which is presented as the essence
of propriety and mutual respect. Significantly, it is a marriage which
was not motivated by love.

Of all the contrasts between the male figures in *Onegin*, perhaps the
most significant is that between Onegin and Prince N: where Tat'iana's
husband has made a good career, served his country well, and integrated
himself into society, thus earning the hand of Tat'iana, the paragon of
Russian beauty (and, in a sense, symbolic of mother Russia herself),
Onegin has remained alienated from all that is Russian. He has ne-

glected his life, his fortune, and his career, and now is punished for his neglect and lack of caring. Of the range of lives and careers presented, the only one that holds out the promise of greater satisfaction than that of Prince N is that of the poet, the narrator of *Onegin*, friend of Onegin (and, presumably, of Prince N too). It is on this figure that we shall concentrate in the next chapter.

Onegin and Pushkin on the Neva embankment. Drawing by Pushkin to illustrate One: XLVII. 1824

6

The Lyrical Essence

In chapter two I discussed the way in which in *Onegin* the 'implied author' (to use Wayne Booth's terminology [1961, 211-21]) is projected into the work itself. As Lotman indicates, all the different 'voices' that go to make up the fabric of the text are subsumed in the single voice of the narrator, who 'adopts,' as it were, the voices in an act of mimickry.[1] There is thus an implied author in the sense which Booth means it, but there is also the author-narrator, and finally the character 'Pushkin,' who has a certain role to play in the novelistic events, and whose function can be compared to the 'editor' of the eighteenth-century epistolary novel. These characters are not necessarily totally identical, but rather overlapping. A number of recent studies of *Onegin* have been devoted to the analysis of this phenomenon, which was, as we have seen, largely ignored by critics, at least until the 1920s. K. Hielscher, for example, distinguishes three distinct characters in the narrative voice, while L. Stepanov sees no need to split the author into different roles.[2] Perhaps the best description of the plasticity of the character 'author-narrator' is to be found in Lotman, who writes: 'The work is narrated as if by several voices which interrupt each other, some of them being outside the events, at a remote distance, like historians or chroniclers, while others are intimately acquainted with the participants, and yet others are themselves included directly in the text. Inasmuch as all these voices are united in the voice of the author and compose the range of its various manifestations, there arises that complex richness of the authorial personality' (1980, 296). Whether or not they agree on the structure of the figure of the author, all recent critics seem united in stressing the importance of the author's presence in the work. In counterbalancing the novelistic elements in the structure, the authorial voice is crucial. It is the prism – the verbal equivalent of the 'magic crystal' that Pushkin mentions – through which we perceive all the events (with the exception of those which are relayed to us directly by document – e.g., letter – although in a deeper sense the reader is reminded that these too have not just been filtered through the author's consciousness, but are also his fictions).

The relationship of the author-narrator to his work is constantly defined and redefined. The ultimate definition is offered in the farewell statement at the end of Eight:

> Prosti zh i ty, moi sputnik strannyi,
> I ty, moi vernyi Ideal,
> I ty, zhivoi i postoiannyi,
> Khot' malyi trud. Ia s vami znal
> Vse, chto zavidno dlia poeta:
> Zabven'e zhizni v buriakh sveta,
> Besedu sladkuiu druzei.
> Promchalos' mnogo, mnogo dnei
> S tekh por, kak iunaia Tat'iana
> I s nei Onegin v smutnom sne
> Iavilisia vpervye mne –
> I dal' svobodnogo romana
> Ia skvoz' magicheskii kristal
> Eshche ne iasno razlichal.

> [*And farewell to you, my strange companion, and to you, my faithful ideal, and to you, lively and constant, though slight work. With you I knew everything that is enviable for a poet: oblivion from the world amid the storms of society, the sweet conversation of friends. Many, many days have hastened by since that time when youthful Tat'iana and with her Onegin first appeared to me in a vague vision – and I glimpsed the distant perspective of a free novel – though not clearly as yet – through my magic crystal.* (Eight: L: 1-14)]

This stanza is crucial in shattering the illusion of the novel and returning the centre of attention back to the narrative voice which the reader has been lulled into forgetting. It makes us newly aware of the 'metavoice' which has provided a constant commentary on the authorial activity throughout the text. It reminds us that the kernel of the work, the 'message' conveyed by the text, is, ultimately, a lyrical one. Tat'iana is the poet's ideal – a symbol of his lyrical concerns, not an observed portrait, for all the novelistic trappings. Lo Gatto's formula for *Onegin – diario lyrico –* is thus not entirely without merit, for the lyrical element is, I would submit, the ultimate one, since it not only frames, but conditions and subsumes, the novelistic events. Failure to understand this has been, as I showed above in chapter one, the principal defect that has vitiated so much writing on *Onegin*. Without the lyrical tone that informs it, the structure of *Onegin* would disintegrate or become a prose novel.

It is frequently thought that the authorial figure is conveyed largely through the digressions.[3] However, we have seen that the digressions, especially those in the first four chapters, are replete with the standard cynical remarks of the romantic anti-hero. They represent the temporary entering of the author-narrator into the orbit of Onegin. The lyrical spirit is rather the point where the converging lines of irony, plot, character, and verse intersect. It is conveyed mostly in the narrative tone, in the asides, even in the choice of epigraphs and the footnotes. As Shaw has shown, the actual nature of the author-narrator changes over the years, since the poem was written and published piecemeal, and since the passage of time and its effect upon the narrator were dramatized, and made significant (1981, 26). This is the 'diario' aspect of the work, though, to be sure, not in the sense that Lo Gatto meant it. The changes in the author's situation, though alluded to only coyly ('And so, at that time I lived in Odessa ...'), are therefore an indispensable backdrop. Since the facts of Pushkin's biography are well enough known, especially to the informed reader, the stylization which they receive, while contributing an air of mystery, is to some extent a narrative device, and tends not to diminish but to heighten the drama of the author-narrator's situation. In particular, it focuses our attention on the author-narrator as a lyrical persona rather than a historical personage.

The discussion in this chapter is centred around the three different guises or roles that the author-narrator assumes in the course of the narrative, although, as I have already said, the structure of the figure is so complex, both in its evolution and in its characterization, that the divisions proposed must be seen as to some extent hypothetical or even as different ways of viewing the same thing:

1. Poet as stylized version or analogue of the historical Pushkin.
2. Poet as *littérateur*, replying to critics, commenting on language and other matters of poetic form, and apostrophizing, often ironically, his fellow poets.
3. Poet as lyrical persona, responding to life in lyrical passages (not necessarily the digressions), and ultimately the hero of the whole work (in opposition to Onegin, who appears as the anti-hero).

The detail given in the text which leads us to speak of a historical Pushkin is sparse indeed: notes 1 and 10, references in One to Pushkin's life in Petersburg before exile, his arrival in Moscow after receiving permission to return from exile at Mikhailovskoe (Seven: XXXVI: 5-11), the descriptions in the Journey of Pushkin's 'typical day' in Odessa (a description which is itself in contrast with Onegin's 'typical day' in One).[4] Moreover, it is given in no particular order, unlike the chronological consequentiality with which we receive the facts of Onegin's life. Generally speaking, the historical facts of Pushkin's life are suppressed or simply hinted at, e.g., 'but the north is dangerous for me' (One: II: 14). Prominence is instead given to the 'creative biography' of the poet, e.g., in the first six stanzas of Chapter Eight. Characteristically, the external events of Pushkin's biography are here given not directly, but as the peregrinations and transformations of Pushkin's muse – from the gardens of Tsarskoe selo, to the bacchanalia of Pushkin's post-lycée sojourn in Petersburg, through the various stages of exile – the Caucasus, the Crimea, Bessarabia, the garden at Mikhailovskoe, and finally the balls and routs of Petersburg. The focus, even in this historical aspect, is thus on Pushkin's poetic history and the development of his poetic talent.

I have already examined one aspect of the author-narrator as *littérateur* in chapters two and five, above, namely the 'battle with the critics' mode contained in the footnotes and in the various prefaces, omitted and otherwise. His use of quotes in the footnotes parallels his insertion of quotations, identified or not, in the text itself. Some of the quotations are clearly ironic, e.g., the burlesqued quotation from Lomonosov in Five: XXV: 1. Others seem to be sincere recognitions of admiration for the work of one poet or another, e.g., the quotation from Viazemskii in note 42. Yet others seem to be entirely neutral, and serve simply to enrich the fabric and perhaps place *Onegin* more firmly in a context, e.g., the quotations from the (banned) play *Woe from Wit* in Eight: XIII: 14 and Six: XII: 12 (which also serve to express Pushkin's solidarity with Griboedov). Some quotations are offered completely without tonal indicators, so that the reader is left unclear how to read them, and whether they are offered in seriousness or in parody, e.g., the quotation from Gnedich in note 8.

Another aspect of the work of the author-narrator in the role of *littérateur* is the amount of commentary on different questions of poetic form and content. This commentary adds up to a meta-text which heightens the reader's awareness of questions of poetics, and focuses the attention in *Onegin* on the work *qua* work, rather than the illusion created. The work of the poet thus becomes material for the poetry in a way that foreshadows modernist writing. In particular, the question of Pushkin's development as a writer is posed, nearly always with irony. Thus, in One: LIX-LX, the poet notes the disappearance in his output of lyric poetry devoted to a real muse: 'Love passed, the Muse appeared.' When all traces of such nostalgia are gone, the author-narrator tells us he will undertake a 'long poem in 25 cantos.' This passage, for all its obvious flippancy, immediately establishes the link between the changing dynamic of the poet's life (cooling towards love) and developments in his art – the projected shift towards the longer form serving as a sort of metaphor for the poet's settling down to a comfortable middle age without love and happiness.

A second mention of the poet's 'creative plans' is in some ways a development of this:

> Unizhus' do smirennoi prozy;
> Togda roman na staryi lad
> Zaimet veselyi moi zakat.

> [I will lower myself to humble prose; then a novel in the old style will occupy my merry old age. (Three: XIII: 6-8)]

Again the longer form is associated with advancing years. All such ironical visions of an old age for the poet are cut off in the last lines of Chapter Eight, where the author-narrator reminds us of the virtues of dying young. Although Pushkin was undoubtedly moving towards prose, he was far from embracing the vast novel-canvas, from which he distanced himself unequivocally in his remarks on Richardson's *Grandison*: 'the inimitable Grandison, who sends us to sleep' (Three: IX: 10-11). The writing of a novel-in-prose, though an idea to be contemplated at some future stage, is, for the Pushkin of *Onegin*, largely a joke, or at best an ironic contemplation of the fate to which the passage of time may bring him willy-nilly. True, *Onegin* does, in a sense, carry out the programme of the sentimental novel, in which virtue is rewarded and the anti-hero (Onegin) is punished. However, the programme is carried out in a totally unexpected way.

As a whole, the description of a 'novel in the old style' (Three: XIII-XIV) is in counterpoint to the plot and structure of *Onegin* (as discussed above, chapter two). In a last mention of the prose/verse opposition, the question is again linked to the passing years:

> Leta k surovoi proze kloniat,
> Leta shalun'iu rifmu goniat

[*The years incline one to stern prose, the years chase away frivolous rhyme* (Six: XLIII: 5-6)]

The time is no longer appropriate, the poet tells us, for the light-heartedness of verse, a sentiment reinforced by the reference in the lines immediately after these to 'other chilling dreams' (an apparent reference to the change in the political climate following the crushing of the Decembrist revolt). The author expresses his surprise at finding that the ritual, conventional content of the elegy, a regret at the passing of youth, which he had mocked in the poetry of the eighteen-year-old Lenskii, is now invested with a real content:

Uzhel' i vpriam, i v samom dele,
Bez elegicheskikh zatei,
Vesna moikh promchalos' dnei?

[*Can it really be and in very truth, without any elegiac embroidering, that the spring of my days has sped away?* (Six: XLIV: 9-10)]

The (metapoetic) question of genre and form is thus intimately linked with the central theme of the dynamic of time, and the choice of genre and medium, prose or verse, is dramatized as the facing of the reality of middle age by the poet.

It can thus be seen that even in the 'metapoetic' mode the image of the poet is essentially a lyric one, in which two principal lyric themes dominate. The first of these concerns the passage of time, and is adumbrated as early as the epigraph from Viazemskii which stands at the head of Chapter One:

I zhit' toropitsia i chuvstvovat' speshit.

[*And one rushes to live, and one hastens to feel.* (PSS, VI, 5)]

It is maintained throughout *Onegin*, so that the last line, 'And so, I lived at that time in Odessa,' by giving us in the past tense what the author-narrator had experienced in Chapter One in the present, conveys an extraordinary sense of this dynamic headlong rush into the future, of the role of memory in making us sense the passage of time, and also, like the poetic imagination (of which memory is one manifestation), of its power to arrest that passage, at least temporarily. Images of time dominate in *Onegin*: the description of Onegin's day, regulated

by the 'unsleeping *breguet*' (One: XV: 13; XVII: 3); the movement of
the seasons in Two to Seven (summer-autumn-winter); the references
to the passage of time (e.g., in Seven: XLII: 2), and so on.[5]

Onegin is, however, carried out not only in time, but also in the
dimension of space: whether micro-space (Tat'iana's rushing from the
house into the garden and down to the bench to get away from Onegin)
or macro-space (Onegin's peregrinations round Russia, which in turn
are in counterpoint to Pushkin's movement from Petersburg to the
Caucasus, Bessarabia, Odessa, Mikhailovskoe, Moscow, and Petersburg
again, and Tat'iana's move from the estate to Moscow and on to Petersburg, the end point where all the paths converge). Such movement
in space is associated with another very important lyrical theme, namely
that of exile – the longing to be where one is not.[6] This theme is
expressed particularly in One, where Pushkin at once looks back with
regret to the Petersburg from which he has been exiled, and at the same
time looks out, beyond the confines of Russia, to Italy and Africa.
Regret at the passage of time is thus linked intimately with regret that
the poet cannot be in those places where he has been happy – or might
be again (e.g., One: XIX, where he recalls the splendours of the Petersburg theatre, and One: XLIX, where he expresses his longing for
the 'waves of the Adriatic'). Time and space are dimensions of the same
thing, and again it is poetry that can traverse the boundaries that separate the poet from a longed-for world (poetry symbolized, for example,
in the Italian opera music which 'recreates' that Italy that the poet
will never see physically).

Space and time converge in the images of headlong speed that characterize many of Onegin's movements in One (and appear as the fulfilment of the suggestion given by the epigraph): 'flying' (*letia* II: 2);
'rushed' (*pomchalsia* XVI: 5); 'flew' (*poletel* XVII: 9); 'galloped headlong' (*stremglav poskakal* XXVII: 3-4); 'flew up like an arrow' (*streloi
vzletel* XXVIII: 2-3); then with Lenskii in Two: 'the friends galloped'
(*poskakali drugi* III: 1); 'they flew home full speed' (*Domoi letiat vo
ves' opor* IV: 2); and in Eight: 'whither does Onegin hasten his speedy
flight?' (*Kuda svoi bystryi beg / Stremit Onegin?* XXXIX: 14-XL: 1).
Striking in all these examples is how close the semantics of movement
in space are to those of movement in time – the headlong gallop of
Onegin and Lenskii symbolizes their haste to live their lives, to spend
them with as little thought as Onegin's father spent his money or
Onegin drains a bottle of champagne. The rapid movement culminates
in the gallop of the horses that pull the sleigh with Lenskii's body from
the field. The heedless gallop of the young men contrasts significantly
with the measured, thoughtful movement of the young reader:

I shagom edet v chistom pole,
V mechtan'ia pogruzias', ona

[*And at a walk she rides across the open field, sunk in reveries*
(Six: XLII: 1-2)]

The passage of time is reflected in the ages of man as they are represented in *Onegin*. Thus, for women the crucial ages are seen to be
thirteen and eighteen (the first age being that at which Tat'iana's nurse
and mother were married, and the latter being that of Tat'iana in Chapters Two through Seven). For the men, the decisive ages are eighteen
and thirty. Lenskii is a young man of eighteen. Onegin is approximately
that age when he enters society. Thirty is the age at which we leave
Onegin. It is the age at which a man is no longer young, by which time
he must have made a successful marriage and be established in his
career.[7] Most important, thirty is the age of the poet at the end of
Chapter Six of *Onegin*:

Uzhel' mne skoro tridtsat' let?
Tak, polden' moi nastal

[*Can it be that I will soon be thirty? So, my mid-day has
arrived* (Six: XLIV: 14-XLV: 1)]

The ages of man can thus be described as youth and middle age.
Childhood is hardly ever described in Pushkin, and the poet never
discusses his own childhood.[8] As for old age, Pushkin gives us a number
of images of that state in *Onegin*, all of them negative: Onegin's father,
his uncle, Dmitrii Larin; the projected view of Lenskii as an old man
(Six: XXXIX); and, most interestingly, the poet himself, in a momentary
glimpse of him as an old man (Two: XL: 14). It is clear that for him
old age is far from a desirable state; hence his categorical declaration
in favour of leaving life's cup undrained:

Blazhen, kto prazdnik zhizni rano
Ostavil, ne dopiv do dna
Bokala polnogo vina,
Kto ne dochel ee romana
I vdrug umel rasstat'sia s nim,
Kak ia s Oneginym moim.

[*Blessed is he who has left life's feast early, without draining to the bottom the cup full of wine, who has not read its novel to the end, and has known how to part with it suddenly, as I have with my Onegin.* (Eight: LI: 9-14)]

Grouped around the theme of youth in *Onegin* are a number of motifs that serve as emblems of it: love, wine – in particular champagne – poetry. To these are contrasted those of middle age: lack of love, bordeaux, and prose. Since I have discussed the problems of love and poetry elsewhere, it is perhaps useful to focus on those of wine. The allusions to wine are so numerous in the text that any modulation in the use of the motif is highly significant. Traditionally, wine in the imagery of anacreontic poetry connotes the pleasures of youth. This role in *Onegin* is played specifically by champagne, to which there are three references in the text: the 'wine of the Comet' (i.e., wine from the year of the mysterious comet of 1811 – a specially good vintage, and one with hidden Napoleonic associations, for the comet was visible well into 1812) which Onegin drinks with Kaverin at Talon's (One: XVI: 8); the Veuve Clicquot or Moët which Onegin and Lenskii drink together in the country and which the author-narrator recalls buying with his last penny to drink with his friends (Four: XLV: 1-10); and the metaphor in the Journey in which the singing at the Italian opera is compared to Ay. Also associated with the carefree days of youth are the (unidentified) wine which Zaretskii drinks on credit three bottles at a time at Véry's in Paris, and the 'light wine' which Pushkin drinks at Automne's in Odessa. In every case the role of France as the purveyor of pleasure is very clear. Hence the domestic Tsimlianskoe (a Russian sparkling wine from the Don region) with which the guests are regaled at Tat'iana's nameday party is a comic modulation of the theme, as is the lingonberry-water which Onegin and Lenskii drink at the Larins' and which disagrees with Onegin. The 'shift' from youth to middle age in Pushkin is marked by a change in his choice of wine:

No izmeniaet penoi shumnoi
Ono zheludku moemu,
I ia *Bordo* blagorazumnyi
Uzh nynche predpochel emu.

[*But it upsets my stomach with its hissing foam, and I have now switched from it to a sensible bordeaux.* (Four: XLVI: 1-4)]

The associations of champagne are more complex than first may appear. Pushkin twice mentions the poetic use of champagne as a metaphor (in Six: XLV and the Journey, *PSS*, VI, 204). According to Lotman, the use of champagne as a metaphor was rejected once by the censor, which helped to bind it further to the associations of 'dangerous youth.'[9] Ay, the author-narrator tells us, is 'like a brilliant, flighty, lively, capricious, and vacuous mistress' (Four: XLVI: 6-8). It is a 'magic stream' that can produce 'jokes and verse, quarrels and merry dreams' (Four: XLV: 13-14). It is, in other words, one way of entering the youthful world of danger, of adventure, of love, and of death. Pushkin's choice of bordeaux thus represents not only a gastronomic decision but a symbolic farewell to that world.

The most significant modulation of the wine motif occurs, however, in the lines from the last stanza of Eight, quoted above, in which the author declares his admiration for those who decide not to drink the cup of life to its dregs. (This image, beyond its obvious metaphorical resonances, recalls the biblical association of Christ begging the Lord not to make him drink the cup: the implication – that for Pushkin, the wine of life has turned to wormwood – has not been noticed in the literature on *Onegin*).[10] Here, as Bocharov points out, 'the traditional epicurean motif is seen from a new point of view, which is complicated by the experience of life. It does not have the former "levity": the author is speaking now not about that conventional poetic death which in the poetry of his youth was earlier depicted in a conventional sense as an insignificant [*legkoe*] event, but about the fact that "some are no more" in very truth [*v samom dele*]. The author is recalling those in whose fate the conventional poetic situation has become reality' (1975, 62). The expression of envy for those who have dared to leave life's feast is consonant with the general tone of the last chapters of *Onegin*: the champagne of youth has been drunk; at best there remains the bordeaux of middle age, and an old age too dismal to be desired. The equation of wine, especially champagne, with poetry and youth is made explicit in the lines in the Journey:

> Smirilis' vy, moei vesny
> Vysokoparnye mechtan'ia,
> I v poeticheskii bokal
> Vody ia mnogo podmeshal.

> [*You have subsided, high-flown reveries of my springtime, and I have mixed a great deal of water into my poetic goblet.* (PSS, VI, 200)]

The contrast between youth, which has passed for the poet, and middle age is expressed by other important metaphors as well, especially by the opposition of the seasons spring and fall.[11] This is particularly evident in the opening of Chapter Seven where the poet discusses his preference for fall over spring, the conventional time of poetry and passion (and traditionally greeted with joy by the poet):

> Kak grustno mne tvoe iavlen'e,
> Vesna, vesna! pora liubvi!

> [*How sad to me is your appearance, spring, spring! time of love!* (Seven: I: 1-2)]

In the following lines the poet rejects spring, especially the conventionality of its role as a time of love and youth:

> Ili, ne raduias' vozvratu
> Pogibshikh osen'iu listov,
> My pomnim gor'kuiu utratu,
> Vnimaia novyi shum lesov;
> Ili s prirodoi ozhivlennoi
> Sblizhaem dumoiu smushchennoi
> My uviadan'e nashikh let,
> Kotorym vozrozhden'ia net?

> [*Or is it that, not jubilant at the return of the leaves which perished in the autumn, we recall a bitter loss as we hear the renewed rustle of the woods; or is it that we with downcast thoughts compare with nature's revival the withering of our years for which there is no rebirth?* (Seven: III: 1-8)]

Spring, then, is associated with the love/youth/poetry/champagne nexus that is rejected by the author-narrator in *Onegin*. It is Lenskii, we note, who bewails the passing of the 'golden days of my spring' in the elegy that he composes on the eve of his death. Pushkin himself draws our attention to the incongruity in Lenskii's choice of theme:

> On pel pobleklyi zhizni tsvet,
> Bez malogo v os'mnadtsat' let.

> [*He sang the faded flower of life, a little short of his eighteenth year.* (Two: X: 13-14)]

It is the imagery of fall that is most lovingly treated in the poem. Already, in the lines quoted above about spring, it is there – in the use of the root 'wither,' the repetition of which becomes a recurrent note in the poem, signalling the poet's approaching middle age.[12] The lyrical descriptions of autumn in Chapter Four, which conveys Onegin's activities in the fall, are an evocation of the beauty of the Russian countryside at that time of year, experienced by Pushkin himself at Mikhailovskoe. They form a singular contrast to Lenskii's 'something, and the misty distance' (Two: X: 8) in the concreteness of the detail and the minor drama of the wolf and his hungry mate:

> Vstaet zaria vo mgle kholodnoi;
> Na nivakh shum rabot umolk;
> S svoei volchikhoiu golodnoi
> Vykhodit na dorogu volk;
> Ego pochuia, kon' dorozhnyi
> Khrapit – i putnik ostorozhnyi
> Nesetsia v goru vo ves' dukh

> [*Dawn arises in the cold gloom; on the meadows the noise of work has fallen silent; the wolf comes out onto the road with his hungry mate; sensing him, the travelling horse snorts – and the cautious wayfarer races up the hill full tilt* (Four: XLI: 1-7)]

The fact that winter (or at least the snow) arrives late – on the night of the second of January – is a kind of wish-fulfilment on the part of Pushkin. Summer, the culmination of the passions stirred in the spring, barely exists for Pushkin:

> No nashe severnoe leto,
> Karrikatura iuzhnykh zim,
> Mel'knet i net

> [*But our northern summer is a caricature of southern winters: it flashes by and is gone* (Four: XL: 1-3)]

If we take the summer as the time when the desires of love conceived in youth are fulfilled, then it is clear that for Pushkin those pleasures are seen to be transitory indeed – as momentary as they are for Tat'iana, who never actually knows love as anything more than a desire, a longing that is left unfulfilled. Tat'iana's 'autumn' – her middle age – begins as soon as she has heard Onegin's 'sermon' at the beginning of Four. It is signalled by the root 'to wither':

Uvy, Tat'iana uviadaet

[*Alas, Tat'iana withers* (Four: XXIV: 1)]

The symbolism of winter is the most interesting of the four seasons, since it can be seen to be ambiguous. Since it follows autumn, the emblem of middle age, one might be tempted to 'read' winter in Pushkin's symbolism as old age. Rather, I would submit, winter is the coming of death (thereby short-circuiting old age). It is winter that transforms everything in the marvellously lyrical passage which opens Five. Winter, the cold, freezes the quickness of water into the rigour of ice (an association that gives a particular overtone to the merry scenes of boys skating and geese slipping and falling). It is winter that has cold hands, recalling the coldness of Lenskii. Winter leads Tat'iana to flirt with the other world (in her dream which I read here as a descent into the underworld, a flirtation with death) and brings Lenskii to his death.

The equation of winter with death, however, if left unmodified, would be an inadequate definition of the complex function of winter, for there is at least one further element involved. It is the notion of winter as the symbol of marriage. Nature, with whom Tat'iana is closely associated, trembles at the onset of winter, which will dress her in white:

Priroda trepetna, bledna,
Kak zhertva pyshno ubrana

[*Nature is trembling, pale, sumptuously adorned, like a sacrifice* (Seven: XXIX: 10-11)]

The coming of the first snow at the beginning of Five is, as it were, a dramatization of Tat'iana's own fate. It is in the winter that Tat'iana is carried off to be married, a notion which, I have suggested, is connected, not with wish-fulfilment, but with sacrifice:

Ne rado ei lish' serdtse Tani.
Neidet ona zimu vstrechat', ...
Tat'iane strashen zimnii put'.

[*Only Tania's heart is not joyful at it* [*the coming of winter*].

> *She does not go to greet the winter ... The winter road is fearful for Tat'iana.* (Seven: XXX: 9-10, 14)]

In a deeper sense, since winter is the symbol of them both, marriage is equated with death – it is passage from the quickness of youth into the dead other world of reason and prose.

As well as signifying death and marriage, the coming of the snows of winter denotes, like both those states, transformation. In his study of the poetics of *Onegin*, Bocharov sees the underlying principle as that of *translation*. This is a creative application of Lotman's notion of *transcoding* to a specific literary context.[13] *Onegin* is a fruitful case for the discussion of the contrastive semiotics of cultures. Indeed, Pushkin himself saw it as such, although he would have used different terms. In his writings on the concept of *narodnost'*, Pushkin showed that he considered that the role of the poet lay in his ability to define the national identity.[14] The whole of *Onegin* can be interpreted as a attempt to do precisely this, through the analysis of the penetration of foreign elements into Russian reality – whether it be fashions, language, literature, imported carriages, or Napoleon himself (and the ideas of revolution, genius, and amoralism which he represented). I would suggest that a better word than *translation* for the mechanics of this phenomenon is *transformation*, since it encompasses the wider theme of the transformation of individuals and character. Seen as transformation, Tat'iana's character moves outwardly in one direction – from Russian *baryshnia*, Tat'iana, to a society lady, Princess N, who would be as much at home in Paris or Vienna as she is in Petersburg. That is to say, superficially she becomes more foreign. Inwardly, however, she moves from an unquestioning acceptance of the (foreign) literary models whose personification she had considered Onegin to be to a rejection of those models (in the form of the fashionable liaison of a married woman with a society rake) in maturity. Onegin, we note, has failed to make the transformation, and is left with an empty shell of 'foreign' behaviour with no 'Russian' content (except for the appreciation of Russian verse). In a nutshell, Tat'iana is Russia trying to understand the foreign, and Onegin is the foreigner trying to understand Russia. The transformation of them both is the core problem of the *fabula*.

It is this idea of transformation that is, I would contend, symbolized by the Russian winter. Nabokov writes of the imagery in *Onegin* as follows: 'Pushkin's composition is first of all and above all a phenomenon of style, and it is from this flowered rim that I have surveyed its sweep of Arcadian country, the serpentine gleam of its imported brooks' (Nabokov, I, 7). Although it is clearly true that Pushkin's descriptions of the Russian landscape owe something to the Western European tradition of pastoral poetry, Nabokov's sweeping statement does much of the landscape description in *Onegin* an injustice. In particular, it is clearly not true of the winterscapes. These are landscapes transformed by the Russian phenomena of snow and winter; there is no snow in Arcadia. It is as a celebration of transformation that we should read the first stanza of Chapter Five, in which Tat'iana awakes to find the landscape that she has known and loved *transformed* by the coming of winter. It is not by chance that we view this transformation from Tat'iana's vantage-point since her own transformation – symbolized by that of nature – is a central theme of the poem. It is thus that the imported poetic myths, characters, and paraphernalia which invited Nabokov's scorn are *made Russian*, just as the poetic motifs of world literature are somehow integrated by Pushkin into a national imagery, and 'Russified.'

Central to the lyrical persona that is projected by Pushkin into *Onegin* is the nature of his muse. Like the other figures – Onegin, Tat'iana, author-narrator – the figure 'muse' is endowed with extraordinary plasticity – 'polysemy,' to use Roman Jakobson's term. The first 'given' in any discussion of the muse is that she does not correspond to a real-life individual: 'Love passed, the muse appeared' (One: LIX: 1), the poet tells us, after taking a whole stanza to deny any tendency to link verse and love in his poetry (even expressing mock-envy at the ability of others to do so). Pushkin's muse, then, is an 'ideal' whose incarnate manifestations may take a variety of forms. This ability is made clear in the first stanzas in Eight, already discussed above, in which she appears in a variety of guises. The figure of the 'muse' is manipulated in quite unexpected ways: she is transformed into Pushkin's old nurse, to whom he reads his latest creations (to what effect is left unsaid):

No ia plody moikh mechtanii
I garmonicheskikh zatei
Chitaiu tol'ko staroi niani,
Podrugi iunosti moei

[*But I read the fruits of my reveries and harmonic undertakings only to my old nurse, the friend of my youth* (Four: XXXV: 1-4)]

The notion of 'muse' is reduced to burlesque when Pushkin, in his next lines, 'suffocates a neighbour with a tragedy.'[15] In refusing to accept the traditional poetic notion of a real-life referent for the figure 'muse,' Pushkin distances himself from the commonly held view of love poetry, to which Lenskii, by contrast, strictly adheres. For Pushkin, 'muse' is simply the incarnation of or metaphor for poetry, and her various guises correspond to the different genres, milieus, and themes that he practised.

The question arises to what extent we may take Tat'iana herself as a hypostasis of Pushkin's muse. Although the question is ultimately unanswerable, there is clearly a considerable affinity between them. Like the muse, Tat'iana is Pushkin's 'ideal.' Like her, she is capable of transformation, in her case from country miss to society queen. The muse figure is, however, much more elastic than Tat'iana, who, on the one hand, represents rather the ideal of femininity expressed in other places in Pushkin's lyric verse by the figure 'angel' or 'madonna,' and is, on the other hand, 'bound' by the novelistic situation in which she is endowed with certain character traits, so that her 'elasticity' is limited to some degree by the requirements of verisimilitude. Admired 'secretly,' 'from afar,' Tat'iana is 'untouchable,' so that Pushkin cannot describe her, as he does his muse, as *rezvaia* (a code-word in Pushkin's poetic vocabulary for a woman of fickle affections and easy virtue).

Of all the transformations that *Onegin* documents, however, the most profound and subtle occur in the lyrical persona of the author/narrator. These can be traced, among other places, in the evolution of the semantics of the words denoting 'freedom.'[16] There are two roots and their derivatives which occupy this semantic field in the text:
1. *Svobod-a* (-*nyi*, -*no*)
2. *vol-ia* (-'*nost*', -'*nyi*)
Four distinct meanings can be distinguished within this semantic field. (Interestingly, the distribution of roots crosses the boundaries between the meanings and is evidently determined by such matters as style, metre, and euphony.)[17] The meanings are as follows:
1. Political freedom (calque of the French *liberté*, as in *liberté, égalité, fraternité*).
In this sense *svoboda* is used twice and *vol'nost'* once, each time with reference to a writer:

Fonvizin, drug svobody

[*Fonvizin, the friend of freedom* (One: XVIII: 3)]

Zashchitnik vol'nosti i prav

[[*Grimm*] *the defender of freedom and rights* (One: XXIV: 13)]

Poklonnik slavy i svobody, ...
Vladimir i pisal by ody,
Da Ol'ga ne chitala ikh.

[*an admirer of fame and freedom ... Vladimir would have written odes, but Ol'ga did not read them.* (Four: XXXIV: 1, 3-4)]

Vladimir (Lenskii) is here identified with the Decembrist poets (cf. the reference to Kiukhel'beker's propaganda in favour of the ode, Four: XXXII: 14-XXXIII: 2). The inclusion of Lenskii in the same 'series' as Grimm and Fonvizin is clearly ironic, as is the association with *slava* (honour, glory) and the ode. It is noteworthy that the three instances of this meaning of freedom occur early in the poem: two in One, the other in Four.

2. Personal freedom from care and responsibility (associated with *dolce far niente*, with the word *nega* – languor, delectation – and, in Pushkin's case, with the untrammmelled life of the poet). This meaning of freedom applies to Onegin:

Vot moi Onegin na svobode

[*Behold my Onegin set free* (One: IV: 5)]

Svobodnyi, v tsvete luchshikh let

[*Free, in the flower of his best years* (One: XXXVI: 10)];

to Pushkin:

Pridet li chas moei svobody?

[*Will the hour of my freedom come?* (One: L: 1)]

Dlia sladkoi negi i svobody

[*for sweet delectation and freedom* (One: LV: 9)]

Svoboden, vnov' ishchu soiuza

[*free, again I seek the union* (One: LIX: 3)];

and to the audience in the theatre:

Gde kazhdyi, vol'nost'iu dysha

[*where everyone, breathing freedom* (One: XVII: 10)]

All the occurrences of this second meaning of freedom occur in Chapter
One. At this point personal freedom is seen by Pushkin as a kind of
possibility for self-indulgence (in his case manifested in poetry-writing)
and the easy life. The linking of this meaning to the theatre audience
is a particularly interesting point, suggesting the liberating force of art.
3. Freedom of manner, rustic simplicity (associated only with Tat'iana):

Imeet sel'skaia svoboda
Svoi schastlivye prava,
Kak i nadmennaia Moskva.

[*Rustic freedom has its happy laws, as does haughty Moscow.*
(Four: XVII: 12-14)]

Gde vse naruzhe, vse na vole

[*In whom everything is visible, everything is free* (Eight: XX:
9)]

Svobodnoi zhivost'iu svoei

[*By her free vivacity* (Eight: XXIII: 14)]

Svobodno doma prinimaet

[*she receives freely at home* (Eight: XXXI: 3)]

The early prefiguring of this quality in Four is realized in that 'rustic'
freedom of manners that Tat'iana manages to preserve in her com-
portment as a society lady.
4. The final meaning that Pushkin arrives at for the notion of freedom
is akin to those mentioned above, but refined and deepened. Thus, the
'external' political notion of *liberté* is rejected, as is the superficial

freedom of the lazy poet or society wastrel. They give way to a concept of inner harmony and independence which is a refinement of that rustic freedom perceived in Tat'iana. This meaning of freedom occurs only three times in the text of *Onegin*, but the location – in Chapter Eight, where the issues have now crystallized and we see poet and creatures at their most mature – suggests its importance as the culmination of the process of definition and distillation:

> Ia dumal: vol'nost' i pokoi
> Zamena schast'iu.
>
> [*I thought that freedom and peace could replace happiness.* (Onegin's letter: *PSS*, VI, 180)]
>
> Sidit pokoina i vol'na.
>
> [[*Tat'iana*] *sits calm and free.* (Eight: XXII: 14)]

In the first instance the doublet ('freedom and peace') is applied to Onegin, in the second to Tat'iana. It occurs for a third time in Pushkin's 1834 lyric 'Pora moi drug, pora ...' ('Tis time, my friend, 'tis time ...):

> Na svete schast'ia net, no est' pokoi i volia.
>
> [*There is no happiness in the world, but there is freedom and peace.* (*PSS*, III, 224)]

This time it is applied to the persona of the poet himself. The concept is, we note, contrasted with happiness, which evidently implies tumult, passion, and eventual woe. Tat'iana, the poet's ideal, lives, isolated, cold, outside warmth and love (which exist for her only as an encapsulated memory). Onegin's confusion at the end of the novel arises because he is unable to live up to such an ideal of independence and lack of human ties. It is Tat'iana's tears and her confession of her love for Onegin during their final tête-à-tête that make her human and admirable. They soften the appearance of external coldness and lack of human ties evoked by Pushkin's formula. Pushkin, in the character of his heroine, modifies what we might otherwise take as his concluding wisdom that happiness is unattainable, and only freedom and peace are desirable goals. Tat'iana's statuesque sublimity is mitigated by her human frailty and her nostalgic recall of her rural haunts.

The refined 'freedom' that is defined in Eight applies not only to

Onegin and Tat'iana in their differing ways, but also, most significantly, to the poet himself. It is hinted at in the reference to the 'distant
prospect of my free novel' ('dal' svobodnogo romana' – Eight: L: 13)
that he makes at the very end of the novel. The implication is not
simply that the novel is 'free form' or 'free from convention' (a notion
that I have discussed already in chapter two), but that in poetry Pushkin
finds the inner freedom he seeks, just as Tat'iana finds it in the memory
of the country places where she grew up and first saw Onegin (Eight:
XLVI: 8-14).[18] Both poet and heroine have found that peace and freedom
in an inner world which is a substitute for happiness. Pushkin's ideal
of the inner freedom which the poet attains through his art is suggested
as early as Chapter One – in the rejection of the real-life person as
muse, poetry ('muse') as substitute for a woman's love, and the escape
from the evils of life in the *grand monde* into a Horatian rural retreat
(evoked by the epigraph to Chapter Two). The difference lies in the
fact that where escape in meaning (2) of 'freedom' had appeared as
ironic self-indulgence on the poet's part, by Eight it seems, against the
sombre hints of friends who are dead or far away, to be a necessity and
a salvation from the grim vicissitudes of life. Of the three, only Onegin,
who is impervious to the charm of the Russian countryside, and who
does not completely master Russian poetry (the two being closely linked
in the semantics of the work), cannot, despite the fact that at the end
he is in love with Tat'iana, maintain his 'peace and freedom,' and must
go on a belated and vain quest for happiness. It is Onegin who, in his
letter, renounces the 'peace and freedom' ideal because he does not
have the inner resources, either the poet's poetry or Tat'iana's deep
love of Russia, to sustain him.

Thus, the notions set out somewhat shallowly and in stereotyped
fashion at the beginning of the text, especially Chapter One, of a sardonic amusement at society, of the rejection of love as a will o' the
wisp, of the desirability of going away from it all to some country
retreat (an option parodied in the figure of Zaretskii), and finally the
notion that happiness, if it exists at all, resides in 'habit' (expressed by
the dictum from Chateaubriand) – all these notions, which had seemed
so facile, are invested by the end of the novel with a real, tough, bitter
content. They are transformed by the infusion of values – in Tat'iana's
case moral ones, in the poet's case – aesthetic. It is this truth, which
Onegin does not have the inner resources to attain, that leaves him
confounded at the end of the novel and constitutes the essential truth
of the work – a truth that Pushkin himself could hardly have foreseen
when he began. It is the deep lyrical kernel of the entire work.

In examining the imagery and semantics of Pushkin's lyrical content in *Onegin*, one is inevitably struck by the extent to which they are structured around oppositions or contrasts. An exhaustive survey of the entire orchestration of the imagery would take a long study, and is perhaps beyond the capability of one person. A preliminary list would, however, have to include the following oppositions, among many more:

> hot : cold
> red : white
> youth : middle age
> free : bound
> water : ice
> passion : peace
> country : city
> verse : prose
> spring : fall
> summer : winter
> South : North
> foreign : Russian
> poetry : novel

Such a listing of contrasts is simple enough: it is the detailed working out of any one item in the imagery that can be, as we have seen in the discussion of the notion of 'freedom,' quite intricate. This intricacy is no doubt explained at least in part by Pushkin's own evolution as a poet in the seven or more years during which he worked at *Onegin*. In the course of that time his imagery developed. While this presents less of a problem when we have to do with separate works, which therefore acquire the status of independent systems, in *Onegin* we have to do with a system that itself changes in time.

On a number of occasions in the course of the text, Pushkin draws the reader's attention to the principle of contrast and opposition in the imagery; for example, in the following lines comparing Onegin and Lenskii:

> Volna i kamen',
> Stikhi i proza, led i plamen'
> Ne stol' razlichny mezh soboi.

[*Wave and stone, verse and prose, ice and flame are not as different from each other.* (Two: XIII: 5-7)]

Here the movement and liveliness of water and flame is contrasted with the immobility of stone and ice. The reference is clear: Lenskii, incarnation of passion, youth, and enthusiasm, is the water (i.e., the waves of the sea, a standard Romantic image) and the flame, while the sceptic Onegin is the stone and the ice. The contrast that is drawn here is related to the statue : living being contrast first discussed by Jakobson (see above, chapter five). The imagery in *Onegin* is thus deeply rooted in the metaphorical structures of the work. (This does not prevent Pushkin from introducing an element of irony in the application of these comparisons quoted here, especially in those applied to Lenskii, since we know from the entire tone of the chapter that Lenskii is a purely conventional poet, whose passion is unreal, a cliché, and whose more usual pose is Wertherian *Weltschmerz*.

The fact that Pushkin 'sets up' such an intricate set of contrasts permits him to manipulate detail in a very significant way. An example of this is the 'moving stream' which rushes between the snowy banks in Tat'iana's dream:

> V sugrobakh snezhnykh pered neiu
> Shumit, klubit volnoi svoeiu
> Kipuchii, temnyi i sedoi
> Potok, ne skovannyi zimoi

> [*Before her among the snowy drifts there babbles and eddies with its wave a boiling, dark and grey stream, unbound by the winter* (Five: XI: 5-8)]

The mention of 'wave' is a reminder of the contrasts which have earlier been 'programmed.' The paradoxical nature of the diabolical stream is stressed by the repeated mentions of the winter. The symbolical nature of the stream as a metaphor for passion, tumult, sex, is heightened by the contrast with previously given mentions of ice. The following description of winter from the preceding chapter is an example:

> I vot uzhe treshchat morozy
> I serebritsia sred' polei ...
> (Chitatel' zhdet uzh rifmy *rozy*;
> Na, vot voz'mi ee skorei!)
> Opriatnei modnogo parketa
> Blistaet rechka, l'dom odeta.
> Mal'chishek radostnyi narod
> Kon'kami zvuchno rezhet led;

Na krasnykh lapkakh gus' tiazhelyi
Zadumav plyt' po lonu vod,
Stupaet berezhno na led,
Skol'zit i padaet; veselyi
Mel'kaet, v'etsia pervyi sneg,
Zvezdami padaia na breg.

[*And lo! the frosts already crackle and gleam like silver amid
the fields ... (The reader is waiting for the rhyme 'roses' – well,
take it quickly!) More perfect than a fashionable parquet
gleams the little river, dressed in ice. A happy crowd of urchins
cuts scrapingly through the ice with their skates; the heavy
goose, thinking to swim on the bosom of the water, steps
carefully onto the ice on its red feet, then slips and falls; the
first snow flashes and whirls merrily, falling like starlets
on the bank.* (Four: XLII: 1-14)]

This stanza, like the initial playing of a motif in a fugue, sets up the
images upon which Pushkin will create the variation in Tat'iana's
dream. It is itself adumbrated by an earlier references to Onegin swimming in the stream and taking baths in water with ice (Four: XXXVI:
6-10; Four: XLV: 3). Onegin's swimming seems almost certainly a
metaphor for sexual freedom, especially when Tat'iana is made to walk
a tottering log-bridge to escape from the bear which pursues her.[19] (The
sexual activities of Onegin in this chapter are hinted at in Four: XXXVIII:
3-4.) The description of the river as being 'dressed in ice' is a modulation
of the transformation of nature by the snow discussed above. The
mention of the 'fashionable parquet' is a foreshadowing of those ball-
rooms where pale Tat'iana, transformed by marriage, will shine. Finally, the image of winter conjured up in these lines ends with the
description of the first snow (which will be described in more detail
in Five: I-II). The contrast 'sexual passion : celibacy' underlined by the
imagery in this stanza is comically alluded to by Pushkin in the
metapoetic mention of rhyme: the rhyme 'frosts' (*morozy*) decidedly
does not lead one to expect the rhyme 'roses' (*rozy*), symbol of passion.
By this comic allusion Pushkin stresses for the aware reader the underlying contrasts in his imagery. The most puzzling image in the
stanza, if we are to assume that it is more than a chance detail, is the
'heavy goose.' I am inclined to see in it a veiled reference to the 'white-
skinned dark-eyed girl' with whom Onegin has had his summer-time
dalliance: surely she is well and truly pregnant by this time, and there-

fore 'heavy.'[20] It is because Pushkin has created a web of metaphorical detail, a 'private vocabulary,' that he is able to weave such elaborate concealed jokes, which the reader must be a sleuth, finely tuned to the nuances of Pushkin's language, to catch. The 'water : ice' contrast is in fact present at many points in the text. It is adumbrated in the waves that wash over the feet of Pushkin's unnamed companion in Chapter One; these are present, transformed, in the comic images of the people and animals sliding on the ice. Tat'iana, who fears, yet dreams, to 'get her feet wet,' takes the tottering bridge in her dream (itself covered with ice), further transformed in Chapter Eight into the parquet of the ballroom floor, which she negotiates perfectly, maintaining her modesty in society just as she maintains her footing on the bridge.

A set of images at least as productive as the 'water : ice' contrast is that associated with the 'sleep : waking' nexus, which is again principally linked with the image of Tat'iana (and as such has been partially discussed in connection with the analysis of the figure of Tat'iana in chapter four). The attentive reader is struck by the large number of references to 'sleep' in the text, especially if he realizes that the Russian *son* can connote 'sleep' or 'dream,' and has a very complicated semantics in Pushkin. The meanings of this word can be summarized as being of three principal kinds:

1. Physical sleep. As such there are numerous references, throughout the novel, to characters sleeping. The information is seldom fortuitous: Onegin's sleeping while others are awake and vice versa in Chapter One is highly significant. Just as significant is the information concerning Tat'iana's sleep, or lack of it, in Three and Four: while she cannot sleep, Onegin is granted 'innocent' (literally 'sin-free') or 'deep' slumber.[21]

2. Dreams. These can be divided into three types:
(a) Erotic dreams – the kind that disturb the sleep of young maidens.
(b) Fearful dreams: the dreams that visit the sleep of one who has killed a man, especially his friend. This is the kind of dream which visits Onegin in Chapter Eight.
(c) Mysterious, ambiguous dreams, the kind that Tat'iana has in Chapter Five. These dreams are a mixture of (a) and (b).[22]

3. Creative activity, poetic imagination (linked with the semantics of the word 'revery' – *mechtan'e*). Practically every use of the word in this meaning is linked with the figure of Pushkin the poet.[23]

In addition to these usages, Pushkin tends to use the term *son* in a figurative sense to denote the oneiric state of one who is in love. This is the application of the term to Tat'iana (recalled by Monsieur Tri-quet's lines 'Réveillez-vous, belle endormie ...'), and to Onegin in the ironic reversal of roles in Chapter Eight.[24]

The intriguing thing about the semantics of 'dream' is the link between dreaming and poetic inspiration. From the lyrical point of view, Pushkin's stress on the dream as the source of inspiration suggests that he is very much in the romantic, 'orphic' stream, seeking his inspiration in the other world of dream (a metaphorical equivalent of death), a world which contrasts with everyday reality. The dreaming of the poet comprises another link between poet and heroine, since she, too, is a dreamer. It is only in Eight that Onegin ceases to be a heavy sleeper and is visited by the fearful dream in which he sees the dead Lenskii and Tat'iana (Eight: XXXVII: 1-14). It is at this point, as we have shown, that he 'almost becomes a poet.' (The semantics of dreaming are related to those of another word – *mechta*, 'revery' – and its derivatives. The difference lies in the fact that *mechta* is a daytime phenomenon, the dreaming and hoping of the young girl, or alternatively the bitter recall of bygone hopes by the poet and his hero, Onegin. As such, *mechta* is imbued with none of the terror which *son* can inflict upon its passive victim.)[25]

In this brief review of some of the essential images and metaphors underlying the lyrical substance of *Onegin* I believe I have been able to show that this aspect of the work is of prime importance and justifies the interpretation that I have offered, namely that first and foremost *Onegin* must be seen as a lyrical poem. To conclude this chapter I will review the essential features of the lyrical persona, as I have called it, which I see drawn in the work. The theme is set in the two stanzas (Six: XLIV-XLV) in which the poet ponders the approach of his thirtieth year, bids farewell to youth, and greets his 'mid-day':

> S iasnoiu dushoiu
> Puskaius' nyne v novyi put'
> Ot zhizni proshloi otdokhnut'.

> [*With a bright soul I now set out on a new path, to rest from my past life.* (Six: XLV: 12-14)]

The 'path' of which the poet speaks might not, it is clear, be a long one. As we have seen (above) in the last stanza of Eight, the author/narrator explicitly rejects the desirability of a lengthy old age. The far from attractive images of old age on the one hand and the ever-present theme of death on the other (represented, for example, in the epigraph to Chapter Six) serve to reinforce this impression.[26] As a contemplation of the vicissitudes of life through the lyrical persona, *Onegin* is a sombre and sobering work. Underlying it all is what Gustafson calls the 'philosophical concern with time irretrievable' (1962, 7).

Faced with the relentless passage of time, the poet sees two possibilities of consolation, of stepping outside time's boundaries. The first of these is memory. If memory can be a source of regret and bitterness for the poet (summarized in the meaning of the word *mechta* discussed above) and reminds him of his spent youth, it also has the power to recreate that past happiness. Already in Chapter One the theme of memory arises (directed from the poet's southern exile towards his life in Petersburg).[27] This use by the poet of memory to relive the past peripeties of youth is shared with the poet's heroine, Tat'iana, and signalled by the presence of the verb *pomnit'*:

> Onegin, pomnite l' tot chas

> [*Onegin, do you remember the time* (Eight: XLII: 10)]

A source of regret and nostalgia, memory is also an escape into what appears – viewed in retrospect – to be a happier time (or at least, a time when happiness seemed attainable). For Onegin, by contrast, far from being an escape, a fertile and redeeming inner world, memory is a torment, since it recalls images of Tat'iana spurned and Lenskii killed (Eight: XXXVII). Memory can thus be a moral force, punishing us for our misdeeds.

Memory is one form of the imagination (*voobrazhenie* in Eight: XXXVII), of which a nobler version is poetry. If memory can arrest time briefly, for one individual, poetry can capture and transfigure the moment eternally. It is this power of poetry to defy time which Pushkin evokes at the end of Two:

> Bez neprimetnogo sleda
> Mne bylo b grustno mir ostavit'.
> Zhivu, pishu ne dlia pokhval;
> No ia by kazhetsia zhelal
> Pechal'nyi zhrebii svoi proslavit',
> Chtob obo mne, kak vernyi drug,
> Napomnil khot' edinyi zvuk.

> [*I would be sad to leave the world without a noticeable trace.*

> *I live and write not for praise; but I think I would like to*
> *make famous my sad fate so that at least one lonely sound*
> *would remind others of me, like a faithful friend.* (Two: XXXIX:
> 8-14)]

True, in the lines immediately following this Pushkin responds ironically to the *exegi monumentum* theme, when he imagines his poetry
and his reputation at the hands of the 'future ignoramus.'[28] Poetry, and
the pleasures and the recall that it provides, are for the intimate few
who understand him, not the ignorant masses (hence the 'hierarchy of
narratees'). Pushkin's poetry is a deeply personal matter; it is defined
by what it is not, for the death of Lenskii surely implies a rejection of
his elegiac poetry, just as Derzhavin's pompous classicism is criticized
in the lines just quoted). The invocation of the image of the poet
wandering above the lake, scaring the wild ducks with his verse, suggests the strangeness and unconventionality of his poetry. By implication, poetry is the highest value in the work, the aesthetic analogue
of memory, an ennobling and moral force that compels the poet to
obey the dictates of inspiration over the transitory blandishments of
a 'successful career.' It is the irreducible kernel of existence.

Roses in the Snow:
The Meaning of *Eugene Onegin*

> When human actions are formed to make an art work, the form that
> is made can never be divorced from the human meanings, including
> the moral judgements, that are implicit whenever human beings act.
> (Wayne Booth, *Rhetoric of Fiction*, 397)

When one surveys the critical literature, some of it brilliant, which
has been produced on *Onegin*, one is, ultimately, left dissatisfied. The
levels of complexity of the work, its technical feats, its repleteness
with literary allusion, and its ironies are so complex that any critic
who feels that he has unravelled even some of them is likely to be
seduced by a sense of achievement into not pursuing the final question
of the meaning of the work. One is inclined to believe that this is not
an accident. Because of its 'battle with the critics' mode, because of
the careful veiling of detail about the author-narrator, because of the
contradictory ironies which are made to resonate, it appears as if the
author has deliberately – or perhaps because of the circumstances of
the creation of *Onegin* – tried to defend himself against any ultimate
judgment about the meaning of it all.

This is not to say that some have not ventured to express themselves
on the subject. Among Western scholars, Shaw and Bayley have offered
insightful interpretations that do attempt the problem of the overall
meaning of the work. In Russian criticism, the attempts to tackle what
appear to be central questions are few and far between: rather we find
isolated modifications of the view in one aspect or another. Some
examples stand out, however. We have seen, for example, the definition
by Ivanov-Razumnik of the joyful, Mozartian tone of the work. There
is indeed a delightful grace to the verse, to much of the structure, with
its repetition of themes, its musicality, the fugue-like intonation of

the stanzas and the echoing of themes and motifs from place to place. The formal delight evoked by the poem is stressed, not surprisingly, by Nabokov: 'This "classical" regularity of proportions is beautifully relieved by the "romantic" device of prolonging or replaying a structural theme in the chapter following the one introducing it' (Nabokov, I, 17). Yet such an 'aesthetic' response is too one-sided, too oriented towards the perfection of the formal categories, for us to accept it as the last – or the only – word.

Some attempts have been made to approach the problem of meaning through the categories of 'comedy' and 'tragedy.' There is in *Onegin* a deep melancholy that leads some to speak of tragedy. Others, e.g., Hoisington and Shklovskii, would see *Onegin* as a comic work. Chumakov tries to resolve the paradox by speaking of the double note of melancholy at the end of Chapter Eight, balanced by the joy of poetic return to the world of youth in Odessa in the Journey. His comment would appear to be as close to a definition of the tone as we could reasonably expect to get. Yet – it *is* only a definition of tone, which is to say that to accept it as all one can say on the subject is to beg a number of important questions which Pushkin's work poses directly or indirectly and which therefore deserve to be answered.

Perhaps one should begin by discussing the irony, since it is the directedness of it, and the bracketing-off of any characters and emotions that are proof against it, that may tell us where to seek the central kernel of positive experience. As Shaw points out, there are certain experiences which Pushkin recalls with enjoyment and which distinguish him from Onegin (who is the centre of the irony): the theatre, Italian music, the Russian countryside, the Russian language (albeit with a French accent). A good part of the aesthetic pleasure of reading *Onegin* derives from the description of these, but mostly it comes from the sheer joy of the Russian verse, its musicality and vitality, which tell us of them. The poem is the celebration of certain pleasures – not all, and not necessarily, Russian, we note – which are, for Pushkin, equated with or serve as metaphors for poetry. More than that, however, it is the power of poetry – to transfix, to compel, to recreate life in memory and imagination – that lies at the heart of the work. Pushkin makes it clear from the stanzas in Eight where Onegin is smitten by love for Tat'iana that for him poetry *is* morality, it is remorse, and it is the overcoming of the formal automatization of life. The ball, the duel, the seduction, the empty and malicious rituals by which humans control and destroy each other – these are the outward forms imposed on life which must be broken through if one is to be truly alive. Poetry is the force which can do this.

The dichotomy of imposed form and life is therefore something that is central to *Onegin*: whether it be in the prose/poetry opposition which I discussed above (in chapter two), or in the behaviour of Onegin with his reverses from natural behaviour to the automatic, or in Tat'iana at the end – loving one man, married to another. The dichotomy is made emblem in the contrast of red and white, flush and pallor, passion and chastity, warmth and cold, south and north, which runs through the work to such an extent that we must consider it a leitmotiv. Lenskii's blood in the snow is emblematic of life petrified by death, the rose on a girl's cheek bitten by frost, Italy exiled to Russia, perhaps even the mix of African and Russian blood in Pushkin's veins.

Beyond these minor manifestations of the categories of opposites which inform *Onegin*, there is one figure who is Pushkin's inspiration in the work, namely Tat'iana (whose opposite is, of course, the eponymous hero). Tat'iana is the personification of the poetic for Pushkin: closely related to the muse-figure, she is Russia, she is constancy, she is the nymph of the birch forests and the lakes. The real drama of the poem is, I would suggest, not Onegin's and Tat'iana's love for each other, but Pushkin's love for Tat'iana – a secret, undemanding love, nurtured from afar. It is Tat'iana who is his 'true ideal.' She overcomes the corrosive negativeness of Onegin and triumphs, although that triumph is a pyrrhic one, for her relationship to it at the end is the analogue of the opposition of Pushkin's poetry and the demonic – keeping it at bay but far from vanquished.

In addition, Tat'iana is the antidote for Pushkin to the visions of the faithless female, the Helen, the adultress whose waywardness destroys her husband. Pushkin, we recall, was switching roles precisely at the time when the last chapter was being written – from young philanderer and seducer of other people's wives to the husband of the beautiful young Natal'ia Goncharova and potential cuckold. Tat'iana is an attempt to realize in concrete form the ideal of womanhood – an ideal in whose existence Pushkin had to believe if he were to survive. Yet Pushkin is curiously reticent about Tat'iana. As I have said, she is an ideal whom he admires from afar, and becomes, after all, the wife of N, not of the poet. The career of Prince N, likewise, is very different from that of the poet and is treated half-ironically, half-enviously as the paradigm of success. The final situation of N and Tat'iana suggests the isolation and exclusion of the poet (and, we might add, of his creation Onegin) – an isolation which is made only more profound by the mention of missing friends.

Ultimately, if one leaves aside the ephemeral pleasures of friendship, wine, the opera, and the theatre, the poet appears as a figure for whom existential happiness is unattainable save in his poetry. The message of the poem is a pessimistic one: love, that chimaera of the poet's world, is in reality either impossible or at best brings not fulfilment but unhappiness. The poetry that makes life so meaningful for Pushkin is likewise that which separates him from so much of it. It is Tat'iana who manages the impossible – to survive in society and yet retain her soul, a feat which seems beyond the poet in a world he so clearly detests. Here the figure of Tat'iana seems to be 'wish fulfilment' on the part of the poet; that is to say, the imposition of an ideal on a less than happy reality. Is such a purity as hers really possible – or desirable? Is it truly possible for Tat'iana to remain free of all the corruptions that surround her? In my reading the Tat'iana of Chapter Eight remains the Madonna, the angel of Pushkin's lyrical symbolism, and the enigmatic qualities that permit her to exist at all in the novel are never really motivated.

A remarkable aspect of *Onegin* is the fact that the poet has been able to weave his narrative out of something so insubstantial. If we were to resume the plot of the novel in a sentence, it would be: 'two people meet and nothing happens.' If we were to imagine ourselves into the position of an outside observer, a frequenter of society gatherings, perhaps, then we would know nothing at all of Onegin's encounters with Tat'iana. We would know that the beautiful Princess N had married, perhaps also that Onegin had killed someone in a duel over her sister, and we might even realize, if we were perspicacious, that Onegin was one of her many admirers. We would know nothing of the inner drama that takes place in the hearts of the two individuals. It is this inner drama, a drama in which nothing happens (but everything happens), that forms the stuff of the novelistic plot. The situation is more than a little reminiscent of David Lean's film *Brief Encounter*, which is equally a film about nothing. Where in the film the camera is the observer, registering the expression on the heroine's face as the express races past, so in *Onegin* Pushkin is our ghostly viewing-piece as he secretly admires her from afar. In this way Tat'iana serves as a metaphor for the intimacy of Pushkin's poetry – the simple external appearance belies the complex inner content. Among other things, the inner drama is suggestive of the poet's own rejection of the search for fame (*slava*) (which had been, we recall, the goal of Lenskii), in favour of a quasi-Horatian withdrawal.

On the question of death and life hereafter, Pushkin seems unequivocal – if we are to seek any fulfilment, then it must be in this world. The oblivion which swallows Lenskii (and which, the author tells us

in the last stanza of Eight, we must be ready to embrace without fear)
is as total as that nothingness which surrounds the few sketchily drawn
episodes of *Onegin*. The brevity and incompleteness of *Onegin* thus
serve as a kind of metaphor for Pushkin's vision of human existence.
Piety, when it exists, is a female quality which Tania finds in her
nurse, but Pushkin insists on the importance of morality, which is 'in
the nature of things' (to quote the epigraph) and is inherent in Pushkin's
notion of the noble life. To ignore it is to court eternal confusion, the
state in which Onegin is left at the end of Eight.

There remains the vexed question of the extent to which we may
trace in *Onegin* Pushkin's political stance in the years after the Decembrist uprising. The contrast between public appearances and private emotions is clearly important here, but so is the attitude of Tat'iana
towards Onegin at the end, for in her refusal of Onegin and her decision
to remain faithful to her husband it is possible to read, as Belinskii
did, a metaphor of the acceptance or acquiescence by Pushkin in the
political realities of Russia under Nicholas I. Such an interpretation
has not been current in Soviet criticism since the publication of the
number of *Literary Heritage (Literaturnoe nasledstvo)* devoted to Pushkin, in 1934. Public acquiescence by Pushkin, private sympathies with
the Decembrists, but a view that all that is past, and moreover, that
to revolt against authority – symbolized here, as Belinskii thought, by
the institution of marriage – is immoral, a quasi-Napoleonic act of self-
aggrandizement: all these can be traced in *Onegin* and serve to shape
its final outcome in Chapter Eight. Pushkin was the scion of a declining
family of nobility, a man poised between his impatience with the
régime and the petty humiliations that it inflicted upon him as a writer
and a person, and his patriotic feelings towards his country. Pushkin
does not find, and does not offer, a solution to these contradictions.
They are enshrined in the final scene between Onegin and Tat'iana:
the predicament of the demon in love with the angel. No outcome is
possible. The demon is petrified into immobility. Similarly, the Pushkin of the 1830s was an individual petrified by the contradictions of
his social and existential circumstances, contradictions that proved
unresolvable by any other outcome than death. I would argue that we
must read *Onegin*, like a lyrical poem, as a sort of map of Pushkin's
existential predicament, and, beyond that, as a symbolic representation
of the dilemma of his whole class – forced to acquiesce in a system to
which they owed their privileges yet which exacted a heavy price for
them in terms of the abasement of that individualism and self-assertion
which they imbibed from Western European culture.

This ideological clash, between the individualistic values of bourgeois Europe, with its stress on personal happiness and the right of the individual to fulfilment, and the traditional, autocratic, collectivist values of Russia runs through every page of *Onegin*. Pushkin is forced to live the paradox of trying to describe and measure his native land with the values and yardsticks of Western Europe. It is this paradox that explains the bizarre, hybrid genre of *Onegin* – a genre expressive of Pushkin's position between two cultures. Pushkin's own ambivalence towards Western European values – seduced by them, yet tugged by atavistic instincts back towards a grudging acceptance of Russian realities – is perhaps his most Russian attribute. In his dilemma Russians recognize their own position in the half-way house between European individualism and Russian (or should one say 'Asiatic'?) collectivism and authoritarianism. Significantly, for Pushkin the final choice falls, reluctantly, on the latter.

In this sense *Onegin* can be seen as the first statement in a vast cultural effort on the part of nineteenth-century Russia to understand and assimilate the values of Western European individualism (just as Russian society in the second half of the century attempted to adopt capitalism). The rejection by Tat'iana of Onegin can thus be read in a much wider sense as a metaphor for the ultimate rejection by Russia of those values in favour of a return to the authoritarian, collectivist model. Although clearly the claims made by Grigor'ev and Dostoevskii for Pushkin as a prophet and visionary are far-fetched, it seems to me that in *Onegin* Pushkin, with his poet's instinct, catches and expresses the nature of Russia's love/hate relationship with Western values – which led, in the fullness of time, to their rejection in the October revolution.

This is not to say, of course, that Pushkin was a revolutionary – on the contrary, for Pushkin the notion of revolution, symbolized by the figure of Napoleon, is consciously rejected (just as the historical Napoleon was made unwelcome by Moscow). The autocratic régime with which he was forced to come to terms was a reactionary one that derived its support from the nobility, of which Pushkin was, after all, a proud member. The régime that was created in October 1917 was equally autocratic and in many ways reactionary, and had a collectivist base too (i.e., it, like the tsarist régime that preceded it, was hostile to the notions of the primacy of the individual before the state), but its power base was that other enemy of middle-class, bourgeois values (and of capitalism), the working classes. The October revolution signalled the end of the attempt by Russia to adopt the Western model (which went as far as a half-hearted attempt at parliamentary democracy after 1905). These bourgeois, Western institutions were swept away with the Russian middle class when Russia reverted to her atavistic structures and values.

We can reproach Pushkin for not having offered a more satisfactory ending to *Onegin*, but we must realize that to do so would have meant finding a way for himself and those like him out of the impasse in which they found themselves. Pushkin's solution, as it is sketched in *Onegin*, is not revolution, an option which, as I have tried to show in my analysis of the poetic semantics, is rejected, but a retreat into a personal, private world of poetry and memory. Such a retreat is balanced by the poet's pride in rejecting the possibility of a toothless and undignified old age, which the poet rules out in favour of a speedy death. As a novel, *Onegin* clearly does not live up to the expectations of a reader weaned on Tolstoi and Dostoevskii, or Lawrence and Forster, for its presentation of the problems of life is not matched by the anticipated advancement of a solution. There is in Pushkin no Levin experiencing epiphanies as he contemplates the threats that nature presents to his young son. Indeed, for Pushkin, the younger generation serves, not as a symbol of hope, but as a challenge and a *memento mori*:

> Pridet, pridet i nashe vremia,
> I nashi vnuki v dobryi chas
> Iz mira vytesniat i nas!

> [*Our time will come too, and one of these fine days our grandchildren will push us out of the world too!* (Two: **XXXVIII**: 12-14)]

However much we try, it is difficult, if not impossible, to read into *Onegin* the social concerns and involvement of a Turgenev or a Tolstoi. Despite Bakhtin's assertion of the presence of a truly novelistic range of voices in *Onegin*, in fact the author's voice overrides all, and the 'dialogic' conflict of voices and ideologies which we can expect in a good Russian novel is present only in an embryonic way. Even the depiction of Russian reality in the poem, however well done, is mannered and personal, evoking Canaletto (or even, as Pushkin himself reminds us, Breughel) rather than Repin. As an 'encyclopedia of Russian life' it is simply deficient, as Nabokov has pointed out. We would do better to turn to the realists of a generation later for a believable evocation of the Russian landscape.

As a lyrical poem and an *apologia pro vita sua*, *Onegin* fares much better, documenting the intimate life and cares of the poet Pushkin, hinting, also, at the life of the man himself, and serving as the vehicle for flights of Russian poetry that have remained unsurpassed. It is here, I believe, that we must seek the ultimate importance of the work, and the reason that it has succeeded in captivating and fascinating generations of Russian-speakers. As I have tried to show, it is in reading the work as poetry, as a piece whose structure is the analogue of a lyrical poem, that we can penetrate to the heart of it and grasp the uniqueness of a work which, despite its imperfections and contradictions, proved an extraordinary beginning to an extraordinary literary century.

Pushkin (top) and two female acquaintances. Drawing by Pushkin on the manuscript of Two: XI-XII. 1823

Notes

1 Research for this chapter was carried out at the Libraries of the Universities of Cambridge, Helsinki, and Illinois (Urbana-Champaign). The Pushkinist has a rich collection of bibliographical tools at his disposal; practically all the material on Pushkin published in Russia is to be found in the series of bibliographies which was begun by Mezhov and Fomin and carried into the Soviet era under the title *Bibliografiia proizvedenii A.S. Pushkina i literatury o nem*. For more information on Pushkin bibliography, see the article by Levkovich in *Pushkin: Itogi i problemy izucheniia*, 631-9.

2 See the survey by a variety of authors in *Pushkin: Itogi i problemy izucheniia*, 11-148; also useful are the survey by Blagoi 1931, and the introduction to the collection of essays on Pushkin in English, Richards and Cockrell 1976.

3 Debreczeny 1969; Hoisington 1971; Forsyth 1970; Clayton 1980a.

4 Zelinskii, I, 12-19. Wherever possible and desirable, references to criticism contemporary to Pushkin are to the useful collection by Zelinskii (see bibliography).

5 D.V. Venevitinov 1825a. The polemic continued in Polevoi 1825b and Venevitinov 1825b. See also the comments of R. R-n in Zelinskii, I, 30-5, and the refutation of same by NN (ibid., 36-42).

6 Zelinskii, II, 81-92. The identity of the reviewer is given as M.A. Dmitriev in Lotman 1980, 251.

7 Zelinskii, II, 75-80. This review is the first to express the opinion that the work should be called 'Tat'iana Larina.' Other reviews of Chapters One through Six are to be found in Zelinskii, II, 42-129.

8 For more detail on this point see Hoisington 1971, 29-30, and Fomin 1911.

9 For details of the publication of *Onegin*, see Nabokov, I, 74-83.

10 See *Pushkin v pechati*, 161.

11 It was the critic in *Severnaia zvezda* (Zelinskii, II, 128-9).

12 N.N., 'Evgenii Onegin, roman v stikhakh. Sochineniia Aleksandra Push-kina. Glava posledniaia,' *Literaturnye pribavleniia k Russkomu invalidu*, no. 22 (1832), 174-6 (176).

13 All are to be found in Zelinskii, IV: Farnhagen von Ense, 105-25 (*Onegin*: 113-15); *Biblioteka*, 126ff. (*Onegin*: 155-62); and Shevyrev, 186ff. (*Onegin*: 204-15).

14 A ridiculous contrast to Belinskii's well-reasoned and influential essays is to be found in the articles published in *Maiak* (a reactionary journal) by Avksentii Martynov (*Maiak*, 1843, IX, 11-32, 127-49). Martynov's pompous and condescending remarks are aimed at pointing out Pushkin's 'mistakes,' and criticizing his use of foreign words and ideas, and are especially directed at the character of Onegin. A typical criticism by Martynov is directed at the comparison of Ol'ga to 'that stupid moon,' etc., on the grounds that such a comparison is inappropriate since the moon is inanimate! Hoisington is inclined to see in Martynov a forerunner of the critical attitude of Pisarev (and indeed, his criticism harks back to the 'archaizing' Decembrists as well) (Hoisington 1971, 63).

15 Grigor'ev 1859, 166. The same year, 1859, saw the publication of an article by Boris Almazov on Pushkin, in which the author stressed the poetic and noted Pushkin's eschewal of formal philosophical systems. For Al-mazov Tat'iana is the quintessential expression of Pushkin's muse: 'Pushkin's muse was no proclaimer of grand ideas; she struck one neither by the force of her passion, nor by a particular pounding of the heart, nor by the brilliance of her attire. ... Pushkin's muse is Tat'iana, a woman who does not strike one particularly at first glance, but who inspires endless, unreserved respect and deep sympathy. ... Neither by word nor gesture nor glance would she ever betray her quiet feminine grace; she is from head to toe a woman from a good milieu' (Almazov 1859, 183). In some ways Almazov's views were to find an echo later in the writings of Ivanov-Razumnik.

16 See, for example, Forsythe 1970.

17 See *Pushkin: Itogi i problemy izucheniia*, 96-9.

18 A typical title was 'S kogo Pushkin spisal Zaretskogo?' *Russkaia starina*, 1908, II, 409-27.

19 See *Pushkin: Itogi i problemy izucheniia*, 99-104.

20 Ibid., 130.

21 See bibliography under Tynianov 1975 and 1977; also Chudakov 1975, for a brief introduction to the essay.

22 Quoted in *Pushkin: Itogi i problemy izucheniia*, 137.
23 See, for example, G.A. Gukovskii 1957, D. Blagoi 1955, and G. Makogonenko 1963.
24 *Pushkin v vospominaniiakh sovremennikov*, II (1974), 107.
25 Tamarchenko 1961; Nikishov 1972; Meilakh in *Pushkin: Itogi i problemy izucheniia*, 436.
26 Vinokur 1941. Vinokur's article represented a valuable continuation of the work done on the stanza of *Onegin* by Grossman 1924.
27 Chudakov 1975, Tynianov 1975. For a more detailed account of recent Soviet treatments of *Onegin*, see my paper, Clayton 1980b. The survey given here is in part drawn from that article.
28 On the incorporation in this book of material from earlier studies by Lotman, see Clayton 1980b, 215.
29 The book was published in a run of 150,000, whereas Lotman 1976 was printed in only 500 copies.
30 The reader is referred for bibliographical details to Wreath 1976, and, for material in Russian published abroad, to Foster 1970.
31 Mirskii 1926, Wilson 1936. Mention must also be made of the Commentary to Onegin by Dmitrii Chizhevskii (1953), which, although criticized by Nabokov, is still of interest. Chizhevskii, carried away by his comparison of *Onegin* with Mickiewicz's and Slowacki's epics, describes Pushkin's work as an 'epic' also, which it surely is not, despite the vestiges in it of the burlesque tradition (xv). More interesting are Chizhevskii's remarks on Romantic irony and 'sense transformations' in Pushkin's poetic vocabulary (xx, xxi-xxii).
32 On Goethe: Peer 1969 and Riggan 1973; on Dante: Picchio 1976; on Constant: Hoisington 1977 and Riggan 1973; on Chateaubriand: Barrat 1972; and on Byron: Hoisington 1975 and Vickery 1963 and 1968.

CHAPTER TWO

1 See Todd 1974, 73; also Shaw's caveat about making too close an association between the style of *Onegin* and that of the letters (Shaw 1980, 42).
2 On the complex literary currents of the time, see Tynianov 1929a, 107ff.
3 Bayley in Pushkin 1979, *Eugene Onegin*, 15
4 Tynianov 1975 (in Tynianov 1977), 60
5 Siniavskii's view of *Onegin* also places great stress on the 'banter' in the tone of the work: 'The genre of Pushkin's novel in verse is conditioned by the banter; in it the verse becomes a means to wash away the novel and finds in the banter a justification for its limitlessness and unsettledness. ...

Later Pushkin's garrulity was considered high realism. ... Banter for all its general "debonairness" of tone assumed a conscious lowering of the speech into the sphere of private life, which is thus dragged out into the light with the domestic bric-a-brac and the humdrum details of existence' (1975, 84-5).

6 See, especially, Hoisington 1976. Cf. Booth 1961: 'It is a curious fact that we have no terms either for this created "second self" or for our relationship with him. None of our terms for various aspects of the narrator is quite accurate. "Persona," "mask," and "narrator" are sometimes used, but they more commonly refer to the speaker in the work who is after all only one of the elements created by the implied author and who may be separated from him by large ironies. "Narrator" is usually taken to mean the "I" of the work, but the "I" is seldom if ever identical with the implied image of the artist' (73). Booth's observation goes a long way towards clearing up the problem of terminology. I agree with him in seeing the narrator as an entity distinct from the implied author.

7 See Lo Gatto 1955, 1958, and 1962, and the critique of Lo Gatto's position by Stanley Mitchell 1966.

8 'It is a polylogue related in an authorial monologue' (Lotman 1976, 87).

9 Nabokov has another explanation: 'This prolix quotation was no doubt prompted by the fact that our poet was grateful to Gnedich for supervising the publication of *Ruslan and Liudmila* in 1821' (Nabokov, II, 175).

10 See Grombakh 1969 and my paper, Clayton 1971. The epigraph serves as an ironic synthesis by the poet of his hero – placed in a voice which is clearly not intended to be his own, but that of a female. The most important word in the epigraph is 'peut-être' – which sums up the ambiguity of Onegin.

11 See Nabokov, II, 462 and Lotman 1980, 250.

12 See Nabokov, I, 9-14; Grossman 1924; Vinokur 1941.

13 See the quotation from Bayley given above in chapter one.

14 Tynianov 1975, 52-4, and Lotman 1970 both discuss the prose/verse dichotomy in *Onegin*.

15 Generally, the problem has been linked to that of the encoded material that was attributed to a destroyed 'Chapter Ten' (Morozov 1910, Tomashevskii 1934, Nabokov, III, 365-75). Another hypothesis, cogently argued by D'iakonov 1963, places the encoded stanzas at the end of the original Chapter Eight (a truncated version of which appears as Onegin's Journey).

16 The primacy of the role of Onegin's Journey is stressed, following Tynianov, by Chumakov: 'Pushkin did not destroy the composition of *Onegin*, nor did he impoverish its conception. He fulfilled a new ideo-stylistic

objective. The "Excerpts from Onegin's Journey" are not an appendix, but an artistically equally valid part of the novel, subjected to compositional inversion, and form *its true ending*' (Chumakov 1970, 28; Chumakov's emphasis). This view should be compared with that of Nabokov, that the Journey is 'an additional small structure unattached compositionally to the main body of the novel' (Nabokov, I, 58).

17 It is also at the same time a 'quotation' from the beginning of Maturin's gothic novel *Melmoth the Wanderer.*

18 Stilman 1958, 330. The idea is picked up by Lotman 1976, 95.

19 Pushkin 'foregrounds' the border between fiction and reality to the extent that he even introduces a *reader* into the novel (Six: XLI: 5-XLII: 12). The logical conclusion of such convolutions would be to have Onegin himself read the story of his own life! The 'biography' of the 'Pushkin' in *Onegin* is, of course, a stylized, fictionalized one, and the searchings of critics for 'real-life Tat'ianas' and Onegins are simply the confusion of the literary with the real.

20 See Ivanov-Razumnik 1907, 210-11; Gukovskii 1957, 131-7; and Clayton 1979.

21 See above, note 16.

22 I explore some of these hints in my (quixotic!) paper on the epigraph, in which I propose, hypothetically, that it be read as a 'fragment of a letter' from Tat'iana (Princess N) to 'Pushkin' (Clayton 1971).

23 The problem of the digressions is one of the most complex in the work. It has been examined, most notably, by Meijer 1968; see also Shaw 1980.

24 'In these numbers are given as it were the equivalents of lines and stanzas filled with any content; instead of a verbal mass there is a dynamic sign pointing to them; instead of a definite semantic weight there is an indefinite, mysterious semantic hieroglyph, from the angle of vision of which the following stanzas and lines appear complex, semantically burdened' (Tynianov 1975 in Tynianov 1977, 60).

25 Siniavskii 1975, 81. Clearly, the form-directed irony which we find in *Onegin* is related to the romantic irony of the Germans, e.g., the *Illusionsbruch* of Tieck's plays. What one lacks in Pushkin, by comparison with the Germans, is a philosophical or theoretical basis for the irony. Pushkin's appears to have its source solely in aesthetic desiderata, and not in a *Weltanschauung* which viewed the world as chaos and disunity.

CHAPTER THREE

1 This bears out Bayley's observation on *Onegin*: 'The novel turned out to be one of sentiment and not of picaresque episode and adventure. ... Jane

Austen's earliest critics were struck ... by her faithful imitation of daily living. Pushkin's novel has it too, though neither he nor Jane Austen was concerned to record life in the methodological fashion of the nineteenth-century novel, the novel of realism and naturalism. The stylization of their art conveys the real as part of its *insouciance*' (Bayley 1971, 241). Bayley's discriminations, based on English literature, which had a sentimental novel, are important in the context of Russian literature, which is dominated by realism.

2 Nabokov, II, 485-6. On the evolution of the characters in *Onegin* see Lotman 1960.

3 See Clayton 1971. These extrapolations are all based on the familiar novelistic devices which Pushkin hints at in a tantalizing way, but only to 'lay them bare' for inspection.

4 A fascinating discussion of this problem can be found in Tynianov 1974 (in Tynianov 1977, 58). As we have seen (above, chapter one), the question of the ending of *Onegin* was problematical from the outset.

5 This is the scheme given, for example, in Frye 1957, 163.

6 Compare the observation by Freeborn quoted above (chapter one, page 69.

CHAPTER FOUR

1 There is considerable association between Tat'iana and the dawn, especially in Chapters Two and Three, e.g., the stanza beginning 'She loved to await the rising of the dawn on her balcony' (Two: XXVIII: 1-2). This is 'picked up' in the significant comment that, after writing her fatal letter to Onegin, 'she does not notice the dawn' (Three: XXXIII: 1). Apart from the romantic literary associations, the coming of the dawn (pallor followed by fiery redness) has obvious metaphorical meaning for a young girl – chastity followed by passion.

2 The word appears only once in *Onegin*: 'To attract the mocking glances of Moscow rakes and circes' (Seven: XXVII: 11). However, one should also note the related use of the words *volshebnitsa* (in its secondary meaning of a society enchantress, not sorceress)(One: XXXIV: 13); and *izmennitsa* ('traitress' – although one should note the element of 'change' in the root, contrasting with Tat'iana's constancy) (Eight: XXXVII: 11). Related to this semantic group is the reference (One: XXVIII: 14) to 'fashionable wives,' an allusion to the poem 'Modnaia zhena' ('The Fashionable Wife,' 1791) by I.I. Dmitriev, in which the young wife of an old man is almost caught by him on the couch with her young lover.

3 For detailed discussions of Tat'iana's dream, see Gregg 1970, and Matlaw 1959.
4 See, for example, the stimulating article by Snyder 1970.
5 The bear-bridegroom association is mentioned by Matlaw 1959, 487. The man whom Tat'iana will eventually marry is not as yet a reality, but simply the shadowy 'other' evoked in her letter quoted above.
6 For information on the links between Pushkin and the French novel, see Vol'pert 1980 and Akhmatova 1936.
7 See my discussion of this point in the preceding chapter, and also Lotman 1980, 274.
8 The phallic overtones of Onegin's 'long knife' in the dream have been pointed out by Gregg, who assumes that it is Tat'iana who is its potential victim (see Gregg 1970, 504). That Ol'ga's red face is not a chance detail is suggested by the fact that Tat'iana, too, has a red face (also as red as a poppy, an interesting Morphic-oneiric detail) when her nurse enters in the morning after her nocturnal letter-writing (Three: XXXIII: 14).
9 See below, chapter five, for more discussion on this point.
10 It is interesting to note that when Pushkin married Natal'ia Goncharova, he switched the language of their correspondence from French (the conventional language of the salon and adultery) to Russian.
11 Although the word *tsirtseia* meant simply 'enchantress,' Pushkin must surely have been aware of the mythical connotations evoked by its etymology. These circean motifs are examined in more detail in Clayton 1975.

CHAPTER FIVE

1 For more information on the chronology of *Onegin*, see Clayton 1979 and Lotman 1980, 18-23.
2 *A.S. Pushkin v vospominaniiakh sovremennikov*, II, 107.
3 See, for example, *Letters*, 197.
4 See Clayton 1971 and Lotman 1980, 221-4.
5 See the discussion in Clayton 1980a, 171-5.
6 See, for example, the remarks in Lotman 1980, 214, which summarize the entrenched view in Soviet criticism.
7 See Nabokov, I, 37.
8 A traditional statement of the problem is given in Lotman 1980, 26-7.
9 One example of this is Onegin swimming the river 'beneath the hill,' an activity compared to Byron's swimming the Hellespont (Four: XXXVII: 6-10). That Pushkin considered Byron's heroes the personification of the

poet himself is suggested by the comparison, a few lines later, of Onegin to Childe Harold (Four: XLIV: 1-2).

10 The resemblance of Lenskii's poetry to Pushkin's early work is a commonplace of Pushkin scholarship. The assumption is implicit, for example, in Shaw's discussion of *Onegin*.

11 The argument for Pushkin's breakaway from the Karamzinian poetic is given in Tynianov 1929c, 234ff.

12 On the bawdy in *Onegin*, see above, chapter two, and also Nabokov, II, 247, 368, 375.

13 It is interesting to note the use of the word *mashinal'no* ('automatically') to which Pushkin draws attention when Tat'iana has heard out Onegin's sermon and has been transformed from the live creature (with attendant animal imagery) of the previous chapter into an automaton – has been, that is to say, made (temporarily at least) to resemble Onegin himself (Four: XVII: 6).

14 I discuss these portraits as a series or a system in Clayton 1980a.

15 *Letters*, 95. That Pushkin was deeply aware of this problem of career (including marriage) is attested by Lotman 1980, 350.

CHAPTER SIX

1 Lotman 1976, 87. The problem of the unity of the author-narrator was first raised by Rybnikova 1924.

2 Hielscher 1966. See also Semenko 1957 and 1960, and Stepanov 1974. Further bibliography on the subject can be found in Shaw 1981, 36-7.

3 For information on the digressions, the reader is referred to Meijer 1968.

4 See Chumakov 1970, 1976, and 1977.

5 For a more detailed discussion of the symbolism of time and space, see Clayton 1981. Part of the text of that article is included in a revised form in the present chapter.

6 Cf. the epigraph from Griboedov's *Woe from Wit* (*Gore ot uma*) that is placed at the head of Chapter Seven: 'Where is it better? Where we are not.'

7 This question is discussed more fully in Clayton 1979, 486. See also Lotman 1980, 18.

8 The lack of any discussion of children and childhood in Pushkin's work may be explained in part by the facts of his own biography: see Maimin 1981, 4-7. An equally important reason is the lack of precedent in literature: children and childhood were simply not recognized topics. Man (and woman for that matter) existed from puberty to death as far as literature was concerned.

9 See Nabokov, II, 480-2 and Lotman 1980, 253-4.

10 I have in mind Christ's words in the Garden of Gethsemane, the wine of
the Last Supper, and the wine mixed with myrrh (or wormwood) which
he is offered on the cross (Mark 14:36, 15:23). The symbolism of the
'cup of suffering' recurs in Pasternak's poem 'Gamlet' ('Hamlet') in *Doktor
Zhivago*, 532.

11 In the following argument I differ from Gustafson, who sees only two
seasons – spring and winter – as being metaphorically significant in
Onegin (1962, 8). I believe that autumn is an inherent feature in the
metaphorical structure of the work. It is manifested in the metaphorical use of the root 'to wither' (*viad-*), which is continually used to
connote the fading of hopes and youthful enthusiasms, and is clearly
linked to the withering of the leaves in the fall (e.g., in Seven: III: 1-8).
Although I agree with Gustafson that Pushkin offers a Russian rein-
terpretation of the seasons, I differ from him in many points in my
analysis of the metaphorical function of the seasons. Pushkin's avowed
(and famous) love of the fall leads him to make of it a metaphor for
middle age, which is where he is in Chapters Seven and Eight (i.e., about
thirty) (not 'old age' as Gustafson suggests!). Winter is the inevitable
and speedy end of the fall, signifying death for Lenskii (and, it is implied
at the end of Eight, for the author-narrator too) and marriage for
Tat'iana. The fact that we see Onegin in love with Tat'iana in the spring
at the end of the novel is significant because it tells us that Onegin
has still to learn the lesson of life: love is only for the spring of one's
days: its coming in one's autumn (i.e., middle age) is a cruel joke
(cf. Eight: XXIX: 9-11).

12 For a discussion of the imagery of fall in *Onegin*, see Clayton 1981, 46-7.

13 See Bocharov 1974, 71. A discussion of Lotman's coining and use of the
term 'transcoding' may be found in Shukman 1977, 79-82.

14 'O narodnosti v literature' ('On *narodnost*' in literature,' *PSS*, XI, 40).

15 For discussions of the transformations of the muse figure, the reader is
referred to Lotman 1975, 50, and to Khodasevich 1937, 9-38.

16 The evolution of the semantics of the word 'freedom' in Pushkin's oeuvre
is described by Bocharov in the article 'Svoboda i "schast'e" v poezii
Pushkina,' in Bocharov 1974, 3-25. Bocharov attempts to analyse the
semantics of 'freedom' throughout a number of works, especially
'Kavkazskii plennik' and 'Tsygany.' His work begs a number of important
questions, including the problem of the internal, contextual semantics of
each individual work vis-à-vis the semantic system of Pushkin's language
as a whole. His lack of a rigorous definition of the semantic shadings
involved (and his avoidance of the problem of the different words used)
makes his discussion less useful than it might be.

17 In saying this I differ not only from Bocharov (ibid., 16), but also from Lotman and Mints.

18 Bocharov notes the importance of the rhyme 'priroda – svoboda' (ibid., 5).

19 See the interpretations of Tat'iana's dream in Gregg 1970 and Matlaw 1959.

20 There is a parallel to be drawn here between Onegin's sojourn in the country and Pushkin's at Mikhailovskoe, as Nabokov explains: 'there is little doubt that ... our poet camouflaged in the present stanza his own experience – namely an affair he was having that summer at Mihailov-skoe ... with a delicate-looking slave girl, Ol'ga Kalashnikov (b. about 1805). ... In late April, 1826, Pushkin dispatched her, big with child, to Moscow' (Nabokov, II, 462).

21 In analysing the semantics of sleep, I took the information given by the *Slovar' iazyka Pushkina* under the headings of *son, spat', snoviden'e*, and *sonnyi*. There are seventeen uses of these words to denote physical sleep in *Onegin*. The mentions of sleep in relation to Tat'iana are in Three: XVI: 13 and XVII: 1, and Four: XXXIII: 8. The restlessness of a young girl's sleep is clearly linked by Pushkin with erotic frustration.

22 Erotic dreams: Two: X: 4 (their absence in children), XXII: 2 (Ol'ga); Three: VIII: 4 (Tat'iana), XII: 6 (the dream of an adolescent girl), XIII: 13, Tat'iana's letter: line 39, line 43; Four: XLV: 14; Six: VII: 6. Fearful dreams: Six: I: 8, XXVIII: 7 ('fearful, incomprehensible dream'); Eight: XXXVI: 11. Mysterious dreams: Five: V: 3, XI: 1, XXI: 14, XXII: 14, XXIV: 11.

23 Creative reveries: (Pushkin) One: LV: 4, LVII: 4; Six: XLIII: 14, XLVI: 4; Eight: I: 14, L: 10; (Lenskii) Six: XXXVI: 14; (unidentified) Seven: III: 10; Eight: X: 5.

24 'or is it a dream?' (Eight: XX: 10).

25 The semantics of *mechta* (and *mechtatel'nost', mechtatel'*) are fascinating. They may denote the revery of the poet, e.g., 'dreams, dreams' (Six: XLIV: 5), which may become 'cold' with disillusion, e.g., 'empty, black dreams' (Four: XIX: 2). An extension of this is the dreams of memory that Onegin and Pushkin share (One: XLVII: 13). In a young girl the word denotes her dreaming of a lover (e.g., Tat'iana in Three: XV: 10 and XXVI: 4). The juxtaposition of the poet's activity with that of the girl is made comic in the image of Lenskii (Two: VI: 11).

26 I discuss in more detail the motifs of death in *Onegin* in Clayton 1981, 49-51.

27 I give a more detailed analysis of the 'memory' theme in Clayton 1981, 44-5.

28 There is more than a slight prefiguring of Pushkin's ironical *exegi monumentum* in Two: XXXIX-XL.

Bibliography

Akhmatova, Anna. 1936. ' "Adol'f" Benzhamena Konstana v tvorchestve Pushkina.' In Akhmatova 1977, 50-88
– 1970. 'Boldinskaia osen' (8-ia glava "Onegina").' In Akhmatova 1977, 174-91
– 1977. *O Pushkine: stat'i i zametki.* Leningrad: Sovetskii pisatel'
Almazov, B.N. 1859. 'O poezii Pushkina.' *Utro: Literaturnyi sbornik* (Moscow: Tipografiia Barfknekhta), 139-92
Bakhtin, M. 1965. 'Slovo v romane.' *Voprosy literatury*, no. 8, 84-90 [reprinted in Bakhtin 1975, 410-17]
– 1975. *Voprosy literatury i estetiki: issledovaniia raznykh let.* Moscow: 'Khudozhestvennaia literatura'
Barrat, Glynn R. 1972. 'Chateaubriand in Russia, 1800-1830.' *Comparative Literature Studies*, IX: 2, 152-72
Bayley, John. 1971. *Pushkin: A Comparative Commentary.* Cambridge: Cambridge University Press
Belinskii, V.G. 1843-46. 'Sochineniia Aleksandra Pushkina.' In Belinskii, *Estetika i literaturnaia kritika v dvukh tomakh* (Moscow: GIKhL, 1959), II, 130-569
Blagoi, D.D. 1929. *Sotsiologiia tvorchestva Pushkina: Etiudy.* Moscow: 'Federatsiia'
– 1931. 'Kritika o Pushkine.' In *Putevoditel' po Pushkinu* (Moscow-Leningrad: Goslitizdat), 189-210
– 1955. *Masterstvo Pushkina.* Moscow: Sovetskii pisatel'
Bocharov, S.G. 1967. 'Forma plana (Nekotorye voprosy poetiki Pushkina).' *Voprosy literatury*, no. 12, 115-36
– 1974. *Poetika Pushkina: ocherki.* Moscow: 'Nauka'
– 1975. 'Poeticheskoe predanie i poetika Pushkina.' In *Pushkin i literatura narodov sovetskogo soiuza* (Erevan: Izdatel'stvo Erevanskogo universiteta), 54-73

Booth, Wayne C. 1961. *The Rhetoric of Fiction*. Chicago: University of Chicago Press

Boyd, Alexander F. 1972. 'The Master and the Source: Alexander Pushkin and *Eugene Onegin*.' In Boyd, *Aspects of the Russian Novel* (Totowa, N.J.: Rowman and Littlefield), 1-23

Bürger, Gottfried August. *Lenore*. In *Sturm und Drang*, II (München: Winkler Verlag, 1971), 1612-18

Burtsev, V.L. 1934. *Kak Pushkin khotel izdat' 'Evgeniia Onegina' i kak izdal*. Paris: Zeliuk

Chizhevskii, Dmitrii. 1953. *Evgenij Onegin*. The Russian text, edited with an introduction and commentary by Dmitrij Čiževskij. Cambridge, Mass.: Harvard University Press

– 1968. *Comparative History of Slavic Literatures*. Vanderbilt University Press, 1971

Chudakov, A.P. 1975. 'Stat'ia Iu.N. Tynianova "O kompozitsii 'Evgeniia Onegina' ".' In *Pamiatniki kul'tury, novye otkrytiia: Pis'mennost', iskusstvo, arkheologiia. Ezhegodnik 1974* (Moscow: 'Nauka'), 121-3

Chumakov, Iu.N. 1969. 'O sostave i granitsakh teksta "Evgeniia Onegina".' *Russkii iazyk v kirgizskoi shkole*, no. 1, 32-3

– 1970. 'Sostav khudozhestvennogo teksta "Evgeniia Onegina".' In E.A. Maimin, ed. *Pushkin i ego sovremenniki*, (Pskov: LGPI), 20-33

– 1976. ' "Otryvki iz puteshestviia Onegina" kak khudozhestvennoe edinstvo.' In *Voprosy poetiki literaturnykh zhanrov: sbornik nauchnykh statei*, vyp. 1 (Leningrad: LGPI), 3-12

– 1977. ' "Den' Onegina" i "Den' avtora".' In *Voprosy poetiki literaturnykh zhanrov: sbornik nauchnykh trudov*, vyp. 2 (Leningrad), 3-10

Clayton, J. Douglas. 1971. 'The Epigraph of *Eugene Onegin*: A Hypothesis.' *Canadian Slavic Studies*, V: 2, 226-33

– 1975. 'Emblematic and Iconographic Patterns in Pushkin's *Eugene Onegin*: A Shakespearean Ghost?' *Germano-Slavica*, I: 6, 53-66

– 1979. 'Considérations sur la chronologie interne de *Evgenii Onegin*.' *Canadian Slavonic Papers*, XXI: 4, 479-88

– 1980a. 'Pushkin, Faust and the Demons.' *Germano-Slavica*, III: 3, 165-87

– 1980b. 'New Directions in Soviet Criticism on *Evgenii Onegin*.' *Canadian Slavonic Papers*, XXII: 2, 208-19

– 1981. '*Evgenij Onegin*: Symbolism of Time and Space.' *Russian Language Journal*, XXXV, no. 120, 43-58

Debreczeny, Paul. 1969. 'Reception of Pushkin's Poetic Works in the 1820's: A Study of the Critic's Role.' *Slavic Review*, XXVIII: 3, 394-415

D'iakonov, I. 1963. 'O vos'moi, deviatoi i desiatoi glavakh "Evgeniia Onegina".' *Russkaia literatura*, no. 3, 37-61

Dobroliubov, N.A. 1858a. 'Aleksandr Sergeevich Pushkin.' In Dobroliubov, *Sobranie sochinenii v deviati tomakh*, I (Moscow-Leningrad: GIKhL, 1961), 287-301

– 1858b. 'O stepeni uchastiia narodnosti v razvitii russkoi literatury.' In Dobroliubov, *Sobranie sochinenii v deviati tomakh*, II (Moscow: GIKhL, 1962), 218-72

Dostoevskii, F.M. 1880. 'Pushkin. Ocherk. Proizneseno 8 iiunia v zasedanii Obshchestva liubitelei rossiiskoi slovesnosti.' In Dostoevskii, *Dnevnik pisateliia na 1877 god* (Paris: YMCA Press [n.d.]), 510-27

Druzhinin, A.V. 1855. 'A.S. Pushkin i poslednee izdanie ego sochinenii.' In Druzhinin, *Sobranie sochinenii*, VII (St Petersburg, 1865), 30-82

Eikhenbaum, B.M. 1921. 'Problema poetiki Pushkina.' In Eikhenbaum, *Skvoz' literaturu: sbornik statei* (Leningrad, 1924; reprint: 'S-Gravenhage: Mouton, 1962), 157-70

Fomin, A.G. 1911. 'Pushkin i zhurnal'nyi triumvirat 30-ykh godov.' In A.S. Pushkin, [*Sochineniia*], V (St. Petersburg), 451-92

Forsyth, J. 1970. 'Pisarev, Belinsky and *Yevgeniy Onegin*.' *Slavonic and East European Review*, XLVIII, 163-80

Foster, L.A. 1970. *Bibliografiia russkoi zarubezhnoi literatury 1918-1968*. Boston, Mass.: G.K. Hall

Freeborn, Richard. 1973. '*Eugene Onegin*.' In Freeborn, *The Rise of the Russian Novel from 'Eugene Onegin' to 'War and Peace'* (Cambridge: Cambridge University Press), 13-68

Frye, Northrop. 1957. *Anatomy of Criticism*. New York: Atheneum, 1970

Golovin [Orlovskii], K.A. 1897. *Russkii roman i russkoe obshchestvo*. 2nd ed. St Petersburg: Marks, [1904]

Gregg, R.A. 1970. 'Tat'yana's Two Dreams: The Unwanted Spouse and the Demonic Lover.' *Slavonic and East European Review*, XLVIII, 492-505

Grigor'ev, A.A. 1859. 'Vzgliad na russkuiu literaturu so smerti Pushkina: Stat'ia pervaia: Pushkin. – Griboedov. – Gogol'. – Lermontov.' In Grigor'ev, *Literaturnaia kritika* (Moscow: 'Khudozhestvennaia literatura,' 1967), 157-203

Grombakh, S.M. 1969. 'Ob epigrafe k "Evgeniiu Oneginu".' *Izvestiia Akademii Nauk SSSR: Seriia literatury i iazyka*, XXVIII: 3, 211-19

Grossman, Leonid. 1924. *Oneginskaia strofa*. [Reprint: Letchworth: Prideaux, 1977]

Gukovskii, G.A. 1957. *Pushkin i problemy realisticheskogo stilia*. Moscow: Goslitizdat

Gustafson, Richard F. 1962. 'The Metaphor of the Seasons in *Evgenij Onegin*.' *Slavic and East European Journal*, VI: 1, 6-20

Hielscher, K.O. 1966. *A.S. Puškins Versepik: Autorenich und Erzählstruktur.*
München: Sagner

Hoisington, Sona S. 1971. *Early Critical Responses to 'Evgenii Onegin', 1825-1845.* Ph.D. Diss. Yale University

– 1975. 'Eugene Onegin: An Inverted Byronic Poem.' *Comparative Literature,*
XXVII: 2, 136-52

– 1976. 'The Hierarchy of Narratees in *Eugene Onegin*.' *Canadian-American Slavic Studies,* X, 242-9

– 1977. 'Eugene Onegin: Product of or Challenge to *Adolphe*.' *Comparative Literature Studies,* XIV, 205-13

Ivanov-Razumnik, R.V. 1907. 'Evgenii Onegin.' In A.S. Pushkin, [*Sochineniia*],
III (St Petersburg), 205-34

Jakobson, Roman. 1937a. 'The Statue in Puškin's Poetic Mythology.' In
Jakobson 1975, 1-44

– 1937b. 'Marginalia on *Eugene Onegin*.' In Jakobson 1975, 51-7

– 1975. *Puškin and His Sculptural Myth.* The Hague: Mouton

Katkov, M.N. 1856. 'Pushkin.' *Russkii vestnik*, vol. I (Ianvar', kn. 1 i 2),
155-72; and vol. II (Mart, kn. 2), 281-320

Khodasevich, Vl.F. 1937. *O Pushkine.* Berlin: Petropolis

Kireevskii, I. 1828. 'Nechto o kharaktere poezii Pushkina.' In Kireevskii,
Polnoe sobranie sochinenii (Moscow, 1911; reprint: Farnborough, Hunts.,
1970), II, 1-13

Kliuchevskii, V.O. 1887. ' "Onegin" i ego predki.' In Kliuchevskii, *Sochineniia,*
VII (Moscow: Sotsekgiz, 1959), 403-22

Konkin, S.S. 1972. 'Pushkin v kritike Pisareva.' *Russkaia literatura*, no. 4,
50-74

Kotliarevksii, N.A. 1907. 'Evgenii Onegin.' In Kotliarevskii, *Literaturnye napravleniia aleksandrovskoi epokhi* (St. Petersburg), 210-36

Laclos, Pierre Choderlos de. *Les Liaisons dangéreuses.* Paris: Garnier-Flammarion, 1964

Lafayette, Madame de. *La Princesse de Clèves.* Paris: Garnier-Flammarion,
1966

Levkovich, Ia.L. 1974. 'Nabroski poslaniia o prodolzhenii "Evgeniia Onegina".'
In N.V. Izmailov, ed. *Stikhotvoreniia Pushkina 1820-1830-kh godov*
(Leningrad: AN SSSR), 255-77

Lo Gatto, Ettore. 1955. 'L'*Onegin* come "diario lirico" di Puškin (Appunti
per una interpretazione).' *Analecta slavica: A Slavonic Miscellany*
(Amsterdam: De Bezige Bij), 91-108

– 1958. 'Su di un problema formale dell'*Onegin*.' *Ricerche Slavistiche*, VI,
41-83

– 1962. 'Sull' elemento lirico-autobiografico nell' *Evgenij Onegin* di Puškin.'
In Z. Folejewski, ed. *Studies in Russian and Polish literature in Honor*

of Waclaw Lednicki ('S-Gravenhage: Mouton; Slavistic Printings and Reprintings, 27), 105-13

Lotman, Iurii M. 1960. 'K evoliutsii postroeniia kharakterov v romane "Evgenii Onegin".' *Pushkin: Issledovaniia i materialy*, III (Moscow-Leningrad: AN SSSR), 131-73

– 1966. 'Khudozhestvennaia struktura "Evgeniia Onegina".' *Trudy po russkoi i slavianskoi filologii*, 9 (*Uchenye zapiski Tartuskogo universiteta*, vyp. 184), 5-22

– 1970. 'K strukture dialogicheskogo teksta v poemakh Pushkina (problema avtorskikh primechanii k tekstu).' In E.A. Maimin, ed. *Pushkin i ego sovremenniki*, (Pskov: LGPI), 101-10

– 1973. 'Theater and Theatricality in the Order of Early Nineteenth Century Culture.' In Henryk Baran, ed. *Semiotics and Structuralism: Readings from the Soviet Union* (White Plains, N.J.: International Arts and Sciences Press, [1976]), 33-63

– 1975. *Roman v stikhakh Pushkina 'Evgenii Onegin'*. Spetskurs, vvodnye lektsii v izuchenie teksta. Tartu: Tartuskii Gosudarstvennyi Universitet

– 1980. *Roman A.S. Pushkina 'Evgenii Onegin': Kommentarii*. Leningrad: 'Prosveshchenie'

Maimin, E.A. 1981. *Pushkin. Zhizn' i tvorchestvo*. Moscow: 'Nauka'

Makogonenko, G.P. 1963. *Roman Pushkina 'Evgenii Onegin'*. Moscow: Goslitizdat

Marchenko, N.V. [N. Narokov]. 1957. 'Kalendar' "Evgeniia Onegina".' *Vozrozhdenie*, LXII, 53-62

Matlaw, R.E. 1959. 'The Dream in *Evgeny Onegin*, with a Note on *Gore ot uma*.' *Slavonic and East European Journal*, XXXVII, 487-503

Meijer, Jan M. 1968. 'The Digressions in *Evgenij Onegin*.' In A.G.F. van Holk, ed. *Dutch Contributions to the Sixth International Congress of Slavists* (The Hague: Mouton), 122-52

Merezhkovskii, D.S. 1897. *Vechnye sputniki: Pushkin*. 3rd edition. St. Petersburg, 1906 [Reprint: Letchworth, 1971]

Miliukov, A.P. 1847. 'Evgenii Onegin.' In Miliukov, *Ocherk istorii russkoi poezii* (St. Petersburg), 167-88

Mirskii, D.S. 1926. *Pushkin*. New York: Dutton, 1963

– 1934. 'Problema Pushkina.' *Literaturnoe nasledstvo*, 16-18 (Moscow: Zhurnal'no-gazetnoe ob"edinenie), 91-112

Mitchell, Stanley. 1966. 'The Digressions of *Yevgeniy Onegin*: Apropos of Some Essays by Ettore lo Gatto.' *Slavonic and East European Review*, XLIV, 51-65

Morozov, P. 1910. 'Shifrovannoe stikhotvorenie Pushkina.' *Pushkin i ego sovremenniki*, IV, vyp. XIII, 1-12

Nabokov, Vladimir. 1975. *Eugene Onegin: A Novel in Verse by Aleksandr*

Pushkin. Translated from the Russian, with a commentary, by Vladimir Nabokov. Revised edition. 4 volumes. Princeton University Press

Nesaule, Valda. 1968. 'Tat'jana's Dream in Puškin's *Evgenij Onegin.' Indiana Slavic Studies*, IV, 119-24

Nezelenov, A.I. 1890. ' "Evgenii Onegin." Roman Pushkina.' In Nezelenov, *Shest' statei o Pushkine* (St.Petersburg, 1892)

Nikishov, Iu.M. 1972. 'Onegin i Tat'iana.' *Filologicheskie nauki*, no. 3, 16-26

Ovsianiko-Kulikovskii, D.N. 1906. 'Evgenii Onegin vo vtoroi polovine 20-kh godov.' In Ovsianiko-Kulikovskii, *Istoriia russkoi intelligentsii: Itogi russkoi khudozhestvennoi literatury XIX v.* [*Sobranie sochinenii*, VII] (St Petersburg, 1914), 70-90

– 1909. 'Evgenii Onegin.' In Ovsianiko-Kulikovskii, *Pushkin* [*Sobranie sochinenii*, IV] (St Petersburg, 1912), 85-113

Pasternak, B.L. 1957. *Doktor Zhivago*. Milano: Feltrinelli

– 1958. *Doctor Zhivago*. London: Collins

Peer, Larry H. 1969. 'Pushkin and Goethe Again: Lensky's Character.' *Papers on Language and Literature*, V, 267-72

Picchio, Riccardo. 1976. 'Dante and J. Malfilâtre as Literary Sources of Tat'jana's Erotic Dream (Notes on the Third Chapter of Puškin's *Evgenij Onegin.'* In *Alexander Puškin: A Symposium on the 175th Anniversary of His Birth* (New York: New York University Press), 42-55

Pisarev, D.I. 1865. 'Pushkin i Belinskii: "Evgenii Onegin".' In Pisarev, *Sochineniia*, III (Moscow: GIKhL, 1956), 306-64

Polevoi, N.A. 1825. ' "Evgenii Onegin," roman v stikhakh Aleksandra Pushkina." In Zelinskii, I, 12-19

Pospelov, G. 1941. ' "Evgenii Onegin" kak realisticheskii roman.' In *Pushkin: sbornik statei* (Moscow: Goslitizdat), 75-154

Pushkin, A.S. *The Letters of Alexander Pushkin*. Three Volumes in One. Translated with Preface, Introduction, and Notes by J. Thomas Shaw. Madison: University of Wisconsin Press, 1967

– 1979. *Eugene Onegin*. Translated by Charles Johnston. Introduction by John Bayley. Penguin

Pushkin: Itogi i problemy izucheniia. 1966. Leningrad: 'Nauka'

Pushkin v pechati: 1814-1837. Compiled by N. Siniavskii and M. Tsiavlovskii. Moscow: L.E. Bukhgeim, 1914

Pushkin v vospominaniiakh sovremennikov. M.: 'Khudozhestvennaia literatura,' 1974

Reeve, Franklin D. 1966. '*Eugene Onegin.'* In Reeve, *The Russian Novel* (New York: McGraw), 14-44

Richards, D.J. and C.R.S. Cockrell, eds. and translators. 1976. *Russian Views of Pushkin.* Oxford: Willem A. Meeuws

Riggan, William. 1973. '*Werther, Adolphe,* and *Eugene Onegin*: The Decline of the Hero of Sensibility.' *Research Studies* (Washington State University), XLI, 252-67

Rybnikova, M.A. 1924. 'Avtor v "Evgenii Onegine".' In Rybnikova, *Po voprosam kompozitsii* (Moscow: Izd. T-va)

Semenko, I. 1957. 'O roli obraza "avtora" v "Evgenii Onegine".' *Trudy Leningradskogo bibliotechnogo instituta im. N.K. Krupskoi,* 2, 127-46

Sergievskii, I. 1934. 'O nekotorykh voprosakh izucheniia Pushkina.' *Literaturnoe nasledstvo,* 16-18 (Moscow: Zhurnal'no-gazetnoe ob"edinenie), 113-34

Shakespeare, William. *Romeo and Juliet.* Penguin, 1967

Shaw, J. Thomas. 1966. 'Recent Soviet Scholarly Books on Puškin: A Review Article.' *Slavic and East European Journal,* X: 1, 64-84

– 1981. 'The Problem of Unity of Author-Narrator's Stance in Puškin's *Evgenij Onegin*.' *Russian Language Journal,* XXXV, no. 120, 25-42

Shklovskii, V. 1923. ' "Evgenii Onegin" (Pushkin i Stern).' In *Ocherki po poetike Pushkina* (Berlin: Epokha), 197-220

Shukman, Ann. 1977. *Literature and Semiotics: A Study of the Writings of Yu.M. Lotman.* Amsterdam: North-Holland

Siniavskii, Andrei [Abram Tertz]. 1975. *Progulki s Pushkinym.* London: Overseas Publications Interchange

Sipovskii, V.V. 1899a. *Pushkin, Bairon i Shatobrian (iz literaturnoi zhizni Pushkina na iuge Rossii).* St Petersburg

– 1899b. 'Onegin, Lenskii i Tat'iana (k literaturnoi istorii Pushkinskikh "tipov").' *Russkaia starina,* no. 5, 311-29 and no. 6, 559-80

Skovajsa, Kornel J. 1971. *Vladimir Nabokov's 'Eugene Onegin': A Critical Study.* Ph.D. Diss. U. of Oregon

Snyder, Susan. 1970. '*Romeo*: Comedy into Tragedy.' *Essays in Criticism,* XX, 391-402

Stepanov, L.A. 1974. 'Avtor i chitatel' v romane "Evgenii Onegin".' In *Pushkinskie chteniia na verzhnevolzh'e: Sbornik vtoroi* (Kalinin: Kalininskii G.U.), 43-59

Stilman, L.N. 1958. 'Problemy literaturnykh zhanrov i traditsii v "Evgenii Onegine" Pushkina.' *American Contributions to the Fourth International Congress of Slavists* (The Hague: Mouton, 1958), 321-67

Strakhov, N.N. 1874. 'Zametki o Pushkine.' In Strakhov 1897, 35-66

– 1888. 'Pushkinskii prazdnik (Otkrytie pamiatnika Pushkinu v Moskve).' In Strakhov 1897, 105-26

– 1897. *Zametki o Pushkine i drugikh poetakh.* 2nd edition. (Kiev, 1897; reprint: The Hague, 1967)

Tamarchenko, D.E. 1961. 'Roman v stikhakh A.S. Pushkina.' In Tamarchenko,

Iz istorii russkogo klassicheskogo romana; Pushkin, Lermontov, Gogol'
(Moscow-Leningrad: AN SSSR), 18-58

Todd, William Mills III. 1976. *The Familiar Letter as a Literary Genre in the Age of Pushkin.* Princeton: Princeton University Press

Tomashevskii, Boris. 1918. 'Ritmika chetyrekhstopnogo iamba po nabliudeniiam nad stikhom "Evgeniia Onegina".' *Pushkin i ego sovremenniki*, vyp. XXIX-XXX (Petrograd), 144-87

- 1934. 'Desiataia glava "Evgeniia Onegina".' *Literaturnoe nasledstvo*, 16-18 (Moscow: Zhurnal'no-gazetnoe ob"edinenie), 378-420

- 1961. 'Osnovnye etapy izucheniia Pushkina.' In Tomashevskii, *Pushkin: Kniga vtoraia* (Moscow-Leningrad: AN SSSR), 444-76

Tseitlin, A. 1941. ' "Evgenii Onegin" i russkaia literatura.' In *Pushkin – rodonachal'nik novoi russkoi literatury: sbornik nauchno-issledovatel'skikh rabot* (Moscow-Leningrad: AN SSSR), 335-64

Turgenev, I.S. 1880. '[Rech' po povodu otkrytiia pamiatnika A.S. Pushkinu v Moskve].' In Turgenev, *Sochineniia v piatnadtsati tomakh*, XV (Moscow-Leningrad: 'Nauka,' 1968), 66-76

Tynianov, Iu.N. 1924. *Problema stikhotvornogo iazyka.* Leningrad: Academia [reprint: Letchworth, 1974]

- 1929a. 'Arkhaisty i Pushkin.' In Tynianov, *Arkhaisty i novatory* (Leningrad, 1929 [reprint: Munich, 1967]), 87-227

- 1929b. 'Dostoevskii i Gogol'.' Ibid., 412-55

- 1929c. 'Pushkin.' Ibid., 228-291

- 1974. 'O kompozitsii "Evgeniia Onegina".' In *Pamiatniki kul'tury, novye otkrytiia: Pis'mennost', iskusstvo, arkheologiia. Ezhegodnik 1974* (Moscow: 'Nauka,' 1975); and in Tynianov, *Poetika, istoriia literatury, kino* (Moscow: 'Nauka,' 1977), 52-77

Venevitinov, D.V. 1825a. 'Razbor stat'i o "Evgenii Onegine", pomeshchennoi v No.5 Moskovskogo telegrafa.' In Venevitinov 1934, 220-227

- 1825b. 'Otvet g. Polevomu.' In Venevitinov 1934, 228-38

- 1827. 'Ob "Evgenii Onegine".' In Venevitinov 1934, 238-39

- 1934. *Polnoe sobranie sochinenii.* Moscow-Leningrad: Academia

Vickery, W.N. 1963. 'Parallelizm v literaturnom razvitii Bairona i Pushkina.' *American Contributions to the Fifth International Congress of Slavists* (The Hague: Mouton), 371-401

- 1968. 'Byron's *Don Juan* and Puškin's *Evgenij Onegin*: The Question of Parallelism.' *Indiana Slavic Studies*, IV, 181-91

Vinogradov, Ivan. 1934. 'Put' Pushkina k realizmu.' *Literaturnoe nasledstvo*, 16-18 (Moscow: Zhurnal'no-gazetnoe ob"edinenie), 49-90

Vinogradov, V.V. 1934. 'O stile Pushkina.' *Literaturnoe nasledstvo*, 16-18 (Moscow: Zhurnal'no-gazetnoe ob"edinenie), 135-214

- 1935. *Iazyk Pushkina: Pushkin i istoriia russkogo literaturnogo iazyka.* Moscow-Leningrad: Academia [Slavica-Reprint Nr. 25, Düsseldorf, 1969]
- 1941. *Stil' Pushkina*
- 1966. 'Stil' i kompozitsiia pervoi glavy "Evgeniia Onegina".' *Russkii iazyk v shkole,* no. 4, 3-21

Vinokur, G. 1941. 'Slovo i stikh v "Evgenii Onegine".' In A. Egolin, ed. *Pushkin: sbornik statei* (Moscow: Goslitizdat), 155-213

Vol'pert, L.I. 1980. *Pushkin i psikhologicheskaia traditsiia vo frantsuzskoi literature.* Tallinn: Eesti Raamat

Weil, Irwin. 1974. 'Onegin's Echo.' *Russian Literature Triquarterly,* X, 260-73

Wilson, Edmund. 1936. '*Evgeni Onegin*: In Honor of Pushkin 1799-1837.' *New Republic,* 89 (9 December 1936), 165-71

Wreath, Patrick J. and April I. Wreath, compilers. 1976. 'Alexander Pushkin: A Bibliography of Criticism in English.' *Canadian-American Slavic Studies,* X: 2, 279-304

Zelinskii, V. 1903. *Russkaia kriticheskaia literatura o proizvedeniiakh Pushkina.* 3rd edition. Moscow

Index